Nealon's Guide to the

28th Dáil
& Seanad

Election '97

Gill & Macmillan

Gill & Macmillan Ltd
Goldenbridge
Dublin 8
with associated companies throughout the world

© Ted Nealon 1997
0 7171 2675 7 paperback
0 7171 2674 9 hardcover
Editor: Gina Menzies
Original design concept by Elizabeth Fitz-Simon
Print origination by Carole Lynch
Printed by ColourBooks Ltd, Dublin

Photographs on the following pages are
© Tony O'Shea 1997
10, 24, 40, 52, 68, 80, 88, 102, 110,
114, 122, 134, 142, 146, 160, 200

This book is typeset in 8/9 pt Univers 45

Other books by the author:
Ireland: A Parliamentary Directory 1973/74 (0 902173 60 X)
Ted Nealon's Guide to the 21st Dáil and Seanad (0 9505984 0 2 paperback, 0 9505984 1 0 hardback)
Nealon's Guide to the 22nd Dáil and Seanad (0 9505984 3 7 paperback, 0 9505984 2 9 hardback)
Nealon's Guide to the 23rd Dáil and Seanad (0 9505984 4 5 paperback)
Nealon's Guide to the 24th Dáil and Seanad (0 9505984 5 3 paperback, 0 9505984 6 1 hardback)
Nealon's Guide to the 25th Dáil and Seanad (0 9505984 8 8 paperback, 0 9505984 7 X hardback)
Nealon's Guide to the 26th Dáil and Seanad (0 9505984 9 6 paperback)
Nealon's Guide to the 27th Dáil and Seanad (0 7171 2113 5 paperback, 0 7171 2112 7 hardback)

A catalogue record is available for this book from the British Library.

Contents

Acknowledgments

This *Nealon's Guide to the Dáil and Seanad* is the ninth in the series which I started after the 1973 General Election. While no one has done a count, it is a fairly safe assumption that the *Guide* contains at least a quarter of a million pieces of information about the elections, the Dáil and the Seanad. Putting it together still remains a very formidable task, despite the experience gained with previous publications and despite the continuous advances in technology affecting all aspects of publishing.

It is a task that I could not have done without the generous help and co-operation of very many people. For this *Guide*, as for the previous four, Gina Menzies has been an excellent editor. I wish to acknowledge her major contribution to all aspects of the publication and to thank her for her efficiency, enthusiasm and dedication. I also wish to thank Donald Menzies who again undertook some of the most demanding aspects of the work, bringing his special skills to bear on them, and so helping to maintain the qualities that have established *Nealon's Guide to the Dáil and Seanad* as the standard reference book of current Irish politics.

I also sought and got help from many other sources and benefited from the advice and encouragement of many people. I wish to thank Kieran Coughlan, Clerk of the Dáil; Deirdre Lane, Clerk of the Seanad; Jody Blake, Assistant Clerk of the Seanad; Peter Greene, Franchise Section, Department of the Environment and Local Government; Martin Groves and Mairéad McCabe of the Bills Office, Leinster House; Liam Fitzgibbon, Editor, Dáil Debates; Caitríona Meehan and the Fianna Fáil Press Office; Niall Ó Muilleoir, Carl Brophy and the Fine Gael Press Office; Tom Butler and the Labour Party Press Office; Sara Morris and the Progressive Democrats Press Office; Tony Heffernan and the Democratic Left Press Office; Joe Lennon, Government Press Secretary; John Murray, Grace Fagan and Jackie Coogan of the Government Information Services; Síle de Búrca of the Government Secretariat; Colm Larkin, Director and Paul Gormley, Information Policy Co-ordinator, European Commission representation in Ireland; Jim O'Brien, Director and Dermot Scott, Deputy Director, European Parliament Office in Ireland.

I wish to acknowledge a special debt, on the publication of this *Guide*, and indeed the whole series, to Muiris Mac Conghail, Jonathan Williams and Pat Staunton.

Again with this *Guide*, as with the last, I had the very considerable advantage of having Gill & Macmillan as the publishers and I was greatly helped by their knowledge and experience. I thank the following for their highly professional work and service: Fergal Tobin, Publisher; Mairead O'Keeffe, Production Director; Paula Elmore, Senior Production Controller; D Rennison Kunz, Editorial Manager.

As always I received maximum co-operation from members of Dáil Éireann and Seanad Éireann in the completion of the biographical details. I thank them for it.

I wish to express my sincere thanks to our advertisers. Their support has been an essential part of the continued feasibility of the production of this directory.

Finally I want to acknowledge the great understanding I had throughout the work on the *Guide*, as on all other matters, from my wife Jo and from Louise and Feargal.

TED NEALON
September 1997

Foreword

by John Bruton

I congratulate Ted Nealon on producing this authoritative *Guide* to the Dáil. Ted's knowledge of figures is matched by a deep and sympathetic understanding of the people and the issues that decide elections.

In this contribution to the *Guide* I would like to focus on the longer-term policy choices that this Dáil, and its immediate successors, will have to make.

As we enter a new century, having done so well economically, we are freed of the necessity to worry about basic survival. We have a choice as to what to spend money on. In addition to these opportunities, there are threats. I would like to deal with the following issues: Northern Ireland, crime, family and housing policy, education, the reform of our political institution, and, finally, Ireland's role in the world.

The biggest single threat is strife in Northern Ireland. We have seen in other parts of the world how things can go radically wrong where there is an underlying conflict. In the early 1960s, Lebanon was seen as the Switzerland of the Middle East, a haven of peace and multi-ethnic co-existence. Yet within a very short time Lebanon was plunged into a civil war from which it has never fully recovered.

Bosnia enjoyed many years of peace too. There was much intermarriage and good social relations between Croats, Serbs, and Muslims. Yet when the fires of underlying ethnic conflict were fanned, all of that broke down, and there was a descent into brutality of a kind not seen in Europe since the death of Adolf Hitler.

Conflicts of identity that are not handled with care can go horribly wrong. Notwithstanding the welcome ceasefire, we in the Republic live within a few miles of a deeply divided society — a society where there are regular punishment beatings to enforce control of particular areas, where church services are picketed, where gravestones are daubed, and where people march and counter-march to stake out ownership over territory.

Similar passions to those that erupted in Lebanon and in Bosnia are there below the surface in Northern Ireland. The new Dáil must ensure that these passions are calmed. It must not take sides on ethnic or religious lines. There is a big temptation to take the side of one community in a conflict. If you do that you become part of the problem, not part of the solution. We must seek a settlement that is fair to both communities.

The Dáil must make a stark distinction between those who pursue objectives by political methods — however controversial — and those who use or threaten violence. A democratic state cannot allow itself to be drawn into an alliance with any political organisation which threatens or supports the use of violence.

Organised crime represents a really big challenge for Ireland and for Europe. The last Government has put through one of the most far-reaching programmes of reform of the criminal justice system in the history of the state in the last year. The courts, the prison service, the Gardaí and our laws against crime have all been strengthened. But these measures will work only if the people are willing to support them. People must be willing to give information to the Gardaí. People must be willing to deny a market to the produce of crime.

The simplest way to end drug-related crime would be for the rising generation of young people to decide that they were not going to use banned drugs. If that happened, the market for criminals would disappear.

Laws do not make us good. We must do that ourselves. We have only to see how the 'compo' culture has developed to see how good laws can be diverted from the original purpose.

Crime and lawlessness have social roots. Urbanisation, social injustice, the reduced role of the extended family, and the decline in the influence of organised religion — all have reduced some of the controls that inhibited people in the past. It is good that some of the inhibitions are gone, but a price has also had to be paid.

Because of urbanisation, many people don't know their neighbours any more. People do not live near their grandparents as much as they used to. Uncles and aunts may live in another city, or another country. This pushes more stress and responsibility back onto the nuclear family, onto parents on their own (whether single or married).

If we wish to create a society where family ties are to be strengthened, we must have a radical re-examination of our expectations and policies in regard to housing. Can we devise a housing policy that encourages extended families to live closer together? Can we avoid a situation where some housing areas are inhabited by a large number of elderly people with surplus space, while their adult children are living at the other side of the city with few neighbours other than people of their own generation?

Of course we cannot re-create the traditional village culture in urban Ireland, but we can plan our housing so that estates are mixed in the type of house provided and where an age mix is promoted.

Ireland has done exceptionally well in the last thirty years, because we are a young and educated people. Economic growth is a race between education and technology. We have to keep running very fast to stay ahead. All countries are now investing heavily in education. Other countries have a younger age profile than Ireland. Our birth rate has been falling off since 1980. Eventually Ireland will experience the 'greying' of its work force that is already causing problems for countries like Japan and Germany.

Young people in their twenties and thirties are more innovative and flexible than people in their forties and fifties. As a country's work force ages, the country itself becomes potentially less flexible and innovative. One of the challenges for Ireland in the early part of the next century will be to prevent this happening to us. If we are to prevent ourselves from becoming tired and inflexible we must ensure that, throughout life, we are constantly challenged and retrained. We must not settle into a rut.

Rather than set money aside to pay redundancy, firms should be encouraged by the tax code to invest in retraining their employees. Employees should invest in their own retraining too, because that is the best guarantee of a rising salary level.

Third-level institutions must look to the existing work force as people who may need mid-career re-education. Obviously those going to college in mid-career will do so with more focused and limited objectives than those coming straight out of school. Colleges must adapt to needs like this.

The skills in most demand in the future will not simply be about 'how to do' things. In the United States the high incomes are going to those who can organise information — people such as lawyers and software engineers — rather than to those who know how to do particular things. This must be the focus of a

second wave of educational investment by Ireland for the twenty-first century.

Another big task for the Dáil will be to oversee the reinvention of our system of government for the twenty-first century. Whereas in the 1960s a Government might have a week or two to think over a new problem, modern media pressures mean that the Government often has to come up with answers in an hour or two.

In the 1960s a hierarchical system of administration, with numerous grades, was necessary so that public service work could be properly supervised. Now, modern information technology means that fewer supervisors are necessary, and more people can take responsibility for their own work. This means that we do not need the complicated grade structures that exist in many of our public services. Getting rid of grades would create great fears among serving employees and pensioners, but it is necessary if we are to have better public services. In modern management jargon, we need a flatter and leaner system.

Ireland will have to think about its place in the world. The freeing of world trade will speed up the pace of change. An uncompetitive system of agricultural production will not survive for ever in Europe. Ireland's advantage in information technology is not impregnable. The pressure of world population growth will produce more and more economic 'refugees' seeking to share Europe's and Ireland's prosperity.

Europe's political institutions will have to be strengthened. Weak and squabbling European institutions will not have the moral authority or the power to manage a single currency, or to penalise national governments that print too much money.

Ireland must support a stronger Europe, because a common European loyalty will help us overcome local conflicts of allegiance, like those that exist in Northern Ireland. And it will also guarantee us long-term prosperity.

John Bruton was Taoiseach 1994-97 leading a Coalition Government of Fine Gael, Labour and Democratic Left. He has been Leader of Fine Gael since 1990. He served as a Minister in several Departments in Dr Garret FitzGerald's Coalition Governments in the 1980s and as a Minister of State in Liam Cosgrave's Government in the 1970s. He has been a Dáil deputy since 1969.

The 28th Dáil (elected 6 June 1997)

The 28th Dáil has **166 deputies** returned by **41 constituencies**. Position of parties as returned in General Election:

Fianna Fáil	77
Fine Gael	54
Labour	17
Democratic Left	4
Progressive Democrats	4
Green Party	2
Sinn Féin	1
Socialist Party	1
Others	6

Deputy	Party	Constituency
* Ahearn, Theresa	FG	Tipperary South
* Ahern, Bertie	FF	Dublin Central
* Ahern, Dermot	FF	Louth
* Ahern, Michael	FF	Cork East
* Ahern, Noel	FF	Dublin North-West
* Allen, Bernard	FG	Cork North-Central
Ardagh, Seán	FF	Dublin South-Central
* Andrews, David	FF	Dún Laoghaire
* Aylward, Liam	FF	Carlow-Kilkenny
† Barnes, Monica	FG	Dún Laoghaire
* Barrett, Seán	FG	Dún Laoghaire
* Bell, Michael	Lab	Louth
† Belton, Louis J.	FG	Longford-Roscommon
Blaney, Harry	Ind	Donegal North-East
* Boylan, Andrew	FG	Cavan-Monaghan
* Bradford, Paul	FG	Cork East
Brady, Johnny	FF	Meath
Brady, Martin	FF	Dublin North-East
* Brennan, Matt	FF	Sligo-Leitrim
* Brennan, Séamus	FF	Dublin South
* Briscoe, Ben	FF	Dublin South-Central
* Broughan, Tommy	Lab	Dublin North-East
* Browne, John	FG	Carlow-Kilkenny
* Browne, John	FF	Wexford
* Bruton, John	FG	Meath
* Bruton, Richard	FG	Dublin North-Central
* Burke, Liam	FG	Cork North-Central
* Burke, Ray	FF	Dublin North
Burke, Ulick	FG	Galway East
* Byrne, Hugh	FF	Wexford
* Callely, Ivor	FF	Dublin North-Central
* Carey, Donal	FG	Clare
Carey, Pat	FF	Dublin North-West
Clune, Deirdre	FG	Cork South-Central
Collins, Michael	FF	Limerick West
* Connaughton, Paul	FG	Galway East
Cooper-Flynn, Beverley	FF	Mayo
† Cosgrave, Michael J.	FG	Dublin North-East
* Coughlan, Mary	FF	Donegal South-West
* Coveney, Hugh	FG	Cork South-Central
* Cowen, Brian	FF	Laois-Offaly
* Crawford, Seymour	FG	Cavan-Monaghan
* Creed, Michael	FG	Cork North-West
* Cullen, Martin	FF	Waterford
* Currie, Austin	FG	Dublin West
† Daly, Brendan	FF	Clare
† D'Arcy, Michael	FG	Wexford
* Davern, Noel	FF	Tipperary South
* Deasy, Austin	FG	Waterford
* Deenihan, Jimmy	FG	Kerry North
* Dempsey, Noel	FF	Meath
† Dennehy, John	FF	Cork South-Central
* De Rossa, Proinsias	DL	Dublin North-West
* de Valera, Síle	FF	Clare
* Doherty, Seán	FF	Longford-Roscommon
* Dukes, Alan	FG	Kildare South
* Durkan, Bernard	FG	Kildare North
* Ellis, John	FF	Sligo-Leitrim
† Enright, Thomas W.	FG	Laois-Offaly
† Fahey, Frank	FF	Galway West
† Farrelly, John V.	FG	Meath
* Ferris, Michael	Lab	Tipperary South
* Finucane, Michael	FG	Limerick West
* Fitzgerald, Frances	FG	Dublin South-East
* Flanagan, Charles	FG	Laois-Offaly
Fleming, Seán	FF	Laois-Offaly
* Flood, Chris	FF	Dublin South-West
* Foley, Denis	FF	Kerry North
* Fox, Mildred	Ind	Wicklow
Gildea, Thomas	Ind	Donegal South-West
* Gilmore, Éamon	DL	Dún Laoghaire
Gormley, John	GP	Dublin South-East
* Gregory, Tony	Ind	Dublin Central
Hanafin, Mary	FF	Dún Laoghaire
* Harney, Mary	PD	Dublin South-West
* Haughey, Seán	FF	Dublin North-Central
Hayes, Brian	FG	Dublin South-West
Healy-Rae, Jackie	Ind	Kerry South
* Higgins, Jim	FG	Mayo
Higgins, Joe	SP	Dublin West

* Higgins, Michael D.	Lab	Galway West
* Hogan, Philip	FG	Carlow-Kilkenny
* Howlin, Brendan	Lab	Wexford
* Jacob, Joe	FF	Wicklow
* Keaveney, Cecilia	FF	Donegal North-East
Kelleher, Billy	FF	Cork North-Central
* Kemmy, Jim	Lab	Limerick East
* Kenneally, Brendan	FF	Waterford
* Kenny, Enda	FG	Mayo
* Killeen, Tony	FF	Clare
* Kirk, Séamus	FF	Louth
* Kitt, Michael P.	FF	Galway East
* Kitt, Tom	FF	Dublin South
* Lawlor, Liam	FF	Dublin West
* Lenihan, Brian	FF	Dublin West
Lenihan, Conor	FF	Dublin South-West
* Lowry, Michael	Ind	Tipperary North
* McCormack, Pádraic	FG	Galway West
* McCreevy, Charlie	FF	Kildare North
* McDaid, James	FF	Donegal North-East
* McDowell, Derek	Lab	Dublin North-Central
* McGahon, Brendan	FG	Louth
McGennis, Marian	FF	Dublin Central
* McGinley, Dinny	FG	Donegal South-West
* McGrath, Paul	FG	Westmeath
McGuinness, John	FF	Carlow-Kilkenny
* McManus, Liz	DL	Wicklow
* Martin, Micheál	FF	Cork South-Central
* Mitchell, Gay	FG	Dublin South-Central
* Mitchell, Jim	FG	Dublin Central
Mitchell, Olivia	FG	Dublin South
* Moffatt, Tom	FF	Mayo
* Molloy, Robert	PD	Galway West
Moloney, John	FF	Laois-Offaly
* Moynihan, Donal	FF	Cork North-West
Moynihan, Michael	FF	Cork North-West
* Moynihan-Cronin, Breeda	Lab	Kerry South
Naughten, Denis	FG	Longford-Roscommon
Neville, Dan	FG	Limerick West
* Noonan, Michael	FG	Limerick East
Ó Caoláin, Caoimhghín	SF	Cavan-Monaghan
* Ó Cuív, Éamon	FF	Galway West
* O'Dea, Willie	FF	Limerick East
* O'Donnell, Liz	PD	Dublin South
* O'Donoghue, John	FF	Kerry South
O'Flynn, Noel	FF	Cork North-Central
* O'Hanlon, Rory	FF	Cavan-Monaghan

* O'Keeffe, Batt	FF	Cork South-Central
* O'Keeffe, Jim	FG	Cork South-West
* O'Keeffe, Ned	FF	Cork East
† O'Kennedy, Michael	FF	Tipperary North
* O'Malley, Desmond J.	PD	Limerick East
* O'Rourke, Mary	FF	Westmeath
* O'Shea, Brian	Lab	Waterford
* Owen, Nora	FG	Dublin North
* Pattison, Séamus	Lab	Carlow-Kilkenny
* Penrose, Willie	Lab	Westmeath
Perry, John	FG	Sligo-Leitrim
* Power, Seán	FF	Kildare South
* Quinn, Ruairí	Lab	Dublin South-East
* Rabbitte, Pat	DL	Dublin South-West
* Reynolds, Albert	FF	Longford-Roscommon
† Reynolds, Gerry	FG	Sligo-Leitrim
* Ring, Michael	FG	Mayo
† Roche, Dick	FF	Wicklow
* Ryan, Eoin	FF	Dublin South-East
* Sargent, Trevor	GP	Dublin North
* Shatter, Alan	FG	Dublin South
* Sheehan, P.J.	FG	Cork South-West
* Shortall, Róisín	Lab	Dublin North-West
* Smith, Brendan	FF	Cavan-Monaghan
* Smith, Michael	FF	Tipperary North
* Spring, Dick	Lab	Kerry North
* Stagg, Emmet	Lab	Kildare North
Stanton, David	FG	Cork East
Timmins, William	FG	Wicklow
* Treacy, Noel	FF	Galway East
* Upton, Pat	Lab	Dublin South-Central
Wade, Eddie	FF	Limerick East
Wall, Jack	Lab	Kildare South
* Wallace, Dan	FF	Cork North-Central
* Wallace, Mary	FF	Meath
* Walsh, Joe	FF	Cork South-West
* Woods, Michael J.	FF	Dublin North-East
† Wright, G.V.	FF	Dublin North
* Yates, Ivan	FG	Wexford

The 28th Dáil has 166 deputies, the same as the previous Dáil. Of these, 121 (72.89%) were outgoing members of the 27th Dáil, denoted here by an asterisk (*); 13 (7.83%) denoted here by † were previously members of the House, but not of the 27th Dáil, and 32 (19.28%) are new deputies.

The Cabinet

Seated: Mary O'Rourke, TD (Minister for Public Enterprise), Michael J. Woods, TD (Minister for the Marine and Natural Resources), Bertie Ahern, TD (Taoiseach), (President Mary Robinson), Mary Harney, TD (Tánaiste and Minister for Enterprise, Trade and Employment), Ray Burke, TD (Minister for Foreign Affairs), David Andrews, TD (Minister for Defence).

Standing: Micheál Martin, TD (Minister for Education), James McDaid, TD (Minister for Tourism, Sport and Recreation), Dermot Ahern, TD (Minister for Social, Community and Family Affairs), John O'Donoghue, TD (Minister for Justice, Equality and Law Reform), Síle de Valera, TD (Minister for Arts, Heritage, Gaeltacht and the Islands), Joe Walsh, TD (Minister for Agriculture and Food), Noel Dempsey, TD (Minister for the Environment and Local Government), Brian Cowen, TD (Minister for Health and Children), Charlie McCreevy, TD (Minister for Finance), David Byrne (Attorney General), Séamus Brennan, TD (Government Chief Whip), Bobby Molloy, TD (Minister of State to the Government).

Ray Burke resigned as Minister for Foreign Affairs on 7 October 1997. He was replaced on 8 October 1997 by David Andrews, Minister for Defence; Michael Smith, Minister of State, was appointed Minister for Defence.

Taoiseach	Bertie Ahern
Tánaiste and Minister for Enterprise, Trade and Employment	Mary Harney
Minister for the Marine and Natural Resources	Michael J. Woods
*Minister for Foreign Affairs	Ray Burke
Minister for Public Enterprise	Mary O'Rourke
Minister for Defence	David Andrews
Minister for Agriculture and Food	Joe Walsh
Minister for Finance	Charlie McCreevy
Minister for Health and Children	Brian Cowen
Minister for the Environment and Local Government	Noel Dempsey
Minister for Social, Community and Family Affairs	Dermot Ahern
Minister for Arts, Heritage, Gaeltacht and the Islands	Síle de Valera
Minister for Justice, Equality and Law Reform	John O'Donoghue
Minister for Tourism, Sport and Recreation	James McDaid
Minister for Education	Micheál Martin
Attorney General	David Byrne

*Ray Burke resigned as Minister on 7 October 1997. David Andrews, Minister for Defence, was appointed Minister for Foreign Affairs on 8 October 1997. Michael Smith, Minister of State, was appointed Minister for Defence on 8 October 1997.

Ministers of State (appointed 26 June, 1 July and 8 July 1997)

Department	Special Responsibilities	Name
Taoiseach, Defence	Govt Chief Whip	Séamus Brennan
Government, Environment & Local Government	Housing and Urban Renewal	Robert Molloy
*Education, and Enterprise, Trade and Employment	Science and Technology	Michael Smith
Agriculture and Food	Livestock Breeding and Horticulture	Noel Davern
Public Enterprise	Energy	Joe Jacob
Health and Children	Children	Frank Fahey
Education	Adult Education, Youth Affairs and School Transport	Willie O'Dea
Enterprise, Trade and Employment	Labour Affairs, Consumer Rights and International Trade	Tom Kitt
Tourism, Sport and Recreation	Local Development, National Drugs Strategy Team	Chris Flood
Environment and Local Government	Environmental Information and Awareness and Environmental Protection Agency	Dan Wallace
Agriculture and Food	Food	Ned O'Keeffe
Marine and Natural Resources	Aquaculture and Forestry	Hugh Byrne
Justice, Equality and Law Reform	Equality & Disabilities	Mary Wallace
Finance	Office of Public Works	Martin Cullen
Arts, Heritage, Gaeltacht and the Islands	Gaeltacht and the Islands	Éamon Ó Cuív
Foreign Affairs	Overseas Development Assistance and Human Rights	Liz O'Donnell
Health and Children	Food Safety, and Older People	Tom Moffatt

*Michael Smith was appointed Minister for Defence on 8 October 1997. Noel Treacy replaced him as the new Minister of State.

The General Election of 6 June 1997 brought a minority Coalition Government of Fianna Fáil and the Progressive Democrats to power. When the 28th Dáil assembled on 26 June 1997, Bertie Ahern, Leader of Fianna Fáil since 1994, was nominated for appointment by the President as Taoiseach by 85 votes to 78. In addition to the 77 votes of his own party and the 4 votes of the Progressive Democrats, Deputy Ahern was supported by the Independents Harry Blaney, Mildred Fox and Jackie Healy-Rae and by Caoimhghín Ó Caoláin (SF). He was opposed by all 54 votes of Fine Gael, 16 of the 17 votes of Labour (Séamus Pattison (Lab) had been elected Ceann Comhairle), the 4 votes of Democratic Left, the 2 votes of the Green Party, and Tony Gregory (Ind) and Joe Higgins (SP). Two independents, Michael Lowry and Thomas Gildea, abstained. Earlier, the nomination of the outgoing Taoiseach, John Bruton, was defeated by 87 votes to 75.

The motion for approval of the nomination by the Taoiseach of other members of the Government was carried by 84 votes to 76.

The Government that came to power on 12 January 1993, after the 1992 General Election, with Albert Reynolds as Taoiseach, continued until 15 December 1994. It was a Fianna Fáil/Labour Coalition. The Labour Ministers resigned on 17 November 1994 and their portfolios were reassigned on 18 November 1994 to serving Fianna Fáil Ministers. No new appointments were made to Cabinet. The Taoiseach and Government Ministers resigned on 15 December 1994 (Article 28.11.1° of the Constitution) and, for the first time in the history of the State, there was a change of Government without a dissolution of the Dáil.

The Government that came to power on 15 December 1994 was a three-party Coalition Government of Fine Gael, Labour and Democratic Left (the Rainbow Coalition), with the Fine Gael Leader, John Bruton, as Taoiseach and the Labour Leader, Dick Spring, as Tánaiste. It continued in office until 26 June 1997. For details of Ministers and Ministers of State, see page 195.

Bertie Ahern on the Fianna Fáil battle bus.

The June 1997 General Election was declared on 15 May 1997. A total of 484 candidates were nominated for the 166 seats to be contested. The outgoing Ceann Comhairle, Seán Treacy, did not exercise his right to be returned automatically in his constituency and retired. Thirteen registered political parties nominated candidates: Fianna Fáil, Fine Gael, the Labour Party, Progressive Democrats, Green Party - Comhaontas Glas, Democratic Left, Sinn Féin, National Party, Socialist Party, Chrisitan Solidarity Party, the Workers' Party, Socialist Workers' Party and the Natural Law Party. Voting took place on 6 June 1997. Counting began on 7 June and was completed on 14 June.

State of the Parties

Election	FF	FG	Lab	PD	DL	Others
1997	**77**	**54**	**17**	**4**	**4**	**10**
1992	68	45	33	10	4	6
1989	77	55	15	6	—	13
1987	81	51	12	14	—	8
Nov. 1982	75	70	16	—	—	5
Feb. 1982	81	63	15	—	—	7
1981	78	65	15	—	—	8

Line-up

Election	Electorate	Candidates	Seats
1997	**2,741,262**	**484**	**166**
1992	2,557,036	481	166
1989	2,448,813	370	166
1987	2,445,515	466	166
Nov. 1982	2,335,153	364	166
Feb. 1982	2,275,450	365	166
1981	2,275,450	403	166

First-Preference Votes

Election	FF		FG		Lab		PD		DL		Others	
1997	**703,682**	**39.33%**	**499,936**	**27.95%**	**186,044**	**10.40%**	**83,765**	**4.68%**	**44,901**	**2.51%**	**270,657**	**15.13%**
1992	674,650	39.11%	422,106	24.47%	333,013	19.31%	80,787	4.68%	47,945	2.78%	166,352	9.64%
1989	731,472	44.15%	485,307	29.29%	156,989	9.48%	91,013	5.49%	—	—	192,032	11.59%
1987	784,547	44.15%	481,127	27.07%	114,551	6.44%	210,583	11.85%	—	—	186,357	10.49%
Nov. 1982	763,313	45.20%	662,284	39.22%	158,115	9.36%	—	—	—	—	105,008	6.22%
Feb. 1982	786,951	47.26%	621,088	37.30%	151,875	8.12%	—	—	—	—	105,219	6.32%
1981	777,616	45.26%	626,376	36.46%	169,990	9.89%	—	—	—	—	144,229	8.39%

Turnout

Election	Total Poll		Spoiled Votes		Valid Poll	
1997	**1,807,016**	**65.92%**	**18,031**	**1.00%**	**1,789,985**	**65.26%**
1992	1,751,351	68.49%	26,498	1.51%	1,724,853	67.46%
1989	1,677,592	68.51%	20,779	1.24%	1,656,813	67.66%
1987	1,793,406	73.33%	16,241	0.91%	1,777,165	72.69%
Nov. 1982	1,701,393	72.86%	12,673	0.74%	1,688,720	72.32%
Feb. 1982	1,679,500	73.81%	14,367	0.86%	1,665,133	73.18%
1981	1,734,379	76.22%	16,168	0.93%	1,718,211	75.51%

Regional First-Preference Percentages by Euro Constituencies

Constituency	FF	FG	Lab	PD	DL	Others
Connacht-Ulster (all of the counties of Connacht, plus Cavan, Monaghan and Donegal)	42.35%	32.42%	5.78%	3.02%	—	16.43%
Dublin (all of Dublin City and County)	36.38%	22.37%	11.20%	6.59%	5.05%	18.42%
Leinster (all of Leinster, except Dublin City and County)	41.08%	30.15%	13.13%	4.46%	2.20%	8.98%
Munster (all of Munster)	38.56%	28.16%	10.14%	4.23%	2.09%	16.82%

WE'VE RESERVED THE BEST SEAT FOR YOU.

When it comes to comprehensive news, current affairs and event coverage you can trust. When you're looking to see the latest films, the hottest shows, the household names. When you want to be in the thick of the action at the big sports event or in the front row for the gig of the year. Just sit back and we'll bring it to your home.

Seats 5 Quota 9,409	1st Count	2nd Count Transfer of **Aylward's** Surplus	3rd Count Transfer of **Nolan's** (Billy) Votes	4th Count Transfer of **Quinn's** Votes	5th Count Transfer of **Townsend's** Votes	6th Count Transfer of **Hogan's** Surplus	7th Count Transfer of **Gibbons's** Votes	8th Count Transfer of **White's** Votes
*AYLWARD, Liam (FF)	11,849	−2,440 9,409						
*BROWNE, John (FG)	6,834	+87 6,921	+53 6,974	+101 7,075	+699 7,774	+156 7,930	+514 8,444	+934 9,378
GIBBONS, Jim G. (PD)	3,184	+284 3,468	+33 3,501	+122 3,623	+115 3,738	+11 3,749	−3,749 —	
*HOGAN, Phil (FG)	9,642	— —	— —	— —	— —	−233 9,409		
McGUINNESS, John (FF)	5,990	+1,262 7,252	+70 7,322	+125 7,447	+36 7,483	+13 7,496	+1,280 8,776	+534 9,310
NOLAN, Billy (Ind)	416	+46 462	−462 —					
*NOLAN, M.J. (FF)	5,975	+487 6,462	+106 6,568	+95 6,663	+370 7,033	+3 7,036	+861 7,897	+651 8,548
*PATTISON, Séamus (Lab)	5,578	+168 5,746	+38 5,784	+76 5,860	+1,565 7,425	+42 7,467	+315 7,782	+1,244 9,026
QUINN, Michael A. (NP)	870	+13 883	+17 900	−900 —				
TOWNSEND, Jim (Lab)	2,995	+12 3,007	+66 3,073	+29 3,102	−3,102 —			
WHITE, Mary (GP)	3,116	+81 3,197	+45 3,242	+259 3,501	+241 3,742	+8 3,750	+503 4,253	−4,253 —
NON-TRANSFERABLE			34	93	76	—	276	890

Carlow-Kilkenny

Elected

Liam Aylward (FF)*	1st Count
Philip Hogan (FG)*	1st Count
John Browne (FG)*	8th Count
John McGuinness (FF)	8th Count
Séamus Pattison (Lab)*	8th Count

Voting by Party

1st Preference	Number	%	% 1992
Fianna Fáil	23,814	42.19	43.13
Fine Gael	16,476	29.19	27.62
Labour	8,573	15.19	24.59
Prog Democrats	3,184	5.64	—
Green Party	3,116	5.52	—
National Party	870	1.54	—
Others	416	0.74	4.66

Statistics

Population	111,027	
Electorate	85,096	
Total Poll	57,141	67.15
Spoiled Votes	692	1.21
Valid Poll	56,449	66.34
Seats	5	
Quota	9,409	
Candidates	11	

Seats

FF	2
FG	2
Lab	1
No change	

The constituency of Carlow-Kilkenny is slightly smaller than in the 1992 General Election, having lost an area with a population of 3,550 to the constituency of Wicklow.

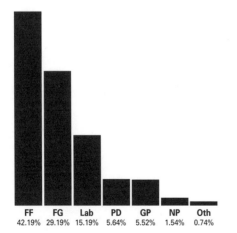

FF	FG	Lab	PD	GP	NP	Oth
42.19%	29.19%	15.19%	5.64%	5.52%	1.54%	0.74%

Liam Aylward (FF)

Home Address
Aghaviller, Hugginstown, Co Kilkenny
Telephone
Home (056) 68703
Birth Place/Date
Knockmoylon, Mullinavat, Co Kilkenny
September 1952
Married
Kathleen Noonan. 2 sons, 2 daughters
Education
St Kieran's College, Kilkenny (Diploma in Building and Construction)
Occupation
Full-time public representative. Formerly laboratory technician

Liam Aylward was Minister of State at the Department of Education February 1992-94, with special responsibility for Youth and Sport. He was Minister of State at the Department of Forestry November 1988-July 1989. He was first elected to the Dáil for Carlow-Kilkenny in 1977.

Member, Parliamentary Assembly of the Council of Europe 1987-88 and 1989-92.

Fianna Fáil spokesperson on Sport, Leisure and Tourism 1995-97.

He served on Kilkenny County Council 1974-92; Kilkenny Health Committee; Kilkenny Scholarship Committee; South-Eastern Health Board (chairman 1986/87); General Council of County Councils.

Member, Gaelic Athletic Association.

He is a son of Bob Aylward, Senator, Agricultural Panel, 1973 until his death in July 1974, and a Dáil candidate in Carlow-Kilkenny constituency in the general elections of 1965, 1969 and 1973.

Philip Hogan (FG)

Home Address
25 The Sycamores, Kilkenny
Business Address
Church Street, Freshford, Co Kilkenny
Telephone
Constituency Office (056) 32318;
Fax (056) 32220
Birth Place/Date
Kilkenny. July 1960
Married
Kathleen Murphy. 1 son
Education
St Joseph's College, Freshford; St Kieran's College, Kilkenny; University College, Cork (BA, HDipEd)
Occupation
Public representative; auctioneer

Phil Hogan was Minister of State at the Department of Finance, with special responsibility for Public Expenditure and the Office of Public Works, December 1994-February 1995, when he resigned. He was first elected to the Dáil in 1989. Fine Gael front bench spokesperson on Regional Affairs and European Development 1993-94. Spokesperson on Consumer Affairs 1991-93, on the Food Industry 1989-91.

Chairman, Fine Gael Parliamentary Party since 1995.

He was a Senator, Industrial and Commercial Panel 1987-89. Fine Gael Opposition spokesperson on Justice in the Seanad 1987-88; Industry and Commerce 1988-89.

Contested Dáil general election in 1987.

Member of Kilkenny County Council since 1982 (chairman 1985/86); South-Eastern Health Board since 1991.

Member, Gaelic Athletic Association; Kilkenny Archaeological Society; Castlecomer Golf Club.

John Browne (FG)

Home Address
Ballinacarrig, Carlow
Telephone
Home (0503) 33033
Birth Place/Date
Kilmihil, Co Clare. October 1936
Married
Nancy Looney. 1 son, 3 daughters
Education
St Flannan's College, Ennis, Co Clare; St Patrick's Teacher Training College, Drumcondra, Dublin; University College, Galway; St Patrick's College, Maynooth (NT, BA, HDipEd, Dipl Soc & Econ Sci)
Occupation
Full-time public representative. Formerly teacher

John Browne was first elected to the Dáil in 1989. Fine Gael spokesperson on Justice and Health (including Care of the Aged) 1993-94. Vice-Chairman, Fine Gael Parliamentary Party 1993-94. Fine Gael Group Leader, Dáil Select Committee on Legislation and Security 1993-94 and Government Convener 1994-97. Member, European Affairs Committee and of Comhchoiste don Ghaeilge 1993-97. Senator, Taoiseach's Nominee 1983-87. Fine Gael Seanad spokesman on Communications 1983-87.

Member of Carlow County Council since 1979 (chairman 1986/87); Carlow ACOT; South-Eastern Health Board 1984-89; Carlow County Library Committee 1979-85.

Former chairman, North Carlow Branch, Irish National Teachers' Organisation.

Former Chairman and secretary, Bord na nÓg and former chairman, BLOE.

John McGuinness (FF)

Home Address
Windsmoor, Brooklawn, Ballyfoyle Road, Kilkenny
Constituency Office
O'Loughlin Road, Kilkenny
Business Address
Fastmac Express Delivery Service, Unit 21, Hebron Industrial Estate, Hebron Road, Kilkenny
Telephone
Fax (056) 70674; *Constituency Office* (056) 70672/73; *Fax* (056) 62706
Birth Place/Date
Kilkenny. March 1955
Married
Margaret Redmond. 3 sons, 1 daughter
Education
Kilkenny CBS (Diploma in Business Management)
Occupation
Full-time public representative. Transport company director

John McGuinness is a new Dáil deputy. This was the first time he contested a general election.

Member, Kilkenny Corporation since 1979 (Mayor of Kilkenny 1996/97, the third generation of his family to serve as Mayor of the borough). Member, Kilkenny County Council since 1991; Kilkenny Enterprise Board; Kilkenny Chamber of Commerce and Industry; Kilkenny Tourism Council; Kilkenny Third-Level Education Committee; Watergate Theatre Board; Association of Municipal Authorities of Ireland.

Séamus Pattison (Lab)

Home Address
6 Upper New Street, Kilkenny
Business Address
Leinster House, Dublin 2
Telephone
Home (056) 21295; *Business* (01) 618 4343
Birth Place/Date
Kilkenny. April 1936
Education
St Kieran's College, Kilkenny; University College, Dublin, extra-mural (Diploma in Social and Economic Science)
Occupation
Ceann Comhairle of Dáil Éireann. Formerly trade union official

Séamus Pattison was unanimously elected Ceann Comhairle at the first meeting of the 28th Dáil in June 1997. He was Minister of State at the Department of Social Welfare December 1983-January 1987. He has been a deputy for Carlow-Kilkenny since 1961 and is now Father of the House. He was a member of the European Parliament 1981-83. He was chairman, Select Committee on Social Affairs 1993-97. Member, British-Irish Parliamentary Body 1993-97.

Member, British-Irish Parliamentary Body 1991-97; Council of Europe 1989-90. Former Labour spokesperson on Justice 1991-92, on Energy and Forestry 1989-91, on Defence and Marine Affairs, 1987. He was Labour spokesman on Lands 1972-73, on Justice 1967-72 and on Education 1963-67. Panel of Temporary Chairmen of the Dáil 1973-77 and 1987-97.

Alderman, Kilkenny Corporation 1964-97 and Mayor of Kilkenny 1967/68, 1976/77 and 1992/93. Member, Kilkenny County Council 1964-97 (chairman 1975/76 and 1980/81); Kilkenny Vocational Education Committee 1964-97.

Member, Irish Transport and General Workers' Union (now SIPTU) since 1956.

He is the son of James P. Pattison, Dáil deputy 1932-51 and 1954-57.

Nuala O'Faolain, John Waters,
Fintan O'Toole, Mary Holland,
Vincent Browne, Dick Walsh
Garret FitzGerald, Máire Geoghegan-Quinn,
Kevin Myers and Martyn Turner.

(Whether you like them or not.)

Opinions you can't ignore. Every day in The Irish Times.

THE IRISH TIMES

FOR THE TIMES WE LIVE IN
http://www.irish-times.com

Seats 5
Quota 9,925

	1st Count	2nd Count Transfer of Ó Caoláin's Surplus	3rd Count Transfer of Duffy's Votes	4th Count Transfer of McGinn's and Flood's Votes	5th Count Transfer of Gallagher's Votes	6th Count Transfer of O'Reilly's Votes	7th Count Transfer of Cotter's Votes
*BOYLAN, Andrew (FG)	4,894	+62 4,956	+7 4,963	+177 5,140	+366 5,506	+2,692 8,198	+1,508 9,706
COTTER, Bill (FG)	4,665	+109 4,774	+5 4,779	+141 4,920	+476 5,396	+461 5,857	−5,857 —
*CRAWFORD, Seymour (FG)	6,552	+99 6,651	+9 6,660	+136 6,796	+377 7,173	+627 7,800	+2,488 10,288
DUFFY, Joseph (Ind)	99	+35 134	−134 —				
FLOOD, Gene (CSP)	1,024	+127 1,151	+30 1,181	−1,181 —			
GALLAGHER, Ann (Lab)	2,359	+176 2,535	+22 2,557	+178 2,735	−2,735 —		
LEONARD, Ann (FF)	6,564	+317 6,881	+17 6,898	+361 7,259	+379 7,638	+148 7,786	+395 8,181
McGINN, Larry (CSP)	1,001	+61 1,062	+18 1,080	−1,080 —			
Ó CAOLÁIN, Caoimhghín (SF)	11,531	−1,606 9,925					
*O'HANLON, Rory (FF)	7,325	+367 7,692	+8 7,700	+320 8,020	+374 8,394	+221 8,615	+936 9,551
O'REILLY, Paddy (FG)	4,532	+57 4,589	+4 4,593	+206 4,799	+331 5,130	−5,130 —	
*SMITH, Brendan (FF)	8,998	+196 9,194	+2 9,196	+355 9,551	+182 9,733	+701 10,434	— —
NON-TRANSFERABLE		—	12	387	250	280	530

Cavan-Monaghan

Elected

Caoimhghín Ó Caoláin (SF)	1st Count
Brendan Smith (FF)*	6th Count
Seymour Crawford (FG)*	7th Count
Andrew Boylan (FG)*	7th Count
Rory O'Hanlon (FF)*	7th Count

Voting by Party

1st Preference	Number	%	% 1992
Fianna Fáil	22,887	38.44	44.26
Fine Gael	20,643	34.67	34.96
Labour	2,359	3.96	8.28
Sinn Féin	11,531	19.37	7.65
Christian Solidarity	2,025	3.40	—
Workers' Party	—	—	0.29
Others	99	0.17	4.57

Statistics

Population	104,089	
Electorate	83,005	
Total Poll	60,145	72.46
Spoiled Votes	601	1.00
Valid Poll	59,544	71.74
Seats	5	
Quota	9,925	
Candidates	12	

Seats

FF	2
FG	2
SF	1
SF gain from FF	

The constituency of Cavan-Monaghan is unchanged since the 1992 General Election.

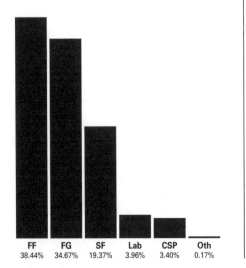

FF	FG	SF	Lab	CSP	Oth
38.44%	34.67%	19.37%	3.96%	3.40%	0.17%

Caoimhghín Ó Caoláin (SF)

Home Address
Mullaghdun, Monaghan
Constituency Office
21 Dublin Street, Monaghan
Telephone
Constituency Office (047) 82917; *Fax* (047) 71849
Birth Place/Date
Monaghan. September 1953
Married
Briege McGinn. 4 daughters
Education
St Mary's CBS, Monaghan
Occupation
Full-time public representative. Formerly bank official

Caoimhghín Ó Caoláin is a new Dáil deputy and is the first Sinn Féin deputy elected since the party abandoned its abstentionist policy. He was a candidate in the general elections of 1987, 1989 and 1992.

Member of Monaghan County Council since 1985 and of Monaghan Urban District Council since 1994. Member, County Monaghan Vocational Education Committee 1985-91.

Member, Sinn Féin Ardchomhairle since 1983; Sinn Féin delegation to the Forum for Peace and Reconciliation; Sinn Féin delegation in direct talks with British Government representatives.

Brendan Smith (FF)

Home Address
3 Carrickfern, Cavan
Telephone
Home (049) 62366; *Fax* (049) 62367; *Business* (01) 618 4400
Birth Place/Date
Cavan. June 1956
Married
Anne McGarry
Education
St Camillus' College, Killucan, Co Westmeath; University College, Dublin (BA)
Occupation
Full-time public representative. Former adviser to Government Minister

Brendan Smith has been a Dáil deputy since 1992. That general election was the first time he ran for public office at any level. Member, British-Irish Parliamentary Body.

He served as adviser to the former Tánaiste John P. Wilson over a period of 15 years during which time Deputy Wilson was Minister for Education, Transport, Posts and Telegraphs, Communications, Tourism and Transport, Marine, Defence and the Gaeltacht.

Member, Co Cavan VEC; Templeport Gaelic Football Club; Cavan GAA Supporters' Club; Cavan Drama Festival; Cumann Seanchais Bhréifne.

Seymour Crawford (FG)

Home Address
Drumkeen, Aghabog, Co Monaghan
Telephone
Home (047) 54038; *Mobile* (088) 254 4886;
Fax (047) 54414
Birth Place/Date
Monaghan. June 1944
Education
Clones High School, Co Monaghan
Occupation
Public representative. Farmer

Seymour Crawford has been a Dáil deputy since 1992. Fine Gael spokesperson on Food and Horticulture 1993-94 and on Food, Horticulture and Disadvantaged Areas 1994.

Member, Monaghan County Council since June 1991 and of subsidiary committees. Member, British-Irish Parliamentary Body 1993-97.

Member, Irish Farmers' Association since 1965 and representative for Co Monaghan on National Council 1965-79, chairman of National Livestock Committee 1979-84, vice-president Ulster/North Leinster 1984-88. He represented the Livestock Committee on COPA in Brussels 1979-86 and chairman of EC Beef and Veal Advisory Committee 1981-86.

Board member of CBF (Irish Livestock and Meat Board) 1979-86. Chairman, Aghabog Buddy Bear Trust and board member of Dungannon Buddy Bear Trust.

Received Bastow Award for service in meat and livestock matters in 1986.

Andrew Boylan (FG)

Home Address
Derrygarra, Butlersbridge, Co Cavan
Constituency Office
11 Rossa Place, Coleman Road, Cavan
Telephone
Home (049) 31747; *Office* (049) 32279; *Fax* (049) 61021
Birth Place/Date
Butlersbridge. January 1939
Married
Margo Galligan. 4 sons, 1 daughter
Education
Rockwell College, Cashel, Co Tipperary
Occupation
Public representative. Farmer

Andrew Boylan has been a Dáil deputy since 1987. Fine Gael spokesperson on Environmental Protection 1993-94 and Social Welfare 1994. Assistant Chief Whip Fine Gael 1988-93.

Convenor, Oireachtas Joint Committee on European Affairs 1994-97. Member, New Ireland Forum.

Member, Cavan County Council since 1974 (chairman 1984/85 and 1991/92); Cavan Urban District Council. He has served on the General Council of County Councils; General Council of Committees of Agriculture; North-West Regional Review Committee.

Chairman of Parents' Committee, Cavan Vocational School.

Rory O'Hanlon (FF)

Home Address
Mullinarry, Carrickmacross, Co Monaghan
Business Address
Dáil Éireann, Leinster House, Dublin 2
Telephone
Home (042) 61530; *Fax* (041) 63220;
Business (01) 618 3570; *Fax* (01) 618 4111
Birth Place/Date
Dublin. February 1934
Married
Teresa Ward. 4 sons, 2 daughters
Education
St Mary's College, Dundalk, Co Louth;
Blackrock College, Dublin; University College, Dublin (MB, BCh, BAO, DCh, LM)
Occupation
Leas-Cheann Comhairle. Formerly medical practitioner

Dr Rory O'Hanlon was elected Leas-Cheann Comhairle of Dáil Eireann in July 1997. He was Minister for the Environment November 1991-February 1992; Minister for Health 1987-November 1991; Minister of State, Department of Health and Social Welfare, October-December 1982. He was first elected to the Dáil for Cavan-Monaghan in 1977. He contested a by-election in the then constituency of Monaghan in 1973. Fianna Fáil spokesman on Health 1983-87.

Chairman, Fianna Fáil Parliamentary Party since 1995.

Member, Oireachtas Joint Committee on Foreign Affairs. Member, British-Irish Parliamentary Body since 1992. He served as a member of the Oireachtas Joint Committee on Marriage Breakdown and the Oireachtas Joint Committee on Women's Rights. Member, New Ireland Forum. Former chairman of Cross-Border Development Committee, Eastern Region.

Member of Monaghan County Council 1979-87.

Medical representative on the North-Eastern Health Board from its inception in 1970 to 1987.

Clare

Seats 4 Quota 9,378	1st Count	2nd Count Transfer of **Aston's** and **McInerney's** Votes	3rd Count Transfer of **Makowski's** Votes	4th Count Transfer of **O'Connor's** Votes
ASTON, Joe (CSP)	499	−499 —		
*CAREY, Donal (FG)	7,781	+76 7,857	+110 7,967	+154 8,121
DALY, Brendan (FF)	7,420	+91 7,511	+55 7,566	+95 7,661
*de VALERA, Síle (FF)	8,025	+79 8,104	+113 8,217	+186 8,403
*KILLEEN, Tony (FF)	8,169	+88 8,257	+120 8,377	+150 8,527
McINERNEY, Michael (Ind)	234	−234 —		
MAKOWSKI, Brigid (Ind)	944	+38 982	−982 —	
MANNION, Mary (PD)	3,250	+30 3,280	+60 3,340	+105 3,445
MEANEY, Brian (GP)	1,682	+67 1,749	+151 1,900	+133 2,033
O'CONNOR, Rita (NP)	876	+149 1,025	+120 1,145	−1,145 —
TAYLOR-QUINN, Madeleine (FG)	6,325	+77 6,402	+70 6,472	+95 6,567
TWIST, Brídín (Lab)	1,684	+26 1,710	+99 1,809	+73 1,882
NON-TRANSFERABLE		12	84	154

5th Count	6th Count	7th Count	8th Count	9th Count
Transfer of **Twist's** Votes	Transfer of **Meaney's** Votes	Transfer of **Mannion's** Votes	Transfer of **Killeen's** Surplus	Transfer of **de Valera's** Surplus
+543 8,664	+414 9,078	+555 9,633	— —	— —
+70 7,731	+107 7,838	+530 8,368	+422 8,790	+252 9,042
+128 8,531	+292 8,823	+886 9,709	— —	−331 9,378
+115 8,642	+260 8,902	+1,035 9,937	−559 9,378	
+86 3,531	+298 3,829	−3,829 —		
+246 2,279	−2,279 —			
+633 7,200	+455 7,655	+505 8,160	+137 8,297	+79 8,376
−1,882 —				
61	453	318	—	—

Clare

Elected

Tony Killeen (FF)*   7th Count
Síle de Valera (FF)*   7th Count
Donal Carey (FG)*   7th Count
Brendan Daly (FF)   9th Count

Voting by Party

1st Preference	Number	%	% 1992
Fianna Fáil	23,614	50.36	51.76
Fine Gael	14,106	30.08	25.65
Labour	1,684	3.59	11.46
Prog Democrats	3,250	6.93	6.98
Green Party	1,682	3.59	—
Sinn Féin	—	—	1.03
National Party	876	1.87	—
Christian Solidarity	499	1.06	—
Others	1,178	2.51	3.13

Statistics

Population	88,074	
Electorate	71,491	
Total Poll	47,366	66.25
Spoiled Votes	477	1.01
Valid Poll	46,889	65.59
Seats	4	
Quota	9,378	
Candidates	12	

Seats

FF	3
FG	1

FF gain from Lab

The constituency of Clare is unchanged since the 1992 General Election.

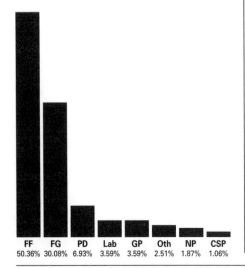

FF	FG	PD	Lab	GP	Oth	NP	CSP
50.36%	30.08%	6.93%	3.59%	3.59%	2.51%	1.87%	1.06%

Tony Killeen (FF)

Home Address
Kilnaboy, Corofin, Co Clare
Constituency Office
Upper Market Street, Ennis, Co Clare
Telephone
Office (065) 41500; *Fax* (065) 41514
Birth Place/Date
Clare. June 1952
Married
Lily O'Keeffe. 5 sons
Education
St Flannan's College, Ennis; Mary Immaculate College of Education, Limerick
Occupation
Full-time public representative. Formerly national school teacher

Tony Killeen has been a Dáil deputy since 1992. Fianna Fáil deputy spokesperson on Tourism 1995-97.

Member, Clare County Council 1985-97 (vice-chairman 1987-89 and chairman 1989-91). Member, County Clare Vocational Education Committee 1979-94 (chairman 1991-94).

Former member, Management Boards of Killaloe and Shannon Community Schools and Limerick Regional Technical College.

Founder member, Shannon Status Committee and chairman 1989-91.

Member, GAA; Macra na Feirme; IFA; INTO; Conradh na Gaeilge and other community and cultural organisations.

Former national chairman of Fianna Fáil Councillors' Association.

Síle de Valera (FF)

Home Address
6 Riverdale, Tulla Road, Ennis, Co Clare
Constituency Office
9 Chapel Lane, Ennis, Co Clare
Business Address
Department of Arts, Heritage, Gaeltacht and the Islands, Mespil Road, Dublin 4
Telephone
(01) 667 0788/667 0805; (065) 21100/40208; *Fax* (01) 667 0827, (065) 40695
Birth Place/Date
Dublin. December 1954
Education
Loreto Convent, Foxrock, Co Dublin; University College, Dublin (BA, HDipEd, Dip Career Guidance, D Psych Sci)
Occupation
Government Minister

Síle de Valera was appointed Minister for Arts, Heritage, Gaeltacht and the Islands in June 1997. She was Fianna Fáil front bench spokesperson on Arts, Culture and Heritage 1995-97.

She has been a Dáil deputy for Clare since 1987. She was previously a Dáil deputy 1977-81 for the then constituency of Dublin Mid-County and was at that time the youngest member of the Dáil. She contested the constituency of Dublin South in 1981 and February 1982, and the constituency of Clare in November 1982.

Member, European Parliament 1979-84 and of the Parliament's Committees for Social Affairs and Employment, Youth Education and Sport, and the Ad Hoc Women's Committee.

She is a granddaughter of Éamon de Valera, President of Ireland 1959-73; Taoiseach 1937-48, 1951-54, 1957-59; President of the Executive Council of the Irish Free State 1932-37; President, first Dáil 1919-21; President, second Dáil, 1921-January 1922.

Donal Carey (FG)

Home Address
3 Thomond Villas, Clarecastle, Co Clare
Business Address
Friary Bow, Abbey Street, Ennis, Co Clare
Telephones
Home (065) 29191; *Business* (065) 29683
Birth Place/Date
Ennis. October 1937
Married
Evelyn Ford (deceased). 2 sons, 1 daughter
Education
St Flannan's College, Ennis; University
College, Dublin (BComm)
Occupation
Full-time public representative. Formerly cost
controller

Donal Carey was Minister of State at the
Department of the Taoiseach and the
Department of Arts, Culture and the Gaeltacht
with special responsibility for Western
Development, the Gaeltacht, and Rural
Renewal, 1995-97.

He has been a Dáil deputy since the general
election of February 1982. He was a Fine Gael
candidate in the Clare constituency in the
1981 general election. Member, Seanad
Éireann 1981-February 1982, Labour Panel.
Spokesperson on the Islands, Gaeltacht and
Western Development since 1997. Member,
Fine Gael front bench 1992-94. Chairman,
Fine Gael National Executive 1991-93 and
Director of Organisation 1994-97. Fine Gael
spokesperson on Local Government Reform
1991-92; on Forestry, 1987-91.

Member, Clare County Council 1974-95.

Member, Ennis and District Round Table;
Muintir na Tíre.

Member, Gaelic Athletic Association and
former officer of Clare County Board.

Brendan Daly (FF)

Address
Cooraclare, Kilrush, Co Clare
Telephone
Home (065) 59040
Birth Place/Date
Cooraclare. February 1940
Married
Patricia Carmody. 2 sons, 1 daughter
Education
Kilrush Christian Brothers' School
Occupation
Full-time public representative

Brendan Daly was previously a Dáil deputy
1973-92. Senator 1993-97, Agricultural Panel.

He has served as Minister for Social Welfare,
Minister for Defence, Minister for the Marine,
Minister for Fisheries and Forestry, Minister
of State at the Departments of the Taoiseach
(Heritage Affairs), Finance (Office of Public
Works), Foreign Affairs (Overseas Aid),
Labour.

As first Minister for the Marine, he was
responsible for setting up Roinn na Mara,
establishing a new administrative structure
for dealing with maritime affairs.

Michael Moynihan, a winner for Fianna Fáil in Cork North-West in his first general election, arrives at the gates of Leinster House with his delighted supporters.

Seats 4
Quota 8,616

	1st Count	2nd Count Transfer of **O'Connor's** Votes	3rd Count Transfer of **O'Keeffe's** Surplus	4th Count Transfer of **McCarthy's** Votes	5th Count Transfer of **Scannell's** Votes	6th Count Transfer of **Flavin's** Votes	7th Count Transfer of **Ahern's** Surplus	8th Count Transfer of **Mulvihill's** Votes
*AHERN, Michael (FF)	6,959	+241 7,200	+74 7,274	+391 7,665	+472 8,137	+1,158 9,295	−679 8,616	
*BRADFORD, Paul (FG)	7,859	+48 7,907	+15 7,922	+87 8,009	+293 8,302	+236 8,538	+195 8,733	— —
FLAVIN, J.J. (PD)	1,830	+42 1,872	+6 1,878	+168 2,046	+196 2,242	−2,242 —		
McCARTHY, Kieran (SF)	1,534	+177 1,711	+2 1,713	−1,713 —				
*MULVIHILL, John (Lab)	3,500	+469 3,969	+1 3,970	+328 4,298	+121 4,419	+141 4,560	+109 4,669	−4,669 —
O'CONNOR, Seán (Ind)	1,281	−1,281 —						
*O'KEEFFE, Ned (FF)	8,737	— —	−121 8,616					
SCANNELL, Mairéad (NP)	1,637	+117 1,754	+3 1,757	+155 1,912	−1,912 —			
SHERLOCK, Joe (DL)	4,622	+59 4,681	+17 4,698	+223 4,921	+265 5,186	+171 5,357	+153 5,510	+1,462 6,972
STANTON, David (FG)	5,117	+65 5,182	+3 5,185	+130 5,315	+212 5,527	+293 5,820	+178 5,998	+1,737 7,735
NON-TRANSFERABLE		63	—	231	353	243	44	1,470

Cork East

Elected

Ned O'Keeffe (FF)*	1st Count
Michael Ahern (FF)*	6th Count
Paul Bradford (FG)*	7th Count
David Stanton (FG)	8th Count

Voting by Party

1st Preference	Number	%	% 1992
Fianna Fáil	15,696	36.44	38.08
Fine Gael	12,976	30.12	33.52
Labour	3,500	8.13	13.75
Prog Democrats	1,830	4.25	—
Sinn Féin	1,534	3.56	0.88
Democratic Left	4,622	10.73	12.90
Workers' Party	—	—	0.37
Others	2,918	6.77	0.51

Statistics

Population	80,369	
Electorate	63,653	
Total Poll	43,407	68.19
Spoiled Votes	331	0.76
Valid Poll	43,076	67.67
Seats	4	
Quota	8,616	
Candidates	10	

Seats

FF	2
FG	2

FG gain from Lab

The constituency of Cork East is unchanged since the 1992 General Election.

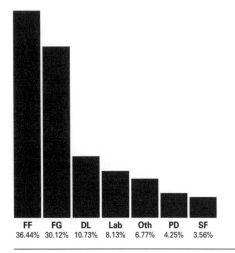

FF	FG	DL	Lab	Oth	PD	SF
36.44%	30.12%	10.73%	8.13%	6.77%	4.25%	3.56%

Ned O'Keeffe (FF)

Home Address
Ballylough, Mitchelstown, Co Cork
Business Address
Department of Agriculture and Food, Kildare Street, Dublin 2
Telephone
Home (022) 25285; *Business* (01) 662 9211/ 607 2000/607 2291, *Fax* (022) 25495, (01) 662 2170
Birth Place/Date
Ballylough, Mitchelstown. August 1942
Married
Ann Buckley. 3 sons, 2 daughters
Education
Darra College, Clonakilty, Co Cork; University College, Cork (Diploma in Social and Rural Science)
Occupation
Minister of State. Formerly company director, farmer

Ned O'Keeffe was appointed Minister of State at the Department of Agriculture and Food, with special responsibility for Food, in July 1997.

He was first elected to the Dáil in November 1982. He was a Senator, Taoiseach's nominee, May-November 1992.

Fianna Fáil spokesperson on Industry 1982-87. Deputy spokesperson on Enterprise and Employment with responsibility for Commerce, Science and Technology and Small Businesses 1994-97.

Member, Cork County Council 1985-97. Chairman, Northern Committee 1985/86; member, Library Committee.

He has served as member, Regional Council and Council of Dairygold Co-operative Society.

Director, Mitchelstown Co-operative Society 1974-82; director, Agricultural Credit Corporation 1980-82. Member, ICOS 1978-81.

Member, Macra na Feirme 1958-71; Irish Farmers' Association 1969-82; chairman, Cork County Executive 1979-82. Member, Gaelic Athletic Association.

Michael Ahern (FF)

Home Address
Libermann, Barryscourt, Carrigtwohill, Co Cork
Telephone
Home (021) 883592; *Fax* (021) 883436
Birth Place/Date
Dungourney, Co Cork. January 1949
Married
Margaret Monahan. 3 daughters
Education
Rockwell College, Cashel, Co Tipperary; University College, Dublin (BA)
Occupation
Public representative. Registered auditor and accountant.

Michael Ahern was Minister of State at the Department of Industry and Commerce, with special responsibility for Science and Technology 1992-93. He was first elected to the Dáil in February 1982. Fianna Fáil deputy spokesperson on Transport 1984-87. Spokesperson on the Office of Public Works and Taxation Policy 1995-97.

Member, Finance and General Affairs Committee 1993-97; Joint Committee on State-Sponsored Bodies 1993-94.

Member, Carrigtwohill Community Council; Dungourney Hurling Club; Midleton Gaelic Football Club; Midleton Rugby Football Club; Muintir na Tíre.

Michael Ahern is a son of the late Liam Ahern, Senator 1957-73 and Dáil deputy for Cork North-East 1973-74.

His grand-uncle, John Dineen, was Farmers' Party Dáil deputy 1922-27.

Paul Bradford (FG)

Home Address
Mourne Abbey, Mallow, Co Cork
Telephone
Home (022) 29375; *Business* (022) 42181
Birth Place/Date
Mallow. December 1963
Education
Patrician Academy, Mallow
Occupation
Full-time public representative. Farmer.

Paul Bradford has been a Dáil Deputy since 1989. Spokesperson on Health - Food Safety and Older People since 1997. Front bench spokesperson on Defence and Marine 1994. Special assistant to Fine Gael party leader on Northern Ireland with special responsibility for developing contacts with Northern Ireland political parties 1994. Joint chairperson, British-Irish Interparliamentary Body 1994-97. Fine Gael spokesperson on Poverty, Integration of Tax and Social Welfare Codes (also dealing with Problems of Persons with a Disability), 1993-94. Spokesperson on Food and Horticulture, 1991-93; on Science and Technology 1989-91.

Senator, Agricultural Panel, 1987-89; he was the youngest ever elected senator. He contested the Dáil general election in 1987 in Cork East.

Fine Gael Opposition spokesperson in Seanad on Communications and Energy 1987-89.

Member, Cork County Council since 1985; Cork County Committee of Agriculture 1985-88; Cork Vocational Education Committee since 1990.

He was the youngest ever member of Cork County Council when elected in June 1985 at the age of 21.

David Stanton (FG)

Home Address
Coppingerstown, Midleton, Co Cork
Telephone
Home (021) 632867; *Fax* (021) 632867
Birth Place/Date
Cork. February 1957
Married
Mary Lehane. 4 sons
Education
St Colman's Vocational School, Midleton; Sharman Crawford Technical Institute, Cork; University College, Cork (BA, MEd, Diploma in Career Guidance, Diploma in Educational Administration)
Occupation
Full-time public representative. Formerly teacher, career guidance counsellor

David Stanton is a new Dáil deputy. This was the first general election he contested. He won a seat held since 1992 by John Mulvihill for Labour, and before that by Joe Sherlock for the Workers' Party. Fine Gael spokesperson on Labour Affairs, Consumer Rights and Trade since 1997.

Formerly a commissioned officer in An Fórsa Cosanta Áitiúil. Director and Public Relations Officer, Midleton and District Day Care Centre.

Cork North-Central

Seats 5 Quota 7,335	1st Count	2nd Count Transfer of **Allen's** Surplus	3rd Count Transfer of **Homan's** Votes	4th Count Transfer of **Mullins's** Votes	5th Count Transfer of **Mulcahy's** Votes
*ALLEN, Bernard (FG)	7,746	−411 7,335			
*BURKE, Liam (FG)	5,527	+234 5,761	+55 5,816	+87 5,903	+84 5,987
HOMAN, Jimmy (WP)	545	+7 552	−552 —		
KELLEHER, Billy (FF)	5,419	+15 5,434	+17 5,451	+55 5,506	+52 5,558
*LYNCH, Kathleen (DL)	3,146	+48 3,194	+89 3,283	+22 3,305	+162 3,467
MULCAHY, Paddy (Ind)	899	+6 905	+68 973	+45 1,018	−1,018 —
MULLINS, Eddie (CSP)	777	+2 779	+13 792	−792 —	
O'FLYNN, Noel (FF)	4,943	+18 4,961	+33 4,994	+46 5,040	+82 5,122
O'LEARY, Con (NP)	1,114	+9 1,123	+46 1,169	+231 1,400	+119 1,519
O'LEARY, Don (SF)	1,654	+5 1,659	+78 1,737	+17 1,754	+129 1,883
O'SULLIVAN, Sheila (Lab)	2,321	+25 2,346	+29 2,375	+14 2,389	+69 2,458
POWER, Jane (GP)	1,340	+5 1,345	+33 1,378	+57 1,435	+139 1,574
*QUILL, Máirín (PD)	3,304	+17 3,321	+9 3,330	+67 3,397	+55 3,452
*WALLACE, Dan (FF)	5,273	+20 5,293	+49 5,342	+120 5,462	+66 5,528
NON-TRANSFERABLE		—	33	31	61

6th Count	7th Count	8th Count	9th Count	10th Count	11th Count
Transfer of **O'Leary's** (Con) Votes	Transfer of **Power's** Votes	Transfer of **O'Leary's** (Don) Votes	Transfer of **O'Sullivan's** Votes	Transfer of **Quill's** Votes	Transfer of **Wallace's** Surplus
+166 / 6,153	+209 / 6,362	+186 / 6,548	+996 / 7,544	— / —	— / —
+89 / 5,647	+101 / 5,748	+246 / 5,994	+198 / 6,192	+1,009 / 7,201	+116 / 7,317
+169 / 3,636	+369 / 4,005	+331 / 4,336	+996 / 5,332	+538 / 5,870	+25 / 5,895
+136 / 5,258	+50 / 5,308	+228 / 5,536	+124 / 5,660	+708 / 6,368	+107 / 6,475
−1,519 / —					
+140 / 2,023	+162 / 2,185	−2,185 / —			
+81 / 2,539	+274 / 2,813	+209 / 3,022	−3,022 / —		
+185 / 1,759	−1,759 / —				
+101 / 3,553	+196 / 3,749	+116 / 3,865	+178 / 4,043	−4,043 / —	
+264 / 5,792	+145 / 5,937	+298 / 6,235	+159 / 6,394	+1,189 / 7,583	−248 / 7,335
188	253	571	371	599	—

Cork North-Central

Elected

Bernard Allen (FG)*	1st Count
Liam Burke (FG)*	9th Count
Dan Wallace (FF)*	10th Count
Billy Kelleher (FF)	11th Count
Noel O'Flynn (FF)	11th Count

Voting by Party

1st Preference	Number	%	% 1992
Fianna Fáil	15,635	35.53	28.26
Fine Gael	13,273	30.16	22.74
Labour	2,321	5.27	22.29
Prog Democrats	3,304	7.51	11.56
Green Party	1,340	3.04	1.82
Sinn Féin	1,654	3.76	1.38
Democratic Left	3,146	7.15	4.00
National Party	1,114	2.53	—
Christian Solidarity	777	1.77	—
Workers' Party	545	1.24	2.64
Others	899	2.04	5.31

Statistics

Population	100,829	
Electorate	71,873	
Total Poll	44,416	61.80
Spoiled Votes	408	0.92
Valid Poll	44,008	61.23
Seats	5	
Quota	7,335	
Candidates	14	

Seats

FF	3
FG	2

FF gains from PD and DL

The constituency of Cork North-Central is unchanged since the 1992 General Election.

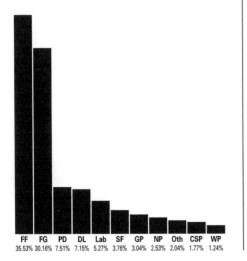

FF	FG	PD	DL	Lab	SF	GP	NP	Oth	CSP	WP
35.53%	30.16%	7.51%	7.15%	5.27%	3.76%	3.04%	2.53%	2.04%	1.77%	1.24%

Bernard Allen (FG)

Home Address
Mount Prospect, Shanakiel, Cork
Telephone
Home (021) 303068
Birth Place/Date
Cork. September 1944
Married
Marie Dorney. 3 daughters
Education
North Monastery CBS, Cork; Cork Regional Technical College; University College, Cork (Diploma in Chemical Technology)
Occupation
Full-time public representative. Formerly laboratory technologist

Bernard Allen was Minister of State at the Department of Education, with special responsibility for Youth and Sport, 1994-97; Minister of State at the Department of the Environment, with special responsibility for Local Government Reform and Urban Traffic Management, 1994-97.

He was first elected to the Dáil in June 1981. Fine Gael front bench spokesperson on Tourism, Sport and Recreation since 1997; on Social Welfare 1993-94; on Health 1987-88; spokesperson on Environmental Protection 1982.

Alderman, Cork City Council 1979-95 (Lord Mayor, 1988/89); Southern Health Board 1982-95. Former chairman, Southern Health Advisory Board. He also served on the Board of Management, North Infirmary, Cork.

Member, Pitch and Putt Union of Ireland; Bol-Chumann na hÉireann; Golfing Union of Ireland.

Liam Burke (FG)

Home Address
The Grove, Douglas Hall, Cork
Business Address
Constituents' Advice Centre, 9 Lavitt's Quay, Cork
Telephone
Business (021) 276116; *Mobile* (087) 241 4860; *Fax* (021) 276117
Birth Place/Date
Cork. February 1928
Married
Noreen Casey. 2 daughters
Education
Christian Brothers' College, Cork (DLitt [*hon. causa*], University College, Cork)
Occupation
Full-time public representative. Formerly garage proprietor, auctioneer

Liam Burke was first elected to the Dáil, for Cork City North-West, in 1969 and represented the constituency until 1977. He was an unsuccessful candidate in the 1977 general election in the newly formed Cork City constituency but regained a Dáil seat in a by-election in the same constituency in November 1979. Dáil deputy Cork North-Central 1981-89 when he was an unsuccessful candidate in the general election. He regained his seat in the general election of 1992. He was a Senator, Administrative Panel, 1977-79 and Taoiseach's Nominee, June-July 1977.

Member, Cork City Council since 1967 (Lord Mayor 1984/85); City of Cork Vocational Education Committee. He served on Cork Health Authority; Southern Health Board; Board of Management, South Infirmary, Cork (former chairman); South-West Regional Development Authority.

Member, Na Piarsaigh Hurling and Football Club, Cork. Greyhound owner and breeder.

He is a nephew of the late Tadhg Manley, Fine Gael deputy for Cork South 1954-61.

Dan Wallace (FF)

Home Address
13 Killeens Place, Farranree, Cork
Business Address
Department of the Environment and Local Government, Custom House, Dublin 1
Telephone
Home (021) 307465; *Business* (01) 679 3377; *Fax* (01) 671 3630, (021) 279107
Birth Place/Date
Cork. June 1942
Married
Ethel Sutton. 2 sons, 3 daughters
Education
North Presentation Convent, Cork; North Monastery CBS, Cork; College of Commerce, Cork
Occupation
Minister of State. Formerly customs clerk with Henry Ford Ltd

Dan Wallace was appointed Minister of State at the Department of the Environment and Local Government with special responsibility for Environment Information and Awareness and the Environmental Protection Agency, in July 1997. He was Minister of State at the Department of the Environment, with special responsibility for Urban Renewal, February 1992-January 1993. He has been a Dáil Deputy since November 1982.

Chariman, Select Committee on Legislation and Security 1993-95. He has served on the Women's Rights Committee; Oireachtas Joint Committee on the Secondary Legislation of the European Communities; Committee on Crime, Lawlessness and Vandalism; Select Committee on Finance and General Affairs.

Member, Cork City Council 1979-92 (Alderman 1985-92 and Lord Mayor 1985/86). He has served on the Corporation's Housing (former chairman), Environment, Community Development, Travellers, Finance and Planning, Roads, Transportation and Safety Committees. Former member, Southern Health Board.

Billy Kelleher (FF)

Home Address
Ballyphilip, White's Cross, Glanmire, Co Cork
Constituency Office
28 Ballyhoolley Road, Dillons Cross, Cork
Telephone
Home (021) 821045; *Constituency Office* (021) 502289; *Mobile* (087) 258 0521; *Fax* (021) 502356
Birth Place/Date
Cork. January 1968
Education
Sacred Heart College, Carignavar, Co Cork; Agricultural College, Limerick
Occupation
Full-time public representative. Farmer

Billy Kelleher is a new Dáil deputy. He was a Senator, Taoiseach's Nominee, 1992-97. He was a candidate in the 1992 general election in Cork North-Central, losing out on the last seat by 25 votes. He was also a candidate in the by-election in the same constituency in 1994, caused by the death of Gerry O'Sullivan (Lab).

Fianna Fáil spokesperson on Social Welfare in the Seanad, 1993-97.

Cork North-Central was one of four constituencies where Fianna Fáil won three seats.

Noel O'Flynn (FF)

Home Address
Melvindale House, Coolowen, Blarney, Co Cork.
Constituency Office
Kilnap, Mallow Road, Cork
Telephone
Home (021) 382500; *Constituency Office* (021) 305677; *Mobile* (086) 246 4856; *Fax* (021) 300527
Birth Place/Date
Cork. December 1951
Married
Frances O'Keeffe. 3 sons
Education
Regional Technical College, Cork
Occupation
Full-time public representative. Company director, Noel O'Flynn Ltd, Kilnap, Mallow Road, Cork

Noel O'Flynn is a new Dáil deputy. This was the first time he contested a general election.

Member, Cork Corporation since 1991. He has served as chairman of the Environmental and PSV Committee of the Corporation, on Housing Committee, Arts Committee and Travellers' Committee. Member, Cork Chamber of Commerce.

Former member, Cork Harbour Commissioners; Director, Cork Regional Sports Complex.

Member, Institute of Motor Industry; Institute of Road Transport Engineers; Society of Irish Motor Industry.

Cork North-West

Seats 3 Quota 8,691	1st Count	2nd Count Transfer of **Howard's** and **Cashin's** Votes	3rd Count Transfer of **Creed's** Surplus
CASHIN, Bill (Lab)	2,574	−2,574 —	
***CREED**, Michael (FG)	8,041	+1,326 9,367	−676 8,691
***CROWLEY**, Frank (FG)	6,253	+1,092 7,345	+568 7,913
HOWARD, Donie (Ind)	1,729	−1,729 —	
***MOYNIHAN**, Donal (FF)	7,867	+566 8,433	+108 8,541
MOYNIHAN, Michael (FF)	8,299	+950 9,249	— —
NON-TRANSFERABLE		369	—

Elected

Michael Creed (FG)*	2nd Count
Michael Moynihan (FF)	2nd Count
Donal Moynihan (FF)*	3rd Count

Voting by Party

1st Preference	Number	%	% 1992
Fianna Fáil	16,166	46.50	41.25
Fine Gael	14,294	41.12	44.02
Labour	2,574	7.40	14.19
Others	1,729	4.97	0.54

Statistics

Population	60,353	
Electorate	47,119	
Total Poll	35,164	74.63
Spoiled Votes	401	1.14
Valid Poll	34,763	73.78
Seats	3	
Quota	8,691	
Candidates	6	

Seats

FF 2
FG 1
FF gain from FG

The constituency of Cork North-West is slightly smaller than in the 1992 General Election, an area with a population of 502 having been transferred to the constituency of Cork South-West

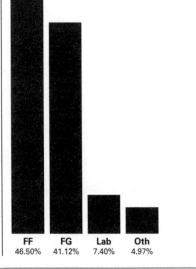

FF	FG	Lab	Oth
46.50%	41.12%	7.40%	4.97%

Michael Creed (FG)

Home Address
Codrum, Macroom, Co Cork
Telephone
Home (026) 41177
Birth Place/Date
Cork. June 1963
Education
St Colman's College, Fermoy, Co Cork; De La Salle College, Macroom; University College, Cork (BA, HDipEd)
Occupation
Full-time public representative. Formerly farmer

Michael Creed was first elected to the Dáil in 1989. That was the first Dáil election which he contested. Front bench spokesperson on Arts, Culture and the Gaeltacht 1994. Spokesperson on Health 1989-93, on Youth and Sport 1993-94.

Chairman, Joint Committee on Small Businesses and Services 1995-97. Chairman, Fine Gael Parliamentary Party Committee on Enterprise and Economic Strategy 1993-94; on Health 1989-93.

Co-opted to Cork County Council in March 1985 and a member since then. Member, Southern Health Board since 1985.

Member, Macroom Macra na Feirme; won County and Munster National Debating Titles in 1987. Playing member of Macroom Gaelic Athletic Association Club

Son of Donal Creed, Dáil deputy for Mid-Cork 1965-81 and for Cork North-West 1981-89, Minister of State at the Department of Education 1982-86, at the Department of Health June-November 1981 and at the Department of the Environment 1981-82.

Michael Moynihan (FF)

Home Address
Meens, Kiskeam, Mallow, Co Cork
Constituency Office
Kanturk, Co Cork
Telephone
Home (029) 76200;
Constituency Office (029) 51299; *Fax* (029) 51300
Birth Place/Date
Cork. January 1968
Education
Boherbue Comprehensive School, Mallow
Occupation
Full-time public representative. Farmer

Michael Moynihan is a new Dáil deputy. This was the first time he contested a general election.

In winning a second Dáil seat for Fianna Fáil (along with outgoing Deputy Donal Moynihan) in Cork North-West he changed a pattern of representation that existed since the present 3-seat constituency was formed in 1981. In all the previous 6 elections in the constituency, Fianna Fáil won 1 seat and Fine Gael 2 seats.

Donal Moynihan (FF)

Home Address
Gortnascorty, Ballymakeera, Macroom, Co Cork
Telephone
Home (026) 45019
Birth Place/Date
Ballymakeera. October 1941
Married
Catherine Twomey. 4 sons, 5 daughters
Education
Ballyvourney Vocational School, Co Cork
Occupation
Public representative. Farmer

Donal Moynihan has been a Dáil deputy for Cork North-West since 1992, when he regained a seat he had previously held in the constituency November 1982-89. He contested the 1989 general election.

Member, Cork County Council since 1970, making him the longest-serving Fianna Fáil member of the County Council.

Member, Cork Vocational Education Committee; Southern Health Board; General Council of County Councils; South Infirmary Board of Management. Chairman of Comhaltas Cosanta Chúil Aodha.

Cork South-Central

Seats 5 Quota 9,174	1st Count	2nd Count Transfer of **Martin's** Surplus	3rd Count Transfer of **Coveney's** Surplus	4th Count Transfer of **Ahern's, Luck's, Twomey's** and **Murphy's** Votes
AHERN, Seán (Ind)	112	+1 113	— 113	−113 —
BOYLE, Dan (GP)	3,622	+28 3,650	+16 3,666	+385 4,051
CANTY, Derry (Ind)	1,497	+4 1,501	+4 1,505	+35 1,540
CLUNE, Deirdre (FG)	4,602	+20 4,622	+159 4,781	+79 4,860
COTTER, Sylvester (FG)	2,701	+11 2,712	+82 2,794	+59 2,853
COUGHLAN, Tom (PD)	2,304	+35 2,339	+8 2,347	+53 2,400
*****COVENEY**, Hugh (FG)	9,524	— —	−350 9,174	
DENNEHY, John (FF)	6,524	+158 6,682	+12 6,694	+94 6,788
LUCK, Nora Anne (NLP)	182	+1 183	— 183	−183 —
*****MARTIN**, Micheál (FF)	9,652	−478 9,174		
MURPHY, Tim (Ind)	663	+2 665	+1 666	−666 —
O'CALLAGHAN, Matty (Ind)	1,254	+9 1,263	+5 1,268	+176 1,444
*****O'KEEFFE**, Batt (FF)	7,279	+183 7,462	+16 7,478	+107 7,585
*****O'SULLIVAN**, Toddy (Lab)	4,908	+25 4,933	+46 4,979	+111 5,090
TWOMEY, Seán P. (Ind)	215	+1 216	+1 217	−217 —
NON-TRANSFERABLE		—	—	80

5th Count	6th Count	7th Count	8th Count	9th Count
Transfer of **O'Callaghan's** Votes	Transfer of **Canty's** Votes	Transfer of **Coughlan's** Votes	Transfer of **Cotter's** Votes	Transfer of **Boyle's** Votes
+324 / 4,375	+213 / 4,588	+296 / 4,884	+300 / 5,184	−5,184 / —
+179 / 1,719	−1,719 / —			
+149 / 5,009	+187 / 5,196	+280 / 5,476	+1,798 / 7,274	+1,195 / 8,469
+82 / 2,935	+113 / 3,048	+134 / 3,182	−3,182 / —	
+73 / 2,473	+63 / 2,536	−2,536 / —		
+150 / 6,938	+180 / 7,118	+733 / 7,851	+273 / 8,124	+851 / 8,975
−1,444 / —				
+227 / 7,812	+607 / 8,419	+775 / 9,194	— / —	— / —
+139 / 5,229	+181 / 5,410	+102 / 5,512	+542 / 6,054	+1,582 / 7,636
121	175	216	269	1,556

Cork South-Central

Elected

Voting by Party

1st Preference	Number	%	% 1992
Fianna Fáil	23,455	42.62	36.08
Fine Gael	16,827	30.57	18.23
Labour	4,908	8.92	18.03
Prog Democrats	2,304	4.19	12.54
Green Party	3,622	6.58	2.18
Sinn Féin	—	—	1.10
Democratic Left	—	—	4.74
Workers' Party	—	—	0.32
Natural Law Party	182	0.33	—
Others	3,741	6.80	6.78

Statistics

Population	107,608	
Electorate	84,288	
Total Poll	55,401	65.73
Spoiled Votes	362	0.65
Valid Poll	55,039	65.30
Seats	5	
Quota	9,174	
Candidates	15	

Seats

FF	3
FG	2
FF gain from Lab	

The constituency of Cork South-Central is unchanged since the 1992 General Election.

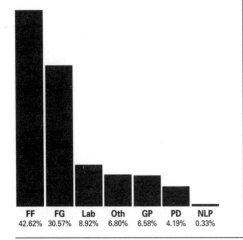

FF	FG	Lab	Oth	GP	PD	NLP
42.62%	30.57%	8.92%	6.80%	6.58%	4.19%	0.33%

Micheál Martin (FF)

Home Address
Lios Laoi, 16 Silver Manor, Ballinlough, Cork
Business Address
Department of Education, Marlborough Street, Dublin 1
Telephone
Home (021) 295218; *Business* (01) 878 6595/ 878 7484; *Constituency Office* (01) 878 8583; *Fax* (021) 320089, (01) 872 9093
Birth Place/Date
Cork. August 1960
Married
Mary O'Shea. 1 son, 1 daughter
Education
Coláiste Chríost Rí, Cork; University College, Cork (BA, HDipEd, MA)
Occupation
Government Minister. Formerly secondary school teacher

Micheál Martin was appointed Minister for Education in June 1997. He was first elected to the Dáil in 1989. He was a candidate in the 1987 general election.

Fianna Fáil front bench spokesperson on Education and the Gaeltacht 1995-97.

Member, Cork City Council 1985-97; (Lord Mayor, 1992/93, Alderman from 1991); chairman, Arts Committee 1987/88. Former chairman, City of Cork VEC. He has served on Governing Body of UCC, Governing Body of Cork RTC.

Chairman, Oireachtas All-Party Committee on the Irish Language 1989-92. Chairman, Dáil Committee on Solicitors Bill.

He has served as a member, Association of Secondary Teachers of Ireland (shop steward); Nemo Rangers Hurling and Football clubs.

National chairman, Ógra Fianna Fáil.

Hugh Coveney (FG)

Home Address
Laharn, Minane Bridge, Co Cork
Constituency Office
17 Halldene Drive, Bishopstown, Cork
Telephone
Home (021) 887227; *Constituency Office* (021) 341926; *Fax* (021) 345822
Birth Place/Date
Cork. July 1935
Married
Pauline Brown. 6 sons, 1 daughter
Education
Christian Brothers' College, Cork; Clongowes Wood College, Co Kildare
Occupation
Public representative. Formerly chartered quantity surveyor in private practice

Hugh Coveney was Minister for Defence and Minister for the Marine December 1994-May 1995 when he resigned. Minister of State at the Department of Finance, with special responsibility for the Office of Public Works and Public Expenditure, May 1995-97. Member, Cabinet Budget Committee 1995-97. Member, Government ministerial team for the Peace Process 1996-97. Front bench spokesperson on Agriculture and Food since 1997.

He was a Dáil deputy 1981-February 1982 and November 1982-87, and since November 1994 when he won a by-election in Cork South-Central.

Lord Mayor of Cork 1982/83, Elected Alderman, Cork Corporation in his first election June 1979. President, Cork Chamber of Commerce 1981. Former member, Higher Education Authority; Cork Harbour Commissioners; Cork-Kerry Tourism; Commissioner of Irish Lights.

Hugh Coveney captained the Irish Admiral's Cup sailing team 1979. Played rugby with Cork Constitution 1st team.

Batt O'Keeffe (FF)

Home Address
8 Westcliffe, Ballincollig, Co Cork
Constituency Office
Commercial Park, Ballincollig, Co Cork
Telephone
Home/Office (021) 871393; *Fax* (021) 871393
Birth Place/Date
Cullen, Mallow, Co Cork. April 1945
Married
Mary Murphy. 1 son, 3 daughters
Education
St Brendan's College, Killarney, Co Kerry;
University College, Cork (BA, HDipEd)
Occupation
Public representative. Lecturer in Cork
Regional Technical College

Batt O'Keeffe has been a Dáil deputy since
1992 and previously 1987-89. Senator, Labour
Panel, 1989-92. He was a candidate in the
1989 general election.

Chairman, Sustainable Development
Committee during 27th Dáil. Member, Public
Accounts Committee.

Member, Cork County Council since 1985;
Cork Vocational Education Sports Advisory
Committee; Higher Education Committee;
Southern Health Board.

Member, Gaelic Athletic Association and Cork
Handball Board. Vice-chairman, Ballincollig
Community Centre Management Committee.

Cork footballer and holder of Munster medals
at under-21, junior and senior levels. Cork
Intermediate Handball Champion, 1980.

John Dennehy (FF)

Home Address
Avondale, 13 Westside Estate, Togher, Cork
Telephone
Home (021) 962908; *Mobile* (087) 239 2517;
Fax (021) 320799
Birth Place/Date
Togher, Cork. March 1940
Married
Philomena Martin. 5 sons, 2 daughters
Education
Sharman Crawford Technical College, Cork;
Cork School of Commerce (Dip Supervisory
Studies [IMI])
Occupation
Full-time public representative. Formerly
engineering supervisor

John Dennehy was previously a Dáil deputy
1987-92, representing Cork South-Central. He
was a candidate in Cork-Mid constituency in
the 1977 general election, in a by-election in
Cork City in 1979 and in the general election
of 1992 in Cork South-Central.

He was Assistant Government Chief Whip
1989-92. Co-chairman of the Committee of
the British-Irish Interparliamentary Body,
dealing with Environment, Culture, Education.

Member, Cork City Council since 1974,
Alderman since 1985, and Lord Mayor of Cork
1983/84. Chairman, Southern Health Board
1984-86 and 1995-97, and chairman of its
Committee on Drugs and Alcohol Prevention
and Treatment since 1995.

Deirdre Clune (FG)

Home Address
Adare, Rochestown, Cork
Constituency Office
Douglas, Cork
Telephone
Home (021) 364934; *Constituency Office*
(021) 890000; *Mobile* (087) 244 7027;
Fax (021) 365229
Birth Place/Date
Cork. June 1959
Married
Conor Clune. 4 sons
Education
Ursuline Convent, Blackrock, Cork; University
College, Cork; Trinity College, Dublin (BE,
Diploma in Management for Engineers,
Higher Diploma in Environmental Engineering)
Occupation
Public representative. Mother working in
the home

Deirdre Clune is a new Dáil deputy. This
was the first time she was a candidate in a
general election. Fine Gael spokesperson on
Environmental Information and Protection
since 1997.

Member, Women's Political Association.
Member of European Movement.

Deirdre Clune is a daughter of Peter Barry,
Dáil deputy for Cork constituencies 1969-97,
Tánaiste 1987, Minister for Foreign Affairs
1982-87, Minister for the Environment 1981-
82, Minister for Transport and Power 1973-76,
Minister for Education 1976-77, and Deputy
Leader of Fine Gael 1979-87 and 1989-93.

She is a grand-daughter of Anthony Barry, Dáil
deputy 1954-57 and 1961-65.

Cork South-West

Seats 3	1st Count	2nd Count	3rd Count
Quota 8,749		Transfer of **Ahern's, Ní Chonaill's** and **Giles's** Votes	Transfer of **Heaney's** and **Calnan's** Votes
AHERN, Seán (Ind)	199	*−199* —	
CALNAN, Michael (Lab)	2,361	*+355* 2,716	*−2,716* —
GILES, Paula (GP)	1,221	*−1,221* —	
HEANEY, Theresa (NP)	1,792	*+244* 2,036	*−2,036* —
NÍ CHONAILL, Áine (Ind)	293	*−293* —	
O'DONOVAN, Denis (FF)	6,081	*+204* 6,285	*+797* 7,082
***O'KEEFFE,** Jim (FG)	7,454	*+348* 7,802	*+1,326* 9,128
***SHEEHAN,** P.J. (FG)	8,008	*+225* 8,233	*+1,312* 9,545
***WALSH,** Joe (FF)	7,586	*+197* 7,783	*+733* 8,516
NON-TRANSFERABLE		140	584

Elected

P.J. Sheehan (FG)*	3rd Count
Jim O'Keeffe (FG)*	3rd Count
Joe Walsh (FF)*	3rd Count

Voting by Party

1st Preference	Number	%	% 1992
Fianna Fáil	13,667	39.05	40.97
Fine Gael	15,462	44.18	40.42
Labour	2,361	6.75	11.28
Green Party	1,221	3.49	4.28
Sinn Féin	—	—	0.99
National Party	1,792	5.12	—
Others	492	1.41	2.06

Statistics

Population	61,210	
Electorate	49,382	
Total Poll	35,314	71.51
Spoiled Votes	319	0.90
Valid Poll	34,995	70.87
Seats	3	
Quota	8,749	
Candidates	9	

Seats

FF	1
FG	2
No change	

The constituency of Cork South-West is slightly larger than in the 1992 General Election, an area with a population of 502 having been transferred from the constituency of Cork South-Central

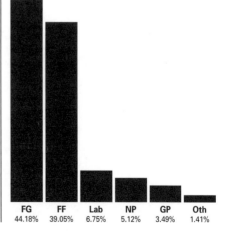

| FG 44.18% | FF 39.05% | Lab 6.75% | NP 5.12% | GP 3.49% | Oth 1.41% |

P.J. Sheehan (FG)

Home Address
Main Street, Goleen, Co Cork
Constituency Office
The Quay, Bantry, Co Cork
Telephone
Home (028) 35236; *Constituency Office*
(027) 52011; *Fax* (028) 35236, (027) 52013
Birth Place/Date
Kilbrown, Goleen. March 1933
Married
Elizabeth Frances Collins. 1 son, 3 daughters
Education
Kilroy's College, Dublin
Occupation
Full-time public representative. Formerly
auctioneer, merchant and farmer

P.J. Sheehan has been a member of the Dáil
since 1981. Fine Gael spokesperson on
Agriculture and Forestry, and Assistant Whip
since 1997; spokesperson on Port
Development, Safety and Inland Waterways
(including Fisheries) 1993-94 and in addition
Public Works 1994; on Disadvantaged Areas
1990-93. He was a Fine Gael candidate in Cork
South-West in the general elections of 1977,
1973 and 1969.

Convenor, Select Committee on Enterprise
and Economic Strategy 1994-97.

Member, Cork County Council since 1967;
Cork County Committee of Agriculture since
1962; Bantry Harbour Authority.

Member, Muintir na Tíre; Irish Farmers'
Association; Irish Creamery Milk Suppliers'
Association; Carberry Agricultural Society
Show Committee; Schull Agricultural Society
Show Committee; Kealkil Show Society;
Munster Agricultural Society Show Committee.

Jim O'Keeffe (FG)

Home Address
Oldchapel, Bandon, Co Cork
Telephone
Home (023) 41399; *Mobile* (087) 259 1694;
Fax (023) 41421
Birth Place/Date
Skibbereen, Co Cork. March 1941
Married
Maeve O'Sullivan. 1 son, 7 daughters
Education
St Fachtna's High School, Skibbereen;
University College, Cork; University College,
Dublin; Law School of the Incorporated Law
Society of Ireland, Dublin
Occupation
Public representative. Solicitor and Notary
Public

Jim O'Keeffe was Minister of State at the
Departments of Finance and the Public
Service, February 1986-March 1987. He was
Minister of State at the Department of
Foreign Affairs with special responsibility for
Development Co-operation 1982-86 and June
1981-March 1982. He was first elected to the
Dáil for Cork South-West in 1977. Fine Gael
front bench spokesperson on Social,
Community and Family Affairs since 1997;
on Foreign Affairs 1990-93; on Justice 1989-
90; on Social Welfare 1988; on Agriculture
1987; on Health 1982; on Security 1980-81;
on Foreign Affairs 1979-80; on Law Reform
1977-79. Chairman, Dáil Consolidation
Committee 1977-81.

Director of Fine Gael Organisation and Policy
Committee and member of front bench 1993-
94. Chairperson, Oireachtas Sub-Committee
on the Constitution 1993-97 and chairperson
of the All-Party Oireachtas Committee on the
Constitution 1997. Convenor, Joint
Committee on Foreign Affairs 1994-97.

Member, Skibbereen Urban District Council
1971-79 and chairman 1975/76; Baltimore
Harbour Commissioners 1974-79.

Joe Walsh (FF)

Home Address
5 Emmet Square, Clonakilty, Co Cork
Business Address
Department of Agriculture and Food,
Kildare Street, Dublin 2
Telephone
Home (023) 33575; *Business* (01) 607 2000;
Fax (01) 661 6263
Birth Place/Date
Ballineen, Co Cork. May 1943
Married
Marie Donegan. 3 sons, 2 daughters
Education
St Finbarr's College, Farranferris, Cork;
University College, Cork (Dairy Science)
Occupation
Government Minister. Formerly dairy manager

Joe Walsh was appointed Minister for
Agriculture and Food in June 1997. He was
Minister for Agriculture, Food and Forestry
January 1993- December 1994. He was
Minister for Agriculture and Food, February
1992-January 1993; Minister of State at the
Department of Agriculture and Food 1987-
February 1992, with special responsibility for
the food industry. He has been a member of
the Dáil since 1977 with the exception of the
period June 1981 to February 1982. He was a
candidate in the June 1981 general election.
He was a Senator August 1981-February
1982.

He was Fianna Fáil front bench spokesperson
on Social Welfare 1995-March 1997 and on
Agriculture 1997.

Former member, Cork County Council; Cork
County Committee of Agriculture (chairman
1976/77, 1985/86); Cork County Vocational
Education Committee.

He was a member, Irish Creamery Managers'
Association; Society of Dairy Technology.

Dick Spring and Róisín Shortall canvassing in Ballymun.

Seats 3
Quota 8,883

	1st Count	2nd Count	3rd Count	4th Count	5th Count
		Transfer of **Devenney's** Votes	Transfer of **Sheridan's** Votes	Transfer of **Doherty's** and **Maloney's** Votes	Transfer of **Keaveney's** Surplus
BLANEY, Harry (Ind)	7,484	+124 7,608	+115 7,723	+1,664 9,387	— —
DEVENNEY, Jim (Ind)	1,657	−1,657 —			
DOHERTY, Pat (SF)	2,881	+36 2,917	+58 2,975	−2,975 —	
***HARTE**, Paddy (FG)	4,969	+891 5,860	+938 6,798	+829 7,627	+102 7,729
***KEAVENEY**, Cecilia (FF)	8,317	+133 8,450	+410 8,860	+852 9,712	−829 8,883
***McDAID**, James (FF)	6,538	+172 6,710	+78 6,788	+1,106 7,894	+350 8,244
MALONEY, Seán (Lab)	1,948	+90 2,038	+140 2,178	−2,178 —	
***McDAID**, James (FF)	6,538	+172 6,710	+78 6,788	+1,106 7,894	+350 8,244
SHERIDAN, Jim (FG)	1,735	+58 1,793	−1,793 —		
NON-TRANSFERABLE		153	54	702	377

Donegal North-East

Elected

Cecilia Keaveney (FF)*	4th Count
Harry Blaney (Ind)	4th Count
James McDaid (FF)*	5th Count

Voting by Party

1st Preference	Number	%	% 1992
Fianna Fáil	14,855	41.81	36.74
Fine Gael	6,704	18.87	22.30
Labour	1,948	5.48	11.34
Green Party	—	—	1.96
Sinn Féin	2,881	8.11	2.62
Others	9,141	25.73	25.05

Statistics

Population	65,841	
Electorate	52,576	
Total Poll	35,951	68.38
Spoiled Votes	422	1.17
Valid Poll	35,529	67.58
Seats	3	
Quota	8,883	
Candidates	8	

Seats

FF	2
Ind	1
Ind gain from FG	

The constituency of Donegal North-East is unchanged since the 1992 General Election.

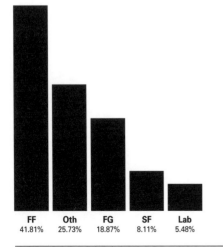

FF	Oth	FG	SF	Lab
41.81%	25.73%	18.87%	8.11%	5.48%

Cecilia Keaveney (FF)

Home Address
Loreto, Moville, Co Donegal
Telephone
Constituency Office (077) 82177; *Fax* (077) 82177
Birth Place/Date
Derry. November 1968
Education
Carndonagh Community School, Co Donegal; University of Ulster at Jordanstown (BMus, MPhil), LTCL, PGCE
Occupation
Full-time public representative. Formerly music teacher

Cecilia Keaveney was first elected to the Dáil at a by-election in Donegal North-East in April 1996, caused by the death of Neil T. Blaney.

Member, Donegal County Council since July 1995 and many of its subsidiary committees, including the North-West Cross-Border Group. Chairperson, Arts Committee 1995/96.

Cecilia Keaveney reached Grade 8 on clarinet, violin, piano and singing, through the Royal Irish Academy of Music, and a Performer's diploma on clarinet through Trinity College, London. As a music teacher, she worked in Nigeria, England and Northern Ireland.

She is a daughter of Paddy Keaveney, Dáil deputy 1976-77.

Harry Blaney (Ind)

Home Address
Rossnakill, Letterkenny, Co Donegal
Telephone
Home (074) 59014; *Mobile* (087) 236 2215; *Fax* (074) 59700
Birth Place/Date
Donegal. February 1928
Married
Margaret Conaghan. 2 sons, 5 daughters
Occupation
Full-time public representative. Farmer

Harry Blaney is a new Dáil deputy. He was a candidate in a by-election in Donegal in April 1996, caused by the death of his brother Neil T. Blaney (Ind).

He has been a member of Donegal County Council for more than 40 years (chairman 1967/68, 1986/87). He has been a member of the North-Western Health Board for over 14 years (chairman 1996/97). Member, Co Donegal Vocational Education Committee; Governing Body of Letterkenny Regional Technical College; Association of Health Boards of Ireland; General Council of County Councils for 18 years.

He is a brother of Neil T. Blaney, Dáil deputy 1948-96 (as a Fianna Fáil representative up to 1971 and afterwards as an independent); MEP 1979-84 and 1989-94, and a former Minister for Posts and Telegraphs, Local Government and Agriculture and Fisheries.

Harry Blaney is son of Neil Blaney, Dáil deputy 1927-38 and 1943-48.

James McDaid (FF)

Home Address
2 Sylvan Park, Letterkenny, Co Donegal
Business Address
Department of Tourism, Sport and Recreation, Kildare Street, Dublin 2
Telephone
Home (074) 21652; *Business* (01) 662 1444
Birth Place/Date
Donegal. October 1949
Married
Marguerite McLoughlin. 3 sons, 1 daughter
Education
St Eunan's College, Letterkenny; University College, Galway (MB, BCh, BAO), MRCGP
Occupation
Government Minister. Formerly medical doctor (GP)

James McDaid was appointed Minister for Tourism, Sport and Recreation in June 1997. He was Fianna Fáil front bench spokesperson on Equality and Law Reform 1997. Spokesperson on North-South Development 1995-97.

He has been a member of the Dáil since 1989. That was the first time he was a candidate for public office.

He has served as a member of the All-Party Committees on Women's Rights and Public Accounts, and the Committee on the Foreign Adoption Bill.

At university he was prominent in sporting activities and captain of UCG soccer team. He was medical officer to Donegal senior Gaelic Athletic Association team 1983-87.

Co-founder of Donegal Hospice (with Dr Tom McGinley, Foyle Hospice, Derry), and has been chairman of the Donegal Hospice Movement since 1988.

For coach travel that's low on cost

yet high on comfort...

Bus Éireann's Expressway Service offers great value fares to a host of destinations around the country. Travel midweek and you can avail of our bargain return fares.

BUS EIREANN/EUROLINES

We operate daily Express Coach Services from most major towns in Ireland to various destinations in Britain from £39.00 with connections to Mainland Europe. There's no better value way to travel to Britain and Europe.

HOLIDAY BREAKS

Three excellent travel inclusive Holiday Options
- Budget Hostel Breakaways from just £23pps
- Bargain B&B Breakaways from just £32pps
- Hotel Breakaways £37pps

This includes overnight hotel accommodation, full Irish breakfast and return coach fare to your choice of destination.

For travel information contact: Central Bus Station (Busaras), Store St., Dublin 1 (01) 8366111; Parnell Place Bus Station, Cork (021) 508188; Colbert Station, Limerick (061) 313333; Ceannt Station, Galway (091) 562000; Plunkett Station, Waterford (051) 879000; Casement Station, Tralee, (066) 23566 or your local Bus Éireann office, Tourist Office or Travel Agent.

RETURN FARES FROM DUBLIN			
WATERFORD	£6.00	ENNIS	£10.00
WEXFORD	£7.00	LETTERKENNY	£10.00
BALLINA	£8.00	LIMERICK	£10.00
GALWAY	£8.00	BELFAST	£10.50
SLIGO	£8.00	CORK	£12.00
DONEGAL	£10.00	TRALEE	£14.00

Fares correct at time of going to press.

...you're better off on

BUS EIREANN

A subsidiary of **Córas Iompair Éireann**

Seats 3 Quota 8,111	1st Count	2nd Count Transfer of **Kennedy's** Votes	3rd Count Transfer of **Brennan's** Votes	4th Count Transfer of **Cullen's** Votes	5th Count Transfer of **O'Kelly's** Votes	6th Count Transfer of **Kelly's** Votes
BONNER, Enda (FF)	5,742	+9 5,751	+81 5,832	+114 5,946	+54 6,000	+745 6,745
BRENNAN, Manus (Lab)	1,361	+6 1,367	−1,367 —			
*COUGHLAN, Mary (FF)	6,597	+23 6,620	+257 6,877	+315 7,192	+356 7,548	+655 8,203
CULLEN, Elizabeth (GP)	1,366	+21 1,387	+256 1,643	−1,643 —		
GILDEA, Thomas (Ind)	5,592	+59 5,651	+274 5,925	+445 6,370	+119 6,489	+1,494 7,983
KELLY, Paddy (Ind)	4,123	+52 4,175	+75 4,250	+165 4,415	+100 4,515	−4,515 —
KENNEDY, Tom (Ind)	206	−206 —				
*McGINLEY, Dinny (FG)	5,679	+16 5,695	+278 5,973	+249 6,222	+1,212 7,434	+731 8,165
O'KELLY, Frank (FG)	1,774	+9 1,783	+90 1,873	+180 2,053	−2,053 —	
NON-TRANSFERABLE		11	56	175	212	890

Donegal South-West

Elected

Mary Coughlan (FF)*	11th Count
Dinny McGinley (FG)*	11th Count
Thomas Gildea (Ind)	11th Count

Voting by Party

1st Preference	Number	%	% 1992
Fianna Fáil	12,339	38.04	48.67
Fine Gael	7,453	22.97	37.74
Labour	1,361	4.20	—
Green Party	1,366	4.21	—
Sinn Féin	—	—	3.31
Democratic Left	—	—	6.12
Others	9,921	30.58	4.16

Statistics

Population	62,276	
Electorate	51,479	
Total Poll	32,894	63.90
Spoiled Votes	454	1.38
Valid Poll	32,440	63.02
Seats	3	
Quota	8,111	
Candidates	9	

Seats

FF	1
FG	1
Ind	1
Ind gain from FF	

The constituency of Donegal South-West is unchanged since the 1992 General Election.

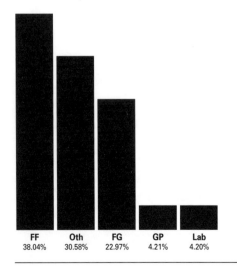

FF	Oth	FG	GP	Lab
38.04%	30.58%	22.97%	4.21%	4.20%

Mary Coughlan (FF)

Home Address
Cranny, Inver, Co Donegal
Telephone
Constituency Office (073) 36002;
Mobile (087) 258 3459; *Fax* (073) 36333
Birth Place/Date
Donegal. May 1965
Married
David Charlton. 1 son
Education
Ursuline Convent, Sligo; University College, Dublin (BSocSc)
Occupation
Full-time public representative. Formerly social worker

Mary Coughlan was first elected to the Dáil in 1987. Spokesperson on Educational Reform 1995-97. Chairperson, Joint Committee on the Irish Language 1993-95.

Member of Donegal County Council since 1986; Donegal County Vocational Education Committee since 1986 (chairperson 1991/92). Chairperson, Board of Management, Abbey Vocational School, Donegal. Member, Board of Management, Killybegs Tourism College.

Honorary secretary Fianna Fáil party since 1996.

Member, Oireachtas Joint Committee on the Irish Language, 1987. Member of British-Irish Parliamentary Body, 1991-92.

President, Killybegs Coast and Cliff Rescue Service.

She is a daughter of the late Cathal Coughlan, Dáil deputy for Donegal South-West 1983-86, and niece of the late Clement Coughlan, Dáil deputy for the same constituency 1980-83.

Dinny McGinley (FG)

Home Address
Bunbeg, Co Donegal
Telephone
Home (075) 31719; *Constituency Office* (075) 31025; *Mobile* (087) 241 4809;
Fax (075) 31025
Birth Place/Date
Gweedore, Co Donegal. April 1945
Education
Coláiste Íosagáin, Ballyvourney, Co Cork; St Patrick's Teachers' Training College, Drumcondra, Dublin; University College, Dublin (BA, HDipEd)
Occupation
Full-time public representative. Formerly principal national school teacher

Dinny McGinley was first elected as a Dáil deputy in February 1982. Spokesperson on Gaeltacht and Emigrants' Welfare 1991-94 and also Youth and Sport 1994. Front bench spokesperson on Gaeltacht 1988-91; spokesperson on Youth Affairs and Sport, 1987-88.

Chairperson, Joint Committee on the Irish Language 1995-97 and vice-chairman 1987-89.

Member, British-Irish Parliamentary Body 1993-97.

Member, Donegal Vocational Education Committee since 1991; Board of Management of Pobalscoil Ghaoth Dobhair since 1991. Member, Irish National Teachers' Organisation since 1965.

Thomas Gildea (Ind)

Home Address
Stranaglough, Glenties, Co Donegal
Constituency Office
The Diamond, Ardara, Co Donegal
Telephone
Home (075) 51757; *Constituency Office*
(075) 41847; *Fax* (075) 41847
Birth Place/Date
Glenties. September 1939
Education
Glenties NS
Occupation
Full-time public representative. Formerly, farm
caretaker, St Columba's Comprehensive
School, Glenties; farmer

Thomas Gildea is a new Dáil deputy. This was
his first election for public office.

He was a candidate on behalf of the Voluntary
Community deflector re-broadcasting system,
seeking the rights to re-broadcast television
channels not directly available, the retention
of the deflector systems in Donegal South-
West and in other parts of the county, and on
behalf of an anti-MMDS campaign.

Chairman of Glenties and Edeninfreagh Parish
Council since 1992. Chairman, Glenties
Community TV Co-operative; Glenties
Anglers' Association. Committee member of
Cumann Traenach na Gaeltactha Láir,
responsible for the restoration of a section of
the old Co Donegal railway as a tourist
attraction.

Dublin Central

Seats 4 Quota 7,149	1st Count	2nd Count	3rd Count	4th Count
		Transfer of **Ahern's** Surplus	Transfer of **Walsh's** and **Shelley's** Votes	Transfer of **Devlin's** Votes
*AHERN, Bertie (FF)	12,175	−5,026 7,149		
BURKE, Christy (SF)	2,377	+264 2,641	+7 2,648	+5 2,653
CONAGHAN, Michael (Ind)	1,343	+69 1,412	+3 1,415	+5 1,420
*COSTELLO, Joe (Lab)	3,035	+227 3,262	+6 3,268	+33 3,301
CUFFE, Ciarán (GP)	1,253	+114 1,367	+12 1,379	+43 1,422
DEVLIN, Kevin (Ind)	307	+67 374	— 374	−374 —
*GREGORY, Tony (Ind)	5,261	+991 6,252	+12 6,264	+94 6,358
JACKSON, Vincent B. (Ind)	650	+52 702	+12 714	+4 718
KAVANAGH, Linda (WP)	509	+28 537	+7 544	+8 552
McGENNIS, Marian (FF)	3,132	+2,977 6,109	+10 6,119	+80 6,199
*MITCHELL, Jim (FG)	5,185	+206 5,391	+10 5,401	+58 5,459
MURPHY, Eamonn (Ind)	432	+22 454	+11 465	+30 495
SHELLEY, Patrick John (Ind)	39	+8 47	−47 —	
WALSH, Aidan (Ind)	43	+1 44	−44 —	
NON-TRANSFERABLE		—	1	14

5th Count	6th Count	7th Count	8th Count	9th Count	10th Count
Transfer of **Murphy's** Votes	Transfer of **Kavanagh's** and **Jackson's** Votes	Transfer of **Cuffe's** Votes	Transfer of **Gregory's** Surplus	Transfer of **Conaghan's** Votes	Transfer of **Burke's** Votes
+33 2,686	+79 2,765	+114 2,879	+33 2,912	+189 3,101	−3,101 —
+20 1,440	+127 1,567	+71 1,638	+38 1,676	−1,676 —	
+24 3,325	+122 3,447	+300 3,747	+183 3,930	+320 4,250	+1,093 5,343
+57 1,479	+80 1,559	−1,559 —			
+69 6,427	+523 6,950	+596 7,546	−397 7,149		
+37 755	−755 —				
+6 558	−558 —				
+101 6,300	+137 6,437	+151 6,588	+63 6,651	+331 6,982	+612 7,594
+53 5,512	+146 5,658	+205 5,863	+80 5,943	+448 6,391	+259 6,650
−495 —					
95	99	122	—	388	1,137

Dublin Central

Elected

Bertie Ahern (FF)*	1st Count
Tony Gregory (Ind)*	7th Count
Marian McGennis (FF)	10th Count
Jim Mitchell (FG)*	10th Count

Voting by Party

1st Preference	Number	%	% 1992
Fianna Fáil	15,307	42.83	39.28
Fine Gael	5,185	14.51	14.08
Labour	3,035	8.49	20.08
Green Party	1,253	3.51	2.55
Sinn Féin	2,377	6.65	3.74
Democratic Left	—	—	1.28
Workers' Party	509	1.42	1.62
Others	8,075	22.59	17.37

Statistics

Population	87,393	
Electorate	64,073	
Total Poll	36,282	56.63
Spoiled Votes	541	1.49
Valid Poll	35,741	55.78
Seats	4	
Quota	7,149	
Candidates	14	

Seats

FF	2
FG	1
Ind	1
FF gain from Lab	

The constituency of Dublin Central is somewhat larger than in the 1992 General Election, having lost areas with populations of 6,577 to the constituency of Dublin North-West and 3,503 to the constituency of Dublin North-Central, and having gained an area with a population of 16,494 from Dublin West.

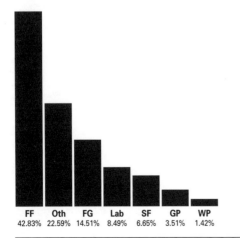

FF	Oth	FG	Lab	SF	GP	WP
42.83%	22.59%	14.51%	8.49%	6.65%	3.51%	1.42%

Bertie Ahern (FF)

Home Address
44 Beresford Avenue, Dublin 9
Business Address
Department of the Taoiseach, Government Buildings, Dublin 2
Constituency Office
St Luke's, 161 Drumcondra Road, Dublin 9
Telephone
Business (01) 662 4888; *Constituency Office* (01) 837 4129; *Fax* (01) 676 4048, (01) 826 8877
Birth Place/Date
Dublin. September 1951
Marital Status
Separated. 2 daughters
Education
St Aidan's CBS, Whitehall, Dublin; Rathmines College of Commerce, Dublin; University College, Dublin; London School of Economics (Diplomas in Taxation, Business Administration and Computer Studies)
Occupation
Taoiseach. Formerly accountant

Bertie Ahern was appointed Taoiseach on 26 June 1997. He was Tánaiste November-December 1994. He was Minister for Finance November 1991-94. He was also Minister for Industry and Commerce January 1993 and Minister for Arts, Culture and the Gaeltacht November-December 1994. Minister for Labour 1987-91. Minister of State at the Department of the Taoiseach and at the Department of Defence and Government Chief Whip March-December 1982. Assistant Government Whip 1980-81; Opposition Chief Whip December 1982-84. Fianna Fáil front bench spokesman on Labour 1984-87; on Youth 1981-82. He was first elected to the Dáil in 1977 for the constituency of Dublin-Finglas and has represented Dublin Central since 1981.

Leader of Fianna Fáil since November 1994.

Member, Dublin City Council, 1978-88 (Lord Mayor 1986/87). He also served on the Eastern Health Board, Dublin Port and Docks Board and the Board of University College, Dublin. Chairman, Dublin Millennium Committee.

Brother of Noel Ahern, Fianna Fáil Dáil deputy for Dublin North-West since 1992.

Tony Gregory (Ind)

Home Address
5 Sackville Gardens, Ballybough, Dublin 3
Telephone
Office (01) 618 3488
Birth Place/Date
Dublin. December 1947
Education
Christian Brothers' O'Connell School, Dublin; University College, Dublin (BA, HDipEd)
Occupation
Full-time public representative. Formerly secondary school teacher

Tony Gregory has been a Dáil deputy since February 1982.

Member, Dublin City Council since 1979. Former member, Dublin Port and Docks Board.

Chairman, North Centre City Community Action Project.

Former member, Official Sinn Féin, and of the Irish Republican Socialist Party.

Member, Association of Secondary Teachers of Ireland (ASTI).

In both March 1982 and March 1987, Tony Gregory's vote was a key factor in the election of Taoiseach. In 1982 he voted for Charles Haughey, and in 1987 his abstention in the vote was crucial in the success of Mr Haughey.

Marian McGennis (FF)

Home Address
44 Bramley Walk, Dublin 15
Telephone
Home (01) 821 2340; *Constituency Office*
(01) 618 3333
Birth Place/Date
Dublin. November 1953
Married
Bryan McGennis. 1 son, 2 daughters
Education
Stanhope Street Convent, Dublin; St Patrick's
College, Maynooth (Diploma in Social Studies;
certificate in Public Relations)
Occupation
Full-time public representative. Mother
working in the home. Formerly civil servant

Marian McGennis is a new Dáil deputy.
Senator, Taoiseach's Nominee 1993-97.
Fianna Fáil spokesperson in Seanad on
Equality and Law Reform and Women's
Affairs 1996-97. Dáil candidate in general
election of 1992 in constituency of Dublin
North.

Member, Dublin County Council 1985-93 and
Fingal County Council since 1993.

She was one of six women elected to the Dáil
for the first time in the 1997 general election.

Jim Mitchell (FG)

Home Address
4 Rathdown Crescent, Terenure, Dublin 6W
Telephone
Business (01) 618 3333
Birth Place/Date
Inchicore, Dublin. October 1946
Married
Patricia Kenny. 2 sons, 3 daughters
Education
James's Street CBS, Dublin; Vocational
School, Inchicore; College of Commerce,
Rathmines, Dublin; Trinity College, Dublin
Occupation
Public representative. Formerly brewery
executive

Jim Mitchell was Minister for Communications
1984-87; Minister for Transport and Minister
for Posts and Telegraphs 1982-84. Minister
for Justice June 1981-March 1982. Member,
EC Council of Ministers of Justice and
Transport (president, Transport Council, 1985).
He was first elected to the Dáil in 1977 for the
3-seat constituency of Dublin Ballyfermot.
Following constituency boundary changes he
was elected for Dublin West 1981-92 and
Dublin Central in 1992. Fine Gael front bench
spokesman on Social Welfare 1992-93; on the
Environment 1990-92; on Labour and
Communications 1989-90; on Labour 1988-89;
on Social Welfare 1987-88; on Justice March-
December 1982; on Labour 1977-81 and also
for the Public Service January-June 1981.
Member, Irish Council of the European
Movement; Parliamentary Assembly of the
Council of Europe since 1993.

Chairman, Public Accounts Committee 1993-
94; Chairman, Select Committee on Finance
and General Affairs 1994-97.

Member, Dublin City Council 1974-81 and
1991-94 (Alderman 1979-81, Lord Mayor
1976/77; he became at 29 the youngest holder
of the office in its 800-year history).

Member, Society of St Vincent de Paul 1964-
74; president, St Paul's Youth Conference,
Inchicore 1964-66; President, Ballyfermot
United Sports and Social Club since 1975.

On the Election Trail '97 . . .

Michael Noonan and Nora Owen in serious mood at a Fine Gael press conference.

Seats 4 Quota 8,232	1st Count	2nd Count Transfer of **Burke's** Surplus	3rd Count Transfer of **Coyle's, Hyland's** and **O'Brien's** Votes	4th Count Transfer of **Keaveney's** and **Ryan's** (Annie) Votes	5th Count Transfer of **Fallon's** Votes	6th Count Transfer of **Wright's** Surplus	7th Count Transfer of **Jenkinson's** and **Daly's** Votes
*BURKE, Ray (FF)	8,901	−669 8,232					
COYLE, Paul (Ind)	42	+4 46	−46 —				
DALY, Clare (SP)	2,971	+26 2,997	+145 3,142	+112 3,254	+46 3,300	+24 3,324	−3,324 —
FALLON, Finian (PD)	1,431	+36 1,467	+19 1,486	+72 1,558	−1,558 —		
HYLAND, Barbara Mary (Ind)	52	+1 53	−53 —				
JENKINSON, Philip (FG)	1,857	+12 1,869	+13 1,882	+80 1,962	+78 2,040	+27 2,067	−2,067 —
KEAVENEY, Angela (CSP)	666	+3 669	+17 686	−686 —			
O'BRIEN, Tim (Ind)	376	+4 380	−380 —				
*OWEN, Nora (FG)	5,956	+18 5,974	+31 6,005	+191 6,196	+149 6,345	+78 6,423	+1,879 8,302
RYAN, Annie (Ind)	669	+12 681	+34 715	−715 —			
*RYAN, Seán (Lab)	5,616	+42 5,658	+69 5,727	+184 5,911	+82 5,993	+46 6,039	+1,203 7,242
*SARGENT, Trevor (GP)	5,614	+38 5,652	+98 5,750	+344 6,094	+362 6,456	+215 6,671	+1,494 8,165
WRIGHT, G.V. (FF)	7,007	+473 7,480	+37 7,517	+334 7,851	+771 8,622	−390 8,232	
NON-TRANSFERABLE		—	16	84	70	—	815

Dublin North

Elected

Ray Burke (FF)*	1st Count
G.V. Wright (FF)	5th Count
Nora Owen (FG)*	7th Count
Trevor Sargent (GP)*	7th Count

Voting by Party

1st Preference	Number	%	% 1992
Fianna Fáil	15,908	38.65	36.51
Fine Gael	7,813	18.98	16.61
Labour	5,616	13.64	34.03
Prog Democrats	1,431	3.48	—
Green Party	5,614	13.64	8.77
Sinn Féin	—	—	0.95
Socialist Party	2,971	7.22	—
Christian Solidarity	666	1.62	
Others	1,139	2.77	3.12

Statistics

Population	81,023	
Electorate	64,030	
Total Poll	41,522	64.85
Spoiled Votes	364	0.88
Valid Poll	41,158	64.28
Seats	4	
Quota	8,232	
Candidates	13	

Seats

FF	2
FG	1
GP	1

FF gain from Lab

The constituency of Dublin North is slightly smaller than in the 1992 General Election, having lost an area with a population of 13,847 to the constituency of Dublin West.

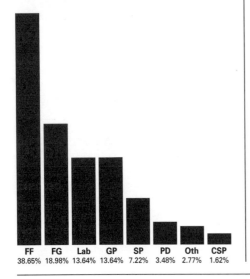

FF	FG	Lab	GP	SP	PD	Oth	CSP
38.65%	18.98%	13.64%	13.64%	7.22%	3.48%	2.77%	1.62%

Ray Burke (FF)

Ray Burke resigned his Dáil seat on 7 October 1997. He was Minister for Foreign Affairs June-October 1997.

He was Minister for Justice 1991-92; Minister for Justice and Minister for Communications 1989-91. Minister for Industry and Commerce and for Communications, November 1988-July 1989. Minister for Energy and for Communications March 1987-November 1988. Minister for the Environment March-December 1982 and October 1980-June 1981. Minister of State at the Department of Industry, Commerce and Energy, 1978-80. He had been a Dáil deputy since 1973.

He was Fianna Fáil front bench spokesperson on Foreign Affairs 1995-97.

Member, Dublin County Council 1967-78 and 1985-87 (chairman 1985-87).

He is a son of the late Patrick J. Burke, Dáil deputy for Dublin County constituencies from 1944 until his retirement in 1973.

G.V. Wright (FF)

Home Address
58 The Moorings, Malahide, Co Dublin
Constituency Office
1 Church Road, Malahide
Telephone
Home (01) 845 2642; *Constituency Office* (01) 845 0710; *Fax* (01) 845 5545
Birth Place/Date
Malahide. August 1947
Married
Monica Kane; 2 sons, 1 daughter
Education
Chanel College, Coolock, Co Dublin
Occupation
Full-time public representative. Formerly businessman, fresh food

G.V. Wright was previously a Dáil deputy 1987-89 for Dublin North constituency. Senator May 1982-January 1983, 1989-93 and 1993-97 (Taoiseach's Nominee).

He was a candidate in the general elections in February and November 1982, 1989, 1992.

He was Assistant Government Chief Whip in the Dáil 1989. Chief Whip in the Seanad 1990-91 and Leader of the House 1991-94. Fianna Fáil Leader, Seanad, 1994-97.

Member, Dublin County Council 1985-92; Fingal County Council since 1993 and Leader of the Fianna Fáil group in the Council. Chairman, Fingal Committee 1988/89.

He served as a director of Bord Iascaigh Mhara, 1980-85.

He played Gaelic football with Dublin County and was an international basketball coach.

Nora Owen (FG)

Home Address
17 Ard na Mara, Malahide, Co Dublin
Telephone
Home (01) 845 1041
Birth Place/Date
Dublin. June 1945
Married
Brian Owen. 3 sons
Education
Dominican Convent, Wicklow; University
College, Dublin (BSc, Diploma in Microbiology)
Occupation
Public representative. Formerly chemist in
industry

Nora Owen was Minister for Justice 1994-97.
She was appointed Deputy Leader of Fine
Gael in March 1993. She has been a Dáil
deputy 1981-87 and since 1989. Front bench
spokesperson on Enterprise, Trade and
Employment since 1997; on Foreign Affairs
1993-94 and European Affairs 1994; on Health
1992-93; on Foreign Affairs 1989-92; on
Overseas Development 1982; chairperson of
Oireachtas Joint Committee on Development
Co-operation, October 1982-January 1987.

British-Irish Parliamentary Body, 1991-92.

Former member, Dublin County Council;
North County Committee (chairperson
1980/81). Chairperson, Fingal Committee of
Dublin County Council 1992/93.

Member, Executive of Trócaire 1987-89.
Secretary and volunteer, Malahide Information
Centre 1976-80. She has also served on
Malahide Community Council; Ard na Mara
Residents' Association; Editorial Committee
of *Malahide News*.

Grandniece of General Michael Collins. Sister
of Mary Banotti, MEP for Dublin since 1984.

Trevor Sargent (GP)

Home Address
37 Tara Cove, Baile Brigín, Co Bhaile Átha
Cliath
Constituency Office
35 Main Street, Swords, Co Bhaile Átha Cliath
Telephone
Home (01) 841 2371; *Office* (01) 890 0360;
Mobile (088) 254 7836; *Fax* (01) 841 2371,
(01) 890 0361; *Dáil* (01) 618 4190
Birth Place/Date
Baile Átha Cliath. Iúil 1960
Education
The High School, Baile Átha Cliath; Coláiste
Oideachais Eaglais na hÉireann, Rath Maonais,
Baile Átha Cliath; Coláiste na Tríonóide,
Baile Átha Cliath (BEd)
Occupation
Full-time public representative. Formerly
national school teacher

Trevor Sargent has been a Dáil deputy since
1992. He contested the Dáil general election
of 1987 as a Green Alliance candidate in the
old 3-seat constituency of Dublin North, and
the 1989 general election as a Green Party
candidate in the same constituency.

Member, Dublin County Council 1991-93.
Cathaoirleach, Fingal Area 1991-92 and of
Coiste Stiúrtha na Gaeilge. Resigned from
Council 1993 in opposition to dual mandate
of Oireachtas and local council.

Former chairman, Tara Cove Residents'
Association; Fingal Council Against Blood
Sports. Member, Fingal committee of An
Taisce; Amnesty International; Irish Wildbird
Conservancy; Greenpeace; Irish Organic
Society; Dublin Food Co-operative; Alternative
Technology Association. Director of Sonairte
(Ecology Centre). Member, Earthwatch.

Cathaoirleach, Craobh Shéamuis Ennis,
Conradh na Gaeilge. Member, Balbriggan
Rugby Club.

Dublin North-Central

Seats 4
Quota 8,634

	1st Count	2nd Count — Transfer of **Callely's** Surplus	3rd Count — Transfer of **Haughey's** Surplus	4th Count — Transfer of **Hunt's** and **Browne's** Votes	5th Count — Transfer of **Lahert's** Votes
BROWNE, Richard (SWP)	698	+19 / 717	+1 / 718	−718 / —	
*BRUTON, Richard (FG)	8,196	+168 / 8,364	+12 / 8,376	+71 / 8,447	+192 / 8,639
*CALLELY, Ivor (FF)	11,190	−2,556 / 8,634			
COSGRAVE, Niamh (FG)	1,713	+30 / 1,743	+3 / 1,746	+25 / 1,771	+78 / 1,849
FAY, Cathy (FG)	1,326	+26 / 1,352	+2 / 1,354	+18 / 1,372	+63 / 1,435
GARVEY, Ronan (PD)	1,424	+144 / 1,568	+16 / 1,584	+18 / 1,602	+40 / 1,642
GREEN, Ita (FF)	1,184	+683 / 1,867	+198 / 2,065	+49 / 2,114	+49 / 2,163
*HAUGHEY, Seán (FF)	7,760	+1,231 / 8,901	−267 / 8,634		
HUNT, Norman (Ind)	36	+1 / 37	— / 37	−37 / —	
LAHERT, Helen (DL)	1,194	+32 / 1,226	+3 / 1,229	+109 / 1,338	−1,338 / —
LOFTUS, Séan Dublin Bay Rockall (Ind)	2,485	+93 / 2,578	+17 / 2,595	+94 / 2,689	+83 / 2,772
*McDOWELL, Derek (Lab)	2,848	+43 / 2,891	+5 / 2,896	+76 / 2,972	+517 / 3,489
McGRATH, Finian (Ind)	1,551	+44 / 1,595	+5 / 1,600	+109 / 1,709	+88 / 1,797
RAWSON, Stephen (GP)	1,650	+42 / 1,692	+5 / 1,697	+137 / 1,834	+155 / 1,989
NON-TRANSFERABLE		—	—	49	73

6th Count	7th Count	8th Count	9th Count	10th Count	11th Count
Transfer of **Fay's** Votes	Transfer of **Garvey's** Votes	Transfer of **McGrath's** Votes	Transfer of **Rawson's** Votes	Transfer of **Cosgrave's** Votes	Transfer of **Green's** Votes
— —	— —	— —	— —	— —	— —
+1,009 2,858	+143 3,001	+192 3,193	+282 3,475	−3,475 —	
−1,435 —					
+23 1,665	−1,665 —				
+54 2,217	+696 2,913	+242 3,155	+334 3,489	+295 3,784	−3,784 —
+85 2,857	+258 3,115	+389 3,504	+924 4,428	+748 5,176	+1,440 6,616
+144 3,633	+85 3,718	+307 4,025	+644 4,669	+1,821 6,490	+502 6,992
+26 1,823	+107 1,930	−1,930 —			
+30 2,019	+194 2,213	+534 2,747	−2,747 —		
64	182	266	563	611	1,842

Dublin North-Central

Elected

Voting by Party

1st Preference	Number	%	% 1992
Fianna Fáil	20,044	46.44	38.96
Fine Gael	11,235	26.03	22.40
Labour	2,848	6.60	23.12
Prog Democrats	1,424	3.30	—
Green Party	1,650	3.82	—
Sinn Féin	—	—	1.40
Democratic Left	1,194	2.77	3.00
Socialist Workers'	698	1.62	—
Others	4,072	9.43	11.11

Statistics

Population	87,600	
Electorate	66,559	
Total Poll	43,621	65.54
Spoiled Votes	456	1.05
Valid Poll	43,165	64.85
Seats	4	
Quota	8,634	
Candidates	14	

Seats

FF	2
FG	1
Lab	1
No change	

The constituency of Dublin North-Central is slightly larger than in the 1992 General Election, having gained an area with a population of 3,503 from the constituency of Dublin Central.

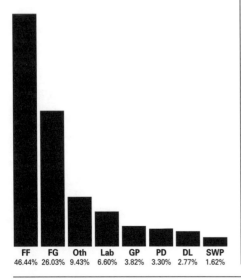

FF	FG	Oth	Lab	GP	PD	DL	SWP
46.44%	26.03%	9.43%	6.60%	3.82%	3.30%	2.77%	1.62%

Ivor Callely (FF)

Home Address
Landsdale House, 7 St Lawrence Road, Clontarf, Dublin 3
Constituency Office
191 Howth Road, Killester, Dublin 3
Telephone
Home (01) 833 0350; *Office* (01) 833 4331; *Mobile* (087) 257 1489
Birth Place/Date
Dublin. May 1958
Married
Jennifer Foley. 2 sons, 1 daughter
Education
St Paul's College, Raheny, Dublin; Fairview College, Dublin (Diplomas in Business Studies, Accountancy, and Sales and Marketing)
Occupation
Full-time public representative. Formerly medical representative

Ivor Callely has been a Dáil deputy since 1989.

Fianna Fáil Assistant Whip and Policy Co-ordinator 1995-97.

Convenor of Committee on Legislation and Security 1993-95.

Member, Dublin City Council since 1985; Eastern Health Board since 1985 (vice-chairman 1987-90, chairman 1990-91). Chairman, Child Care Advisory Committee.

Member, Raheny Gaelic Athletic Association. Member and former honorary secretary, Clontarf Lawn Tennis Club. Member, Killester Sports and Social Club.

Seán Haughey (FF)

Home Address
Chapelfield Lodge, Baskin Lane, Kinsealy, Dublin 17
Constituency Office
5 Mornington Park, Malahide Road, Artane, Dublin 5
Telephone
Home (01) 845 0111; *Office* (01) 831 3988; *Fax* (01) 845 1444
Birth Place/Date
Dublin. November 1961
Married
Orla O'Brien. 1 son, 1 daughter
Education
St Paul's College, Raheny, Dublin; Trinity College, Dublin (BA [Mod])
Occupation
Full-time public representative

Seán Haughey was first elected to the Dáil in 1992. He was a candidate in Dublin North-East constituency in the general elections of 1987 and 1989. Senator, Administrative Panel, 1987-92. Assistant Government Chief Whip in the Seanad 1987-89 and Fianna Fáil spokesperson on Energy 1989-92.

Alderman, Dublin City Council since 1985 (Lord Mayor 1989/90).

National Chairman Ógra Fianna Fáil since 1995.

Director, Dublin and East Regional Tourism Organisation/Dublin Tourism since 1985; Dublin Promotions Organisation since 1986 (chairman 1989/90).

Member, Board of St Vincent's Hospital, Fairview since 1988; Board of Beaumont Hospital 1988-92.

Member, British-Irish Parliamentary Body since 1991; Irish Council of the European Movement.

He is a son of Charles J. Haughey, Taoiseach, December 1979-June 1981, March-December 1982, March 1987-June 1989, Acting Taoiseach June-July 1989, Taoiseach July 1989-February 1992 and Dáil deputy 1957-92.

Richard Bruton (FG)

Home Address
210 Griffith Avenue, Drumcondra, Dublin 9
Telephone
Home (01) 836 8185; *Fax* (01) 836 8185
Birth Place/Date
Dublin. March 1953
Married
Susan Meehan. 2 sons, 2 daughters
Education
Belvedere College, Dublin; Clongowes Wood College, Co Kildare; University College, Dublin; Nuffield College, Oxford (BA, MA, MPhil [Oxon] Economics)
Occupation
Full-time public representative. Formerly economist

Richard Bruton was Minister for Enterprise and Employment 1994-97. He was Minister of State at the Department of Industry and Commerce September 1986-March 1987. Fine Gael front bench spokesperson on Education, Science and Technology, and Relations with the Social Partners, since 1997; on Enterprise and Employment 1993-94 and Director of Policy 1994; Employment 1992-93; Health 1990-92; Energy and Natural Resources 1989-90; Energy and Communications 1987-89. He was first elected to the Dáil in February 1982. He was a Senator, Agricultural Panel, August 1981-February 1982.

Member, Dublin City Council 1991-94.

Member, Meath County Council 1979-82.

Author of *Irish Public Debt* (1979); joint author of *Irish Economy* (1975) and of *Drainage Policy in Ireland* (1982).

Richard Bruton is a brother of John Bruton, Taoiseach 1994-97, Dáil deputy for Meath since 1969, Leader of Fine Gael since 1990 and former Minister.

Derek McDowell (Lab)

Home Address
3 Dunluce Road, Dublin 3
Business Address
107C Malahide Road, Dublin 3
Telephone
Home (01) 833 6138; *Business* (01) 831 7418/ 831 9029
Birth Place/Date
Dublin. September 1958
Married
Vicki Barrett
Education
Ardscoil Rís, Marino, Dublin; University College, Dublin (BA)
Occupation
Public representative. Solicitor

Derek McDowell has been a Dáil deputy since 1992. He was a candidate in the old Dublin North-Central constituency in the general election of 1989. Labour Party spokesperson on Health and Children since 1997.

Member, British-Irish Parliamentary Body 1993-97.

In the 27th Dáil he served on the Select Committee on Legislation and Security; Select Committee on Finance and General Affairs; Joint Oireachtas Committee on European Affairs.

He was advisor to the Labour Party Delegation at the Forum for Peace and Reconciliation.

Member, Dublin City Council since 1991 and of a number of its subsidiary committees.

Dublin North-East

Seats 4 Quota 7,461	1st Count	2nd Count Transfer of **Fraser's, Burns's** and **Poole's** Votes	3rd Count Transfer of **Creevey's** Votes	4th Count Transfer of **Cooney's** Votes
BRADY, Martin (FF)	5,018	+49 5,067	+68 5,135	+108 5,243
*****BROUGHAN**, Tommy (Lab)	3,447	+69 3,516	+396 3,912	+300 4,212
BURNS, John (NLP)	155	−155 —		
COONEY, Donna (GP)	1,332	+144 1,476	+131 1,607	−1,607 —
COSGRAVE, Michael J. (FG)	4,173	+145 4,318	+94 4,412	+137 4,549
CREEVEY, Anthony (DL)	1,381	+44 1,425	−1,425 —	
*****FITZGERALD**, Liam (FF)	4,394	+39 4,433	+78 4,511	+83 4,594
FOLEY, Mairéad (PD)	2,911	+38 2,949	+79 3,028	+165 3,193
FRASER, Lar (Ind)	39	−39 —		
*****KENNY**, Seán (Lab)	2,986	+50 3,036	+280 3,316	+205 3,521
MAHER, Joan (FG)	2,877	+38 2,915	+70 2,985	+142 3,127
O'TOOLE, Larry (SF)	2,212	+76 2,288	+113 2,401	+155 2,556
POOLE, Owen (Ind)	641	−641 —		
*****WOODS**, Michael J. (FF)	5,735	+96 5,831	+76 5,907	+124 6,031
NON-TRANSFERABLE		47	40	188

Dublin North-East

5th Count	6th Count	7th Count	8th Count	9th Count	10th Count
Transfer of O'Toole's Votes	Transfer of Maher's Votes	Transfer of Foley's Votes	Transfer of Kenny's Votes	Transfer of Woods's Surplus	Transfer of Cosgrave's Surplus
+334 5,577	+53 5,630	+685 6,315	+257 6,572	+52 6,624	+121 6,745
+410 4,622	+291 4,913	+233 5,146	+2,592 7,738	— —	— —
+79 4,628	+2,047 6,675	+447 7,122	+626 7,748	— —	−287 7,461
+343 4,937	+79 5,016	+652 5,668	+372 6,040	+60 6,100	+121 6,221
+102 3,295	+193 3,488	−3,488 —			
+322 3,843	+279 4,122	+191 4,313	−4,313 —		
+32 3,159	−3,159 —				
−2,556 —					
+408 6,439	+147 6,586	+987 7,573	— —	−112 7,461	
526	70	293	466	—	45

Dublin North-East

Elected

Michael J. Woods (FF)*	7th Count
Michael J. Cosgrave (FG)	8th Count
Tommy Broughan (Lab)*	8th Count
Martin Brady (FF)	10th Count

Voting by Party

1st Preference	Number	%	% 1992
Fianna Fáil	15,147	40.61	33.83
Fine Gael	7,050	18.90	13.73
Labour	6,433	17.25	30.08
Prog Democrats	2,911	7.80	5.08
Green Party	1,332	3.57	4.31
Sinn Féin	2,212	5.93	2.72
Democratic Left	1,381	3.70	9.36
Workers' Party	—	—	0.60
Natural Law Party	155	0.42	—
Others	680	1.82	0.29

Statistics

Population	83,170	
Electorate	59,497	
Total Poll	37,669	63.31
Spoiled Votes	368	0.98
Valid Poll	37,301	62.69
Seats	4	
Quota	7,461	
Candidates	14	

Seats

FF	2
FG	1
Lab	1
FG gain from Lab	

The constituency of Dublin North-East is unchanged since the 1992 General Election.

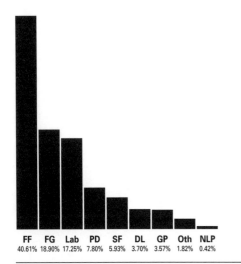

FF	FG	Lab	PD	SF	DL	GP	Oth	NLP
40.61%	18.90%	17.25%	7.80%	5.93%	3.70%	3.57%	1.82%	0.42%

Michael J. Woods (FF)

Home Address
13 Kilbarrack Grove, Raheny, Dublin 5
Business Address
Department of the Marine and Natural Resources, Leeson Lane, Dublin 2
Telephone
Home (01) 832 3357; *Business* (01) 678 5444; *Fax* (01) 661 8214
Birth Place/Date
Bray, Co Wicklow. December 1935
Married
Margaret Maher. 3 sons, 2 daughters
Education
Synge Street CBS, Dublin; University College, Dublin (BAgrSc, MAgrSc, PhD, DSc); Institute of Public Administration (Diploma in Central Administration and Fellowship in Public Administration); Harvard Business School (Diploma in Marketing)
Occupation
Government Minister. Formerly Principal Officer and Head of Glasshouse Crops and Mushroom Department, An Foras Talúntais

Michael Woods was appointed Minister for the Marine and Natural Resources in June 1997. He was Minister for Social Welfare 1993-December 1994 and Minister for Health November- December 1994. He was Minister for the Marine 1992-93; Minister for Agriculture and Food, 1991-92; Minister for Social Welfare 1987-91. He was Minister for Health and Minister for Social Welfare March-December 1982 and 1979-81. He was Minister of State at the Department of the Taoiseach and the Department of Defence and Government Chief Whip in 1979. Fianna Fáil spokesman on Justice 1982-87, on Equality and Law Reform 1993-94; on Social Welfare 1994. He was first elected to the Dáil in 1977.

Former member, Dublin City Council.

He is the author of *Research in Ireland, Key to Economic and Social Development* and numerous technical and scientific papers.

Michael J. Cosgrave (FG)

Home Address
Mangerton, 22 College Street, Baldoyle, Dublin 13
Constituency Office
22A College Street, Baldoyle, Dublin 13
Telephone
Home (01) 832 2554; *Constituency Office* (01) 839 5616
Birth Place/Date
Dublin. February 1938
Marital Status
Separated. 2 sons, 2 daughters
Education
St Joseph's CBS, Fairview, Dublin; School of Management Studies, Rathmines, Dublin; University College, Dublin
Occupation
Full-time public representative. Formerly company director

Michael J. Cosgrave was previously a Dáil deputy 1977-92. He was first elected to the Dáil for Dublin Clontarf in 1977. His present constituency of Dublin North-East covers much the same area. He was a candidate in the general election in 1992.

He served as Assistant Fine Gael Whip.

Member, Dublin City Council 1974-85 and of the Council's Finance and Planning Committees. Member, Dublin County Council since 1985. Former member, Dublin Port and Docks Board.

President, St Lawrence's Pipe Band, Howth. Patron, Baldoyle United Football Club. Former president, Baldoyle Pitch and Putt Club.

Tommy Broughan (Lab)

Home Address
23 Riverside Road, Coolock, Dublin 17
Telephone
Home (01) 847 7634; *Business* (01) 618 4275,
Fax (01) 618 4162
Birth Place/Date
Clondalkin, Co. Dublin. August 1947
Married
Carmel Healy
Education
Moyle Park College, Clondalkin; University
College, Dublin; London University (BA, BSc,
MSc [Econ], HDipEd)
Occupation
Full-time public representative. Formerly
teacher

Tommy Broughan was first elected to the Dáil
in 1992. He was an unsuccessful candidate in
Dublin North-East in the 1989 election.

Labour Party spokesperson on Enterprise and
Employment since 1997.

Member of the Dáil Committees on Finance,
General Affairs, Enterprise and Employment,
Public Accounts, and Joint Oireachtas
Committee on the Irish Language during the
27th Dáil.

Member, Dublin City Council since 1991
(former chairman General Purposes
Committee). Leader of the Labour City
Council Group and chairperson of Civic
Alliance in Dublin City Council.

Founding secretary, Community Enterprise,
Donaghmede and Artane. Founding chairman
of Coolock Development Council. Director,
Northside Centre for the Unemployed.

Member of several north-side Gaelic football
and soccer clubs.

Martin Brady (FF)

Home Address
37 Grangemore Drive, Dublin 13
Telephone
Home (01) 848 4509;
Constituency Office (01) 867 0721
Birth Place/Date
Virginia, Co Cavan. May 1947
Married
Veronica Brady. 3 daughters
Education
Franciscan Brothers' College, Clara, Co Offaly
Occupation
Full-time public representative. Formerly
Telecom Éireann executive

Martin Brady is a new Dáil deputy. He was a
candidate in the Dublin North-East
constituency in the 1992 general election.

He has been a member of Dublin Corporation
since 1991, and of a number of its subsidiary
committees.

He was one of six new Fianna Fáil Dáil
deputies elected in Dublin in the 1997 general
election.

Dublin North-West

Seats 4 Quota 7,340	1st Count	2nd Count	3rd Count	4th Count
		Transfer of **Ahern's** Surplus	Transfer of **Carey's** Surplus	Transfer of **McCool's, Doolan's** and **Fay's** Votes
*AHERN, Noel (FF)	11,075	−3,735 7,340		
BRADY, Brendan (FG)	2,901	+160 3,061	+95 3,156	+9 3,165
CAREY, Pat (FF)	6,188	+2,853 9,041	−1,701 7,340	
*DE ROSSA, Proinsias (DL)	3,701	+139 3,840	+142 3,982	+15 3,997
DOOLAN, Gerard (Ind)	73	+3 76	+31 107	−107 —
DUNNE, John (WP)	489	+22 511	+36 547	+14 561
FAY, T.J. (Ind)	82	+5 87	+23 110	−110 —
*FLAHERTY, Mary (FG)	2,825	+85 2,901	+106 3,016	+11 3,027
McCOOL, Maria (Ind)	13	+1 14	+4 18	−18 —
MacDONOUGH, Joe (NP)	614	+21 635	+68 703	+16 719
MAHER, Kathleen (Ind)	479	+26 505	+39 544	+49 593
*SHORTALL, Róisín (Lab)	4,084	+168 4,252	+208 4,460	+15 4,475
SIMPSON, Tom (GP)	1,525	+78 1,603	+255 1,858	+38 1,896
TAAFFE, Tony (Ind)	1,171	+95 1,266	+434 1,700	+13 1,713
TORMEY, Bill (Ind)	1,479	+79 1,558	+260 1,818	+22 1,840
NON-TRANSFERABLE		—	—	33

5th Count	6th Count	7th Count	8th Count	9th Count	10th Count
Transfer of **Dunne's** Votes	Transfer of **Maher's** and **MacDonough's** Votes	Transfer of **Taaffe's** Votes	Transfer of **Simpson's** Votes	Transfer of **Tormey's** Votes	Transfer of **Flaherty's** Votes
+15 3,180	+94 3,274	+109 3,383	+180 3,563	+406 3,969	+1,864 5,833
+86 4,083	+124 4,207	+209 4,416	+358 4,774	+573 5,347	+586 5,933
−561 —					
+27 3,054	+57 3,111	+160 3,271	+192 3,463	+386 3,849	−3,849 —
+21 740	−740 —				
+58 651	−651 —				
+81 4,556	+178 4,734	+180 4,914	+492 5,406	+625 6,031	+939 6,970
+97 1,993	+277 2,270	+192 2,462	−2,462 —		
+42 1,755	+176 1,931	−1,931 —			
+77 1,917	+204 2,121	+536 2,657	+609 3,266	−3,266 —	
57	281	545	631	1,276	460

Dublin North-West

Elected

Noel Ahern (FF)*	1st Count
Pat Carey (FF)	3rd Count
Róisín Shortall (Lab)*	10th Count
Proinsias De Rossa (DL)*	10th Count

Voting by Party

1st Preference	Number	%	% 1992
Fianna Fáil	17,263	47.04	33.38
Fine Gael	5,726	15.60	12.33
Labour	4,084	11.13	23.06
Green Party	1,525	4.16	2.40
Sinn Féin	—	—	3.21
Democratic Left	3,701	10.08	12.19
Workers' Party	489	1.33	3.29
Others	3,911	10.66	10.15

Statistics

Population	87,762	
Electorate	60,374	
Total Poll	37,203	61.62
Spoiled Votes	504	1.35
Valid Poll	36,699	60.79
Seats	4	
Quota	7,340	
Candidates	15	

Seats

FF	2
Lab	1
DL	1
FF gain from FG	

The constituency of Dublin North-West is slightly larger than in the 1992 General Election, having gained an area with a population of 6,577 from the constituency of Dublin Central.

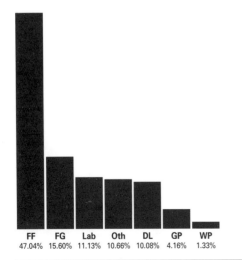

FF	FG	Lab	Oth	DL	GP	WP
47.04%	15.60%	11.13%	10.66%	10.08%	4.16%	1.33%

Noel Ahern (FF)

Home Address
25 Church Avenue, Drumcondra, Dublin 9
Telephone
Home (01) 832 5911; *Mobile* (088) 257 6739; *Fax* (01) 832 5911
Birth Place/Date
Dublin. December 1944
Married
Helen Marnane. 2 sons, 1 daughter
Education
Christian Brothers' O'Connell School, Dublin; University College, Dublin; College of Commerce, Rathmines, Dublin (DPA, MCIT)
Occupation
Full-time public representative. Formerly official with CIE

Noel Ahern was first elected to the Dáil in 1992. That was the first occasion on which he contested a general election.

Fianna Fáil spokesperson on the Environment with special responsibility for Housing 1994-97.

Member, Dublin City Council since 1985 and Alderman since 1991.

Former branch officer and member of National Executive of the Transport Salaried Staffs Association.

He is brother of Bertie Ahern, Taoiseach since 1997, Leader of Fianna Fáil since 1994, former Minister, and Dáil deputy since 1977.

Pat Carey (FF)

Home Address
69 Bourne View, Ashbourne, Co Meath
Telephone
Home (01) 835 0544; *Fax* (01) 835 0430
Birth Place/Date
Castlemaine, Co Kerry. November 1947
Education
Presentation Brothers' College, Milltown, Co Kerry; St Patrick's Teachers' Training College, Drumcondra, Dublin; University College, Dublin; Trinity College, Dublin (BA, HDipEd)
Occupation
Full-time public representative. Formerly primary school teacher, vice-principal

Pat Carey is a new Dáil deputy. He was a candidate in the 1992 general election in Dublin North-West.

Member, Dublin Corporation since 1985. He has served as chairman of a number of its committees dealing with Education, Enterprise, Environment and Culture. Member, City of Dublin Vocational Education Committee since 1985 (chairman 1988-91). Chairman, Council of College of Technology, Bolton Street, Dublin (1985-91). Member, Council of College of Catering, Cathal Brugha Street, Dublin (1985-91). Governing Body of Dublin Institute of Technology (1985-94). Co-Chairman TCD-DIT Liaison Council (1988-91).

Chairman, School Committee of Coláiste Eoin and Coláiste Íde, Finglas since 1985; Plunkett College, Whitehall 1985-91; Coláiste Éanna, Cabra 1985-91; Sports Advisory Committee of City of Dublin VEC 1985-91; City of Dublin Youth Service Board 1985-91. Former chairman, Catholic Youth Council. Council member, NCEA 1991-96. Member, Dublin Regional Authority. Member, EU Monitoring Committee, Dublin Region.

Róisín Shortall (Lab)

Home Address
12 Iveragh Road, Gaeltacht Park, Dublin 9
Telephone
Home (01) 837 0563; *Fax* (01) 618 4163
Birth Place/Date
Dublin. April 1954
Married
Séamus O'Byrne. 3 daughters
Education
Dominican College, Eccles Street, Dublin;
University College, Dublin; St Mary's College of
Education, Marino, Dublin (BA, Dip Teacher of
the Deaf)
Occupation
Full-time public representative. Formerly
primary school teacher for the deaf at St
Joseph's School, Cabra, Dublin

Róisín Shortall has been a Dáil deputy since
1992.

Labour Party spokesperson on Justice since
1997.

Member, Dáil Select Committee on Social
Affairs; Select Committee on Legislation and
Security during the 27th Dáil.

Member, Dublin City Council since 1991;
Eastern Health Board since 1991 (chairperson
1997).

Member, Ballymun Housing Task Force; North
Dublin National School Project. Board member,
Finglas Vocational Education Committee
schools.

Proinsias De Rossa (DL)

Home Address
39 Pinewood Crescent, Ballymun, Dublin 11
Telephone
Business (01) 618 3333
Birth Place/Date
Dublin. May 1940
Married
2 sons, 1 daughter
Education
College of Technology, Kevin Street, Dublin
Occupation
Leader of Democratic Left

Proinsias De Rossa was Minister for Social
Welfare 1994-97 in the Government which his
party formed with Fine Gael and Labour
(15/12/94).

He was first elected to the Dáil in February
1982 as a Workers' Party deputy, and was
elected President and Leader of the Workers'
Party in 1988 on the resignation of Deputy
Tomás Mac Giolla. During the lifetime of the
26th Dáil, 6 of the 7 Workers' Party deputies
formed a new party, which was later called
Democratic Left. Proinsias De Rossa became
the Leader of the new party. Democratic Left
spokesperson on Departments of the
Taoiseach, Foreign Affairs, Social Welfare,
Defence, Marine, and Arts, Culture and the
Gaeltacht, 1993-94. Democratic Left
spokesperson on the Taoiseach, Foreign
Affairs, Social, Community and Family Affairs,
and Defence since 1997.

Elected member of the European Parliament
for Dublin constituency June 1989. Resigned
February 1992. He was a vice-chairman,
Regional Affairs Committee of the European
Parliament 1989-92.

Member, Dublin City Council; Eastern Health
Board, 1985-88.

Member, SIPTU; Campaign for Nuclear
Disarmament (CND); Amnesty International;
Peace Train Organisation.

Proinsias De Rossa, John Bruton and Dick Spring, the leaders of the three outgoing coalition partners, at the launch of their joint campaign.

Seats 5 Quota 9,665	1st Count	2nd Count Transfer of **Dolan's, Doody's, Lyons's** and **Maher's** Votes	3rd Count Transfer of **Kitt's** Surplus	4th Count Transfer of **Buckley's** Votes	5th Count Transfer of **Greene's** Votes	6th Count Transfer of **Ormonde's** Votes	7th Count Transfer of **Brennan's** Surplus	8th Count Transfer of **Boland's** Votes
BOLAND, Gerry (GP)	3,539	+241 3,780	+5 3,785	+356 4,141	+291 4,432	+150 4,582	+236 4,818	−4,818 —
*BRENNAN, Séamus (FF)	8,861	+67 8,928	+113 9,041	+146 9,187	+352 9,539	+2,519 12,058	−2,393 9,665	
BUCKLEY, Christine (Ind)	1,268	+158 1,426	+4 1,430	−1,430 —				
DOLAN, Gerard P. (Ind)	75	−75 —						
DOODY, Johnny Kingsize (Ind)	80	−80 —						
*FITZGERALD, Eithne (Lab)	6,147	+125 6,272	+8 6,280	+205 6,485	+77 6,562	+105 6,667	+89 6,756	+1,402 8,158
GREENE, Richard (Ind)	1,431	+51 1,482	+3 1,485	+100 1,585	−1,585 —			
*KITT, Tom (FF)	9,904	— —	−239 9,665					
LYONS, Jack (NLP)	115	−115 —						
MAHER, Lisa (SP)	624	−624 —						
MITCHELL, Olivia (FG)	8,775	+54 8,829	+8 8,837	+178 9,015	+169 9,184	+158 9,342	+73 9,415	+721 10,136
*O'DONNELL, Liz (PD)	5,444	+47 5,491	+29 5,520	+149 5,669	+115 5,784	+809 6,593	+1,511 8,104	+966 9,070
ORMONDE, Ann (FF)	3,629	+54 3,683	+61 3,744	+93 3,837	+254 4,091	−4,091 —		
*SHATTER, Alan (FG)	8,094	+63 8,157	+8 8,165	+107 8,272	+80 8,352	+204 8,556	+103 8,659	+705 9,364
NON-TRANSFERABLE		34	—	96	247	146	381	1,024

Dublin South

Elected

Tom Kitt (FF)*	1st Count
Séamus Brennan (FF)*	6th Count
Olivia Mitchell (FG)	8th Count
Alan Shatter (FG)*	8th Count
Liz O'Donnell (PD)*	8th Count

Voting by Party

1st Preference	Number	%	% 1992
Fianna Fáil	22,394	38.62	32.64
Fine Gael	16,869	29.09	20.25
Labour	6,147	10.60	28.94
Prog Democrats	5,444	9.39	8.66
Green Party	3,539	6.10	3.79
Sinn Féin	—	—	0.81
Democratic Left	—	—	1.07
Socialist Party	624	1.08	—
Natural Law Party	115	0.20	—
Others	2,854	4.92	3.85

Statistics

Population	111,151	
Electorate	90,050	
Total Poll	58,321	64.77
Spoiled Votes	335	0.57
Valid Poll	57,986	64.39
Seats	5	
Quota	9,665	
Candidates	14	

Seats

FF	2
FG	2
PD	1
FG gain from Lab	

The constituency of Dublin South is slightly smaller than in the 1992 General Election, having lost an area with a population of 7,467 to the constituency of Dublin South-East and having gained an area with a population of 3,539 from the constituency of Dún Laoghaire.

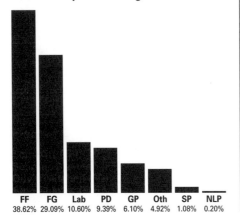

FF	FG	Lab	PD	GP	Oth	SP	NLP
38.62%	29.09%	10.60%	9.39%	6.10%	4.92%	1.08%	0.20%

Tom Kitt (FF)

Home Address
3 Pine Valley Drive, Rathfarnham, Dublin 16
Constituency Office
2 Ashgrove Terrace, Dundrum, Dublin 16
Business Address
Department of Enterprise, Trade and Employment, 65 Adelaide Road, Dublin 2
Telephone
Home (01) 493 8200; *Constituency Office* (01) 298 2304; *Business* (01) 676 4820; *Fax* (01) 493 2207 (H), 298 2460 (C), 676 4902 (B)
Birth Place/Date
Galway. July 1952
Married
Jacinta Burke-Walsh. 3 sons, 1 daughter
Education
St Jarlath's College, Tuam, Co Galway; St Patrick's Teachers' Training College, Drumcondra, Dublin
Occupation
Minister of State. Formerly national school teacher

Tom Kitt was appointed Minister of State at the Department of Enterprise, Trade and Employment, with special responsibility for Labour Affairs, Consumer Rights and International Trade, in July 1997. He was Minister of State at the Department of the Taoiseach and the Department of Foreign Affairs, with special responsibility for European Affairs and Overseas Development Aid, 1993-94. Minister of State at the Department of the Taoiseach with special responsibility for Arts and Culture, Women's Affairs and European Affairs 1992-93. He was elected to the Dáil in 1987.

He was spokesperson on Labour Affairs 1995-97.

He was a member of the British-Irish Parliamentary Body, 1991-92.

Member of Dublin County Council 1979-92. Chairman, Dún Laoghaire-Rathdown District Committee 1986/87.

He is a son of Michael F. Kitt, Dáil deputy for Galway constituencies 1948-51, 1957-75 and brother of Michael Kitt TD, Galway East.

Séamus Brennan (FF)

Home Address
31 Finsbury Park, Churchtown, Dublin 14
Business Address
Department of the Taoiseach, Government Buildings, Dublin 2
Telephone
Constituency Office (01) 295 7171/662 3828; *Fax* (01) 296 2628/676 3533; *Business* (01) 662 4888; *Fax* (01) 676 5757
Birth Place/Date
Galway. February 1948
Married
Ann O'Shaughnessy. 2 sons, 4 daughters
Education
St Joseph's Secondary School, Galway; University College, Galway (BA, BComm); University College, Dublin (MComm)
Occupation
Minister of State, Government Chief Whip. Formerly accountant and management consultant

Séamus Brennan was appointed Minister of State at the Department of the Taoiseach, with special responsibility as Government Chief Whip, and Minister of State at the Department of Defence in June 1997. He was Minister of State at the Department of Enterprise and Employment, with special responsibility for Commerce and Technology, 1993-94. Minister for Education 1992-93. Minister for Tourism, Transport and Communications, 1991-92. Minister for Tourism and Transport 1989-91. Minister of State at the Department of Industry and Commerce with special responsibility for Trade and Marketing 1987-89.

He was Fianna Fáil front bench spokesperson on Transport, Energy and Communications 1995-97. He has been a Dáil deputy for Dublin South since 1981. He was a Senator 1977-81, Taoiseach's Nominee. He was general secretary of Fianna Fáil 1973-80.

Member, Dublin County Council 1985-87.

Olivia Mitchell (FG)

Home Address
18 Ballawley Court, Dundrum, Dublin 16
Telephone
Home (01) 295 3033; *Fax* (01) 295 3033
Birth Place/Date
Birr, Co Offaly. July 1947
Married
James Mitchell. 2 sons, 1 daughter
Education
Dominican Convent, Eccles Street, Dublin;
Trinity College, Dublin (BA, HDipEd)
Occupation
Full-time public representative. Formerly
secondary school teacher

Olivia Mitchell is a new Dáil deputy. She was
a candidate in Dublin South in the 1989 and
1992 general elections. Fine Gael
spokesperson on Local Development,
National Drugs strategy, and Dublin Traffic
since 1997.

Member, Dublin County Council 1985-93 and
of Dún Laoghaire-Rathdown County Council
since 1994 (Cathaoirleach 1995/96).

Member, Eastern Health Board; Dublin
Regional Authority; Dublin Transport Office
Local Advisory Committee.

She was a member of the Fine Gael
delegation to the Forum for Peace and
Reconciliation. Member, Co-ordinating
Committee of the European Sustainable Cities
and Towns Campaign.

Alan Shatter (FG)

Home Address
57 Delbrook Manor, Dundrum, Dublin 16
Business Address
4 Upper Ely Place, Dublin 2
Telephone
Home (01) 298 3045; *Business* (01) 661 0317
Birth Place/Date
Dublin. February 1951
Married
Carol Danker. 1 son, 1 daughter
Education
High School, Dublin; Trinity College, Dublin;
University of Amsterdam; Law School of the
Incorporated Law Society of Ireland (BA
[Mod], Dip EI), Dublin
Occupation
Public representative, solicitor, author

Alan Shatter has been a Dáil deputy since
June 1981. Front bench spokesperson on
Health and Children since 1997; on Equality
and Law Reform 1993-94; Justice 1992-93;
Labour 1990-92; Environment 1988-90; Law
Reform 1987-88.

Chairman, Joint Committee on Foreign
Affairs, 1996-97. He served on the Oireachtas
Joint Committee on Women's Rights;
Committee on Marital Breakdown; Committee
on Building Land; Committee on Child Care
Bill; Committee on Bankruptcy Bill; Select
Committee on Crime.

Member, Dublin County Council 1979-93,
South Dublin County Council since 1993.

Director and former chairman of Free Legal
Advice Centres. Former chairman of CARE
(Campaign for Deprived Children). Member,
Mental Health Association; Irish Council for
the European Movement. President, Irish
Council Against Blood Sports, 1986-93.

The Shatter Bills on Judicial Separation and
Family Law Reform (1989), Adoption (1991)
and Landlord and Tenant (Amendment) 1994
were the only private member's Bills enacted
into law in the last 35 years.

He is author of *Family Law in the Republic of
Ireland* and a novel *Laura* (1989).

Liz O'Donnell (PD)

Home Address
23 Temple Gardens, Dublin 6
Business Address
Department of Foreign Affairs, Iveagh House,
St Stephen's Green, Dublin 2
Telephone
Home (01) 491 0363; *Fax* (01) 491 0369;
Business (01) 478 1063; *Constituency Office*
(01) 478 0822; *Fax* (01) 478 4780
Birth Place/Date
Dublin. July 1956
Married
Michael T. Carson. 1 son, 1 daughter
Education
Salesian Convent, Fernbank, Limerick; Trinity
College, Dublin (BA [Mod], Legal Science)
Occupation
Minister of State. Formerly lawyer

Liz O'Donnell was appointed Minister of State
at the Department of Foreign Affairs, with
special responsibility for Overseas
Development Assistance and Human Rights,
in June 1997. She has been a Dáil deputy
since 1992.

Progressive Democrats spokesperson on
Health and Social Welfare, Justice, and Party
Chief Whip 1993-97. Chairperson of the
Progressive Democrats Policy Development
Committee.

Member, Dublin City Council 1991-94 and a
number of subsidiary bodies. Member, Local
Authority Committee Dublin Transportation
Initiative.

Member, Executive Committee of the
Women's Political Association 1989-91 (vice-
chairwoman and delegate to Council for the
Status of Women 1990-91).

Dublin South-Central

Seats 4 Quota 8,116	1st Count	2nd Count Transfer of **Mitchell's** Surplus	3rd Count Transfer of **Henry's** Votes	4th Count Transfer of **Ó Nualláin's** Votes	5th Count Transfer of **Callanan's** Votes	6th Count Transfer of **Dwyer's** Votes	7th Count Transfer of **O'Reilly's** Votes
ARDAGH, Seán (FF)	4,634	+16 4,650	— 4,650	+4 4,654	+6 4,660	+2 4,662	+9 4,671
*****BRISCOE**, Ben (FF)	4,762	+32 4,794	+4 4,798	+4 4,802	+9 4,811	+5 4,816	+2 4,818
*****BYRNE**, Eric (DL)	4,586	+81 4,667	+2 4,669	+3 4,672	+4 4,676	+1 4,677	+11 4,688
CALLANAN, Colm (Ind)	91	+1 92	+1 93	— 93	−93 —		
DWYER, Michael (NLP)	92	+1 93	+1 94	+1 95	+5 100	−100 —	
GAVIN, Éamonn (Ind)	367	+4 371	+1 372	+2 374	+13 387	+18 405	+18 423
GOODWILLIE, John (GP)	1,603	+14 1,617	+3 1,620	+6 1,626	+9 1,635	+30 1,665	+19 1,684
HENRY, David (Ind)	23	— 23	−23 —				
KEANE, Cáit (PD)	2,031	+19 2,050	+2 2,052	+2 2,054	+7 2,061	+4 2,065	+6 2,071
KELLY, Seán (Ind)	125	+2 127	+1 128	+15 143	+6 149	+4 153	+12 165
KELLY, Shay (WP)	297	+4 301	— 301	— 301	— 301	+4 305	+1 306
KENNA, Martin (SF)	1,937	+6 1,943	— 1,943	+12 1,955	+6 1,961	+3 1,964	+9 1,973
LYDER, André (Ind)	350	+4 354	+1 355	+5 360	+3 363	+6 369	+15 384
McGINLEY, Ruairí (FG)	1,215	+437 1,652	+2 1,654	+3 1,657	+4 1,661	+6 1,667	+9 1,676
*****MITCHELL**, Gay (FG)	8,910	−794 8,116					
MULCAHY, Michael (FF)	4,574	+32 4,606	+1 4,607	+7 4,614	+9 4,623	+2 4,625	+5 4,630
Ó NUALLÁIN, Dean (Ind)	80	+1 81	— 81	−81 —			
O'REILLY, Brendan (Ind)	132	+3 135	— 135	+2 137	+3 140	+5 145	−145 —
SMITH, Bríd (SWP)	218	+4 222	— 222	+1 223	— 223	— 223	+2 225
*****UPTON**, Pat (Lab)	4,224	+130 4,354	+2 4,356	+5 4,361	+3 4,364	+5 4,369	+14 4,383
WALSH, Martin (SP)	328	+3 331	+1 332	+4 336	+2 338	+1 339	+4 343
NON-TRANSFERABLE			1	5	4	4	9

	8th Count	9th Count	10th Count	11th Count	12th Count	13th Count	14th Count	15th Count
	Transfer of **Kelly's** (Seán) Votes	Transfer of **Smith's** Votes	Transfer of **Kelly's** (Shay), **Lyder's, Walsh's** and **Gavin's** Votes	Transfer of **McGinley's** Votes	Transfer of **Goodwillie's** Votes	Transfer of **Keane's** Votes	Transfer of **Kenna's** Votes	Transfer of **Mulcahy's** Votes
	+7 4,678	+1 4,679	+94 4,773	+42 4,815	+100 4,915	+641 5,556	+339 5,895	+2,327 8,222
	+2 4,820	+5 4,825	+91 4,916	+48 4,964	+140 5,104	+569 5,673	+296 5,969	+2,036 8,005
	+7 4,695	+32 4,727	+256 4,983	+309 5,292	+472 5,764	+180 5,944	+467 6,411	+407 6,818
	+20 443	+2 445	−445 —					
	+16 1,700	+15 1,715	+261 1,976	+118 2,094	−2,094 —			
	+5 2,076	+2 2,078	+83 2,161	+90 2,251	+206 2,457	−2,457 —		
	−165 —							
	+10 316	+12 328	−328 —					
	+18 1,991	+33 2,024	+244 2,268	+42 2,310	+186 2,496	+78 2,574	−2,574 —	
	+20 404	+6 410	−410 —					
	+10 1,686	+4 1,690	+86 1,776	−1,776 —				
	+9 4,639	+8 4,647	+89 4,736	+61 4,797	+98 4,895	+424 5,319	+340 5,659	−5,659 —
	+7 232	−232 —						
	+9 4,392	+32 4,424	+184 4,608	+921 5,529	+504 6,033	+267 6,300	+403 6,703	+382 7,085
	+10 353	+71 424	−424 —					
	15	9	219	145	388	298	729	507

Dublin South-Central

Elected

Gay Mitchell (FG)*	1st Count
Seán Ardagh (FF)	15th Count
Ben Briscoe (FF)*	15th Count
Pat Upton (Lab)*	15th Count

Voting by Party

1st Preference	Number	%	% 1992
Fianna Fáil	13,970	34.43	29.56
Fine Gael	10,125	24.95	19.05
Labour	4,224	10.41	29.63
Prog Democrats	2,031	5.01	4.69
Green Party	1,603	3.95	3.22
Sinn Féin	1,937	4.77	1.68
Democratic Left	4,586	11.30	7.43
Socialist Party	328	0.81	—
Workers' Party	297	0.73	1.78
Socialist Workers'	218	0.54	—
Natural Law Party	92	0.23	—
Others	1,168	2.88	2.97

Statistics

Population	88,858	
Electorate	68,146	
Total Poll	41,129	60.35
Spoiled Votes	550	1.34
Valid Poll	40,579	59.55
Seats	4	
Quota	8,116	
Candidates	21	

Seats

FF	2
FG	1
Lab	1
FF gain from DL	

The constituency of Dublin South-Central is slightly larger than in the 1992 General Election, having gained an area with a population of 8,633 from the constituency of Dublin South-East.

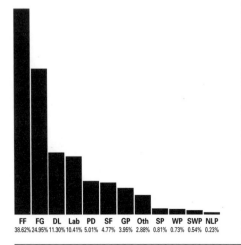

FF	FG	DL	Lab	PD	SF	GP	Oth	SP	WP	SWP	NLP
38.62%	24.95%	11.30%	10.41%	5.01%	4.77%	3.95%	2.88%	0.81%	0.73%	0.54%	0.23%

Gay Mitchell (FG)

Home Address
192 Upper Rathmines Road, Dublin 6
Telephone
Home (01) 490 3744
Birth Place/Date
Inchicore, Dublin. December 1951
Married
Norma O'Connor. 1 son, 3 daughters
Education
St Michael's CBS, Inchicore; Emmet Road Vocational School, Dublin; Rathmines College of Commerce, Dublin; Queen's University, Belfast (MSocSc, FSCA, FIIS, AITI)
Occupation
Full-time public representative

Gay Mitchell was Minister of State at the Department of the Taoiseach with special responsibility for IFSC and Local Government initiatives, and Minister of State at the Department of Foreign Affairs with special responsibility for European Affairs 1994-97. He was first elected to the Dáil in 1981. Front bench spokesperson on Foreign Affairs since 1997; on Justice 1993-94; Public Service and Constitutional Reform 1991-92; Tourism and Transport 1989-91; European Integration 1988-89; Urban Renewal 1987-88; Health Board Reform 1981-82.

Chairman, Dáil Committee of Public Accounts 1987-93. Former vice-chairman, Dáil Committee on Crime, Lawlessness and Vandalism and chairman of Sub-Committee on Motor Insurance. Chaired the Advisory Group on Public Financial Accountability 1987-88.

Member, Dublin City Council 1979-95 (Alderman from 1985, Lord Mayor 1992/93) and of the Council's Finance and Housing Committees (chairman of Finance Committee for 4 years); City of Dublin VEC 1979-85. Chairman, Rathmines College of Commerce 1979-84. Member, board of Our Lady's Hospital for Sick Children, Crumlin.

Founder and president, Dublin International Sports Council 1992.

Seán Ardagh (FF)

Home Address
168 Walkinstown Road, Dublin 12
Constituency Office
168 Walkinstown Road, Dublin 12
Telephone
Home/Office (01) 456 8736; *Fax* (01) 450 1787
Birth Place/Date
Dublin. November 1947
Married
Máire Bhreathnach. 2 sons, 1 daughter
Education
Marian College, Sandymount, Dublin; University College, Dublin; University of Toronto (BSc, Chartered Accountant)
Occupation
Public representative. Partner, Ardagh Holan Chartered Accountants

Seán Ardagh is a new Dáil deputy. This was the first time he contested a general election.

Member, South Dublin County Council since 1991, and Leader of the Fianna Fáil Group on the Council. He is also a member of the Council's subsidiary committees.

Member, Dublin County Council 1985-91.

Director, South Dublin County Enterprise Board.

Member, St Jude's GAA Club; Templeogue Tennis Club.

Ben Briscoe (FF)

Home Address
Shenandoah, Newtown, Celbridge, Co Kildare
Telephone
Home (01) 628 8426; *Fax* (01) 628 8426
Birth Place/Date
Ballybrack, Co Dublin. March 1934
Married
Carol Anne Ward. 2 sons, 2 daughters
Education
St Andrew's College, Dublin (DPolSc [*hon. causa*], North-Eastern University, Boston)
Occupation
Full-time public representative. Formerly businessman

Ben Briscoe first won a seat in the Dáil in 1965, and has been a member since, representing 4 different constituencies in successive Dálaí; Dublin South-West 1965-69, Dublin South-Central 1969-77, Dublin Rathmines West 1977-81 and Dublin South-Central since 1981. He served on the Committee of Public Accounts, Committee of Selection, Committee on Procedure and Privileges, Oireachtas Joint Committee on the Secondary Legislation of the European Communities, Foreign Affairs Committee and as Fianna Fáil Assistant Whip.

Member, Dublin City Council since 1967 (Lord Mayor 1988/89); Eastern Health Board since 1985.

Member, Bone Marrow for Leukaemia Trust since its foundation in 1981; Finance Committee of Cheeverstown House. Council member of Association of Recreation Clubs for the Handicapped.

Distinguished Service Medal, Order of Malta, and Commander of Merit.

He is a son of Bob Briscoe, Dáil deputy 1927-65 and Lord Mayor of Dublin 1956/57 and 1961/62.

Pat Upton (Lab)

Home Address
1 College Drive, Terenure, Dublin 6W
Telephone
Home (01) 490 9653
Birth Place/Date
Kilrush, Co Clare. September 1944
Married
Anne Kent. 3 sons, 1 daughter
Education
St Flannan's College, Ennis, Co Clare; University College, Galway; University College, Dublin (BAgrSc, PhD [Nutrition], FICI)
Occupation
Public representative. University lecturer

Pat Upton was first elected to the Dáil in 1992. Labour Party spokesperson on Science and Technology, and Consumer Affairs, since 1997. He was a candidate in Dublin South-Central constituency in the general election of 1989. Senator, Agricultural Panel, 1989-92 and leader of the Labour Group in the Seanad.

Member, Parliamentary Assembly of the Council of Europe 1994-95.

In the 27th Dáil he served on the Public Accounts Committee, Joint Oireachtas Committee on European Affairs, Joint Oireachtas Committee on the Irish language and Finance and General Affairs Committee.

Member, Dublin County Council 1991-93; South Dublin County Council 1993-94; General Council of County Councils 1991-96; Eastern Health Board since 1996.

Dublin South-East

Seats 4 Quota 7,335	1st Count	2nd Count Transfer of **Harpur's** Votes	3rd Count Transfer of **Gorman's** and **Guerin's** Votes	4th Count Transfer of **Daly's** and **O'Grady's** Votes	5th Count Transfer of **Crilly's** Votes
CRILLY, Tom (WP)	694	+1 695	+12 707	+141 848	−848 —
DALY, Mary (NLP)	231	+3 234	+15 249	−249 —	
DOYLE, Joe (FG)	4,541	— 4,541	+17 4,558	+27 4,585	+82 4,667
***FITZGERALD**, Frances (FG)	5,501	+1 5,502	+22 5,524	+23 5,547	+22 5,569
GORMAN, William D.J. (Ind)	99	+2 101	−101 —		
GORMLEY, John (GP)	4,296	+2 4,298	+42 4,340	+258 4,598	+306 4,904
GUERIN, Joe (Ind)	110	+5 115	−115 —		
HARPUR, John (Ind)	29	−29 —			
KIRRANE, Máire (NP)	1,169	+1 1,170	+7 1,177	+25 1,202	+31 1,233
***McDOWELL**, Michael (PD)	4,022	+2 4,024	+23 4,047	+22 4,069	+26 4,095
O'GRADY, Peadar (SWP)	410	+3 413	+12 425	−425 —	
***QUINN**, Ruairí (Lab)	6,113	+3 6,116	+23 6,139	+92 6,231	+175 6,406
***RYAN**, Eoin (FF)	6,494	+2 6,496	+15 6,511	+34 6,545	+107 6,652
WHELAN, Noel (FF)	2,962	+1 2,963	+17 2,980	+19 2,999	+33 3,032
NON-TRANSFERABLE		3	11	33	66

6th Count	7th Count	8th Count	9th Count	10th Count	11th Count
Transfer of **Kirrane's** Votes	Transfer of **Whelan's** Votes	Transfer of **Ryan's** Surplus	Transfer of **Doyle's** Votes	Transfer of **Fitzgerald's** Surplus	Transfer of **Quinn's** Surplus
+132 4,799	+36 4,835	+51 4,886	−4,886 —		
+83 5,652	+51 5,703	+50 5,753	+3,814 9,567	−2,232 7,335	
+196 5,100	+123 5,223	+270 5,493	+235 5,728	+266 5,994	+807 6,801
−1,233 —					
+223 4,318	+277 4,595	+1,464 6,059	+216 6,275	+175 6,450	+324 6,774
+42 6,448	+116 6,564	+207 6,771	+481 7,252	+1,791 9,043	−1,708 7,335
+250 6,902	+2,475 9,377	−2,042 7,335			
+126 3,158	−3,158 —				
181	80	—	140	—	577

Dublin South-East

Elected

Voting by Party

1st Preference	Number	%	% 1992
Fianna Fáil	9,456	25.79	27.15
Fine Gael	10,042	27.38	21.79
Labour	6,113	16.67	25.79
Prog Democrats	4,022	10.97	11.19
Green Party	4,296	11.71	6.15
Sinn Féin	—	—	2.11
Democratic Left	—	—	2.17
National Party	1,169	3.19	—
Workers' Party	694	1.89	1.42
Socialist Workers	410	1.12	—
Natural Law Party	231	0.63	—
Others	238	0.65	2.23

Statistics

Population	87,353	
Electorate	64,215	
Total Poll	37,032	57.67
Spoiled Votes	361	0.97
Valid Poll	36,671	57.11
Seats	4	
Quota	7,335	
Candidates	14	

Seats

FF	1
FG	1
Lab	1
GP	1

GP gain from PD

The constituency of Dublin South-East is slightly smaller than in the 1992 General Election, having lost an area with a population of 8,633 to the constituency of Dublin South-Central and having gained areas with populations of 7,467 from the constituency of Dublin South and 584 from the constituency of Dún Laoghaire.

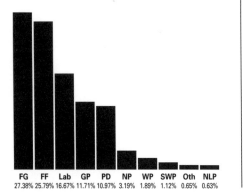

FG	FF	Lab	GP	PD	NP	WP	SWP	Oth	NLP
27.38%	25.79%	16.67%	11.71%	10.97%	3.19%	1.89%	1.12%	0.65%	0.63%

Eoin Ryan (FF)

Home Address
19 Vavasour Square, Sandymount, Dublin 4
Business Address
4 Nassau Street, Dublin 2
Telephone
Home (01) 660 0082; *Business* (01) 618 4375
Birth Place/Date
Dublin. February 1953
Married
Sheila McKeever. 1 son, 2 daughters
Education
St Joseph's, Roscrea, Co Tipperary; St Mary's College, Rathmines, Dublin; College of Commerce, Rathmines; Kildalton Horticultural College, Co Kilkenny
Occupation
Public representative. Formerly retailer and restaurateur

Eoin Ryan has been a Dáil deputy since 1992. Party spokesperson on Ecology and Urban Renewal 1995-97. He contested the general elections of 1987 and 1989 in Dublin South-East constituency. Senator, Taoiseach's Nominee, 1989-92 and Government Whip in the Seanad February-November 1992.

Member, Dublin City Council since 1985; Planning and Development Committee since 1985 (chairman 1985-91) and Youth Committee since 1985 (vice-chairman 1985-91). Member, Dublin Port and Docks Board.

Member, Lansdowne Tennis Club and Shamrock Rovers' Football Club.

Son of former Senator Eoin Ryan and grandson of Dr Jim Ryan, a Minister in the Governments of Éamon de Valera and Seán Lemass.

Frances Fitzgerald (FG)

Home Address
116 Georgian Village, Castleknock, Dublin 15
Telephone
Home (01) 821 1796; *Fax* (01) 618 4143
Birth Place/Date
Croom, Co Limerick. August 1950
Married
Michael Fitzgerald. 3 sons
Education
Sion Hill Convent, Blackrock, Co Dublin; University College, Dublin; London School of Economics (BSocSc; MSc [Social Administration and Social Work])
Occupation
Full-time public representative. Formerly social worker

Frances Fitzgerald has been a Dáil deputy since 1992. Front bench spokesperson on Defence since 1997; on Arts, Culture and the Gaeltacht 1993-94.

Chairwoman, Council for the Status of Women 1988-92. Member, Second Commission on the Status of Women 1990-93. Vice-president, Irish Council of the European Movement 1991-93. Member, All-Party Constitutional Committee 1997; Forum for Peace and Reconciliation 1995-96.

Board member of the Employment Equality Agency 1987-91. Irish representative to European Women's Lobby 1988-92 (vice-president 1992). Chairwoman, Women's Political Association 1987-89 and formerly vice-chairwoman and public relations officer. Board member, Dublin Institute of Adult Education since 1987. Executive Committee member, Institute of European Affairs 1993.

Co-author of *Parenting: A Handbook for Parents*, with Maureen Gaffney, Andy Conway and Father Paul Andrews.

Ruairí Quinn (Lab)

Home Address
23 Strand Road, Sandymount, Dublin 4
Telephone
Home (01) 260 2852; *Fax* (01) 260 2866;
Business (01) 618 4310
Birth Place/Date
Dublin. April 1946
Married
Liz Allman. 1 son and 1 son, 1 daughter by
previous marriage
Education
Blackrock College, Dublin; University College,
Dublin (BArch); Athens Centre of Ekistics,
Greece (HCE)
Occupation
Public representative. Architect and town
planner

Ruairí Quinn was Minister for Finance
1994-97; Minister for Enterprise and
Employment 1993-94. Minister for Labour
December 1983-January 1987; Minister for
the Public Service February 1986-January
1987; Minister of State at the Department of
the Environment with special responsibility for
Urban Affairs and Housing 1982-83. First
elected to the Dáil in Dublin South-East in
1977 but lost his seat in the 1981 general
election. He regained his seat in February
1982. Senator, Industrial and Commercial
Panel, August 1981-February 1982 and June
1976-1977 (selected to fill a vacancy in the
Taoiseach's Nominees). He contested Dublin
South-East in the general election of 1973.

He was elected Deputy Leader of the Labour
Party in July 1989. Spokesperson on Finance
and Economic Affairs 1989-93; on Finance
since 1997.

Labour spokesperson on the Environment and
European Affairs 1987; on the Environment
1977-80; on Foreign Affairs 1980-81. Member,
Oireachtas Joint Committee on the Secondary
Legislation of the European Communities 1987.

Member, Dublin City Council 1974-77 and 1991-
93 (Leader, Labour Group; Leader, Civic Alliance).

Member, Royal Institute of Architects in
Ireland; Royal Institute of British Architects;
Irish Planning Institute; United Arts Club; An
Taisce; World Society of Ekistics; Amnesty
International; Greenpeace.

John Gormley (GP)

Home Address
71 Stella Gardens, Irishtown, Dublin 4
Telephone
Home (01) 660 9148; *Fax* (01) 618 4174
Birth Place/Date
Dublin. August 1959
Married
Penny Stuart
Education
St Munchin's College, Limerick; University
College, Dublin; Freiburg University, Germany
(BA)
Occupation
Full-time public representative. Formerly
director of Academy of European Languages

John Gormley is a new Dáil deputy. He was a
candidate in the general elections of 1992 and
1989 in the Dublin South-East constituency.
With his election and the re-election of Trevor
Sargent in Dublin North, the Green Party for
the first time has more than one deputy in the
Dáil.

Member of Dublin City Council since 1991
and Lord Mayor of Dublin 1994/95.

Author of the *Green Guide for Ireland*
(Wolfhound, 1990). Member of Earthwatch
and ICCL.

'It's all in the swing' — Joan Burton on the canvass trail.

Seats 5 Quota 6,976	1st Count	2nd Count Transfer of **Dowling's, Richards's, Mara's** and **Kinsella's** Votes	3rd Count Transfer of **Tyndall's** Votes	4th Count Transfer of **Federsel's** Votes	5th Count Transfer of **Murphy's** Votes	6th Count Transfer of **McGrath's** Votes	7th Count Transfer of **Crowe's** Votes
CROWE, Seán (SF)	3,725	+113 3,838	+8 3,846	+150 3,996	+444 4,440	+116 4,556	−4,556 —
DOWLING, Denis (Ind)	71	−71 —					
FEDERSEL, Monique Mary (GP)	1,315	+137 1,452	+16 1,468	−1,468 —			
***FLOOD**, Chris (FF)	5,195	+79 5,274	+31 5,305	+94 5,399	+151 5,550	+924 6,474	+872 7,346
***HARNEY**, Mary (PD)	4,713	+76 4,789	+683 5,472	+199 5,671	+120 5,791	+601 6,392	+295 6,687
HAYES, Brian (FG)	6,487	+98 6,585	+38 6,623	+199 6,822	+226 7,048	— —	— —
KINSELLA, Marie (Ind)	509	−509 —					
LENIHAN, Conor (FF)	4,436	+55 4,491	+37 4,528	+81 4,609	+135 4,744	+1,086 5,830	+655 6,485
McGRATH, Colm (FF)	2,898	+27 2,925	+128 3,053	+56 3,109	+110 3,219	−3,219 —	
MARA, Dermot (Ind)	242	−242 —					
MURPHY, Mick (SP)	2,026	+74 2,100	+10 2,110	+139 2,249	−2,249 —		
***RABBITTE**, Pat (DL)	5,094	+89 5,183	+39 5,222	+223 5,445	+458 5,903	+258 6,161	+876 7,037
RICHARDS, Harry (Ind)	76	−76 —					
TYNDALL, Colm (PD)	995	+28 1,023	−1,023 —				
***WALSH**, Eamonn (Lab)	4,070	+61 4,131	+22 4,153	+187 4,340	+362 4,702	+123 4,825	+635 5,460
NON-TRANSFERABLE		61	11	140	243	111	1,223

Dublin South-West

Elected

Voting by Party

1st Preference	Number	%	% 1992
Fianna Fáil	12,529	29.94	29.12
Fine Gael	6,487	15.50	6.13
Labour	4,070	9.72	33.92
Prog Democrats	5,708	13.64	11.64
Green Party	1,315	3.14	2.04
Sinn Féin	3,725	8.90	1.98
Democratic Left	5,094	12.17	8.78
Socialist Party	2,026	4.84	—
Workers' Party	—	—	0.69
Others	898	2.15	5.71

Statistics

Population	110,388	
Electorate	75,646	
Total Poll	42,292	55.91
Spoiled Votes	440	1.04
Valid Poll	41,852	55.33
Seats	5	
Quota	6,976	
Candidates	15	

Seats

FF	2
FG	1
PD	1
DL	1

FF and FG gains from Lab

The constituency of Dublin South-West is unchanged since the 1992 General Election.

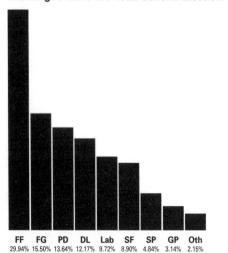

FF	FG	PD	DL	Lab	SF	SP	GP	Oth
29.94%	15.50%	13.64%	12.17%	9.72%	8.90%	4.84%	3.14%	2.15%

Brian Hayes (FG)

Home Address
27 The Dale, Kingswood Heights, Tallaght, Dublin 24
Constituency Office
Leinster House, Dublin 2
Telephone
Home (01) 462 6545; *Office* (01) 618 3333; *Fax* (01) 676 3451
Birth Place/Date
Dublin. August 1969
Education
St Joseph's College, Garbally Park, Ballinasloe, Co Galway; Maynooth College; Trinity College, Dublin (BA, HDipEd)
Occupation
Full-time public representative. Formerly National Youth and Education Officer, Fine Gael, secondary school teacher

Brian Hayes is a new Dáil deputy. This was the first general election he contested. Candidate in by-election in Dublin South-Central, 1994. Fine Gael spokesperson on Housing, House Prices, Urban Renewal since 1997.

Senator, Taoiseach's Nominee December 1995-June 1997 and spokesperson in the Seanad on the Environment.

Member, South Dublin County Council since 1995; South Dublin Enterprise Board; Board of Directors of Virginia House, the Tallaght Community Arts Centre; Board of Management of St Aidan's and St Mark's Community Schools, Tallaght.

He was Fine Gael delegation secretary at the Forum for Peace and Reconciliation. Member, Irish Council for the European Movement.

Chris Flood (FF)

Home Address
22 Birchview Lawn, Kilnamanagh, Tallaght, Dublin 24
Business Address
Department of Tourism, Sport and Recreation, Kildare Street, Dublin 2
Telephone
Home (01) 451 8574; *Fax* (01) 462 6109; *Business* (01) 662 1444; *Constituency Office* (01) 662 9255; *Fax* (01) 662 3810
Birth Place/Date
Westmeath. May 1947
Married
Carmel O'Dwyer. 1 son, 3 daughters
Education
St Norbert's College, Kilnacrott, Ballyjamesduff, Co Cavan
Occupation
Minister of State. Formerly managing director

Chris Flood was appointed Minister of State at the Department of Tourism, Sport and Recreation, with special responsibility for Local Development, in July 1997. He is also Chairman of National Drugs Strategy team. He was Minister of State at the Department of Health 1991-93. He has been a Dáil deputy since 1987, the first time he contested a general election. Party spokesperson on Special Education, Child Care and the Travelling Community 1995-97.

Member, British-Irish Parliamentary Body 1993-97. Member, Select Committee on Enterprise and Economic Strategy 1993-97.

Member, Dublin County Council 1979-91; Eastern Health Board. Former member, Board of Management of Greenhills Community College; Jobstown Community College; Brookfield Community School.

Member, Get Tallaght Working Co-operative, West Tallaght Enterprise Committee.

Member, St Kevin's Hurling and Football Club (vice-president); Kilnamanagh AFC (president).

Pat Rabbitte (DL)

Home Address
56 Monastery Drive, Clondalkin, Dublin 22
Telephone
Home (01) 459 3191; *Business* (01) 618 3980
Birth Place/Date
Mayo. May 1949
Married
Derry McDermott. 3 daughters
Education
St Colman's College, Claremorris, Co Mayo;
University College, Galway (BA, HDipEd, LLB)
Occupation
Full-time public representative. Formerly trade
union official

Pat Rabbitte was Minister of State to the
Government and at the Department of
Enterprise and Employment, with special
responsibility for Commerce, Science and
Technology and Consumer Affairs, 1994-97.
As Minister of State to the Government he
had the right to attend Cabinet meetings but
not to vote. Party Whip since 1997 and
Democratic Left spokesperson on Enterprise,
Trade and Employment, Finance, Education,
Tourism and Transport.

He was first elected to the Dáil in 1989 for the
Workers' Party. During the lifetime of the 26th
Dáil, 6 of the 7 Workers' Party deputies
formed a new party, which was later called
Democratic Left. He served as party
spokesperson on Finance, Enterprise and
Employment, Tourism and Trade, and Health.
He contested Dublin South-West in the general
elections in November 1982 and 1987.

Member, Dublin County Council 1985-95, and
last chairman before it became three separate
administrative counties.

He was a member of the Labour Party until
1976.

Member, Irish Transport and General Workers'
Union (now SIPTU) (formerly National Secretary).

President, UCG Students' Union 1970/71;
President, Union of Students in Ireland 1972-74.

Mary Harney (PD)

Home Address
11 Serpentine Terrace, Ballsbridge, Dublin 4
Business Address
Department of Enterprise, Trade and
Employment, Kildare Street, Dublin 2
Telephone
Home (01) 667 5543; *Fax* (01) 668 9456;
Business (01) 676 1071; *Mobile* (086) 811 2377
Birth Place/Date
Ballinasloe, Co Galway. March 1953
Education
Convent of Mercy, Goldenbridge, Inchicore,
Dublin; Coláiste Bhríde, Clondalkin, Co Dublin;
Trinity College, Dublin (BA [Mod])
Occupation
Tánaiste and Government Minister. Formerly
research worker

Mary Harney was appointed Tánaiste and
Minister for Enterprise, Employment and
Trade in June 1997, becoming the first
woman Tánaiste in the history of the state.
She has been leader of the Progressive
Democrats since 1993 when she became the
first woman leader of a national party.

She was Minister of State at the Department
of the Environment, with special responsibility
for Environmental Protection, 1989-92. She
was first elected to the Dáil in 1981 when she
was a Fianna Fáil candidate. She was a
founder member of the Progressive
Democrats with Desmond O'Malley in 1985.
Senator, Taoiseach's Nominee, 1977-81.
When nominated by the Taoiseach on 25
August 1977, she became the youngest ever
member of the Seanad. She was a candidate
in the 1977 general election in Dublin South-
East.

She was formerly Progressive Democrat
spokesperson on Justice and Social Policy,
Health and Social Welfare, and the party Chief
Whip.

Member, Dublin County Council 1979-91.
Vice-chairperson, County Dublin Vocational
Education Committee 1985.

Conor Lenihan (FF)

Home Address
6 Aylmer Road, Newcastle, Co Dublin
Constituency Office
Greenhills Shopping Centre, Dublin 12
Telephone
Home (01) 458 7276; *Constituency Office* (01)
450 7752
Birth Place/Date
Dublin. March 1963
Married
Denise Russell
Education
Belvedere College, Dublin; University College,
Dublin; Dublin City University (BA, Diploma in
Journalism)
Occupation
Full-time public representative. Formerly
journalist, political correspondent, senior
executive ESAT Digifone

Conor Lenihan is a new Dáil deputy. This was
the first time he contested a general election.

He is a son of Brian Lenihan, a former
Tánaiste, former Minister for Foreign Affairs,
Minister for Agriculture, Minister for Defence,
Minister for Forestry and Fisheries, Minister
for Transport and Power, Minister for
Education, Minister for Justice, a Dáil deputy
for Roscommon-Leitrim 1961-73 and for
Dublin West 1977-95. He is a brother of Brian
Lenihan, Dáil deputy for Dublin West since
1996, and a nephew of Mary O'Rourke,
Minister for Public Enterprise, deputy Leader
of Fianna Fáil and a Dáil deputy since 1982.
Grandson of Patrick Lenihan, Dáil deputy
1965-70.

Dublin West

Seats 4 Quota 8,015	1st Count	2nd Count Transfer of **Malone's, Butler's** and **Lyons's** Votes		3rd Count Transfer of **Mac Giolla's** Votes	4th Count Transfer of **Harmon's** Votes
*BURTON, Joan (Lab)	4,853	+88 4,941		+175 5,116	+313 5,429
BUTLER, Colin (Ind)	96	−96 —			
*CURRIE, Austin (FG)	5,256	+74 5,330		+67 5,397	+938 6,335
GOGARTY, Paul (GP)	1,732	+67 1,799		+127 1,926	+85 2,011
HANRAHAN, Finbarr (FF)	2,216	+30 2,246		+27 2,273	+29 2,302
HARMON, Joanne (FG)	1,532	+54 1,586		+36 1,622	−1,622 —
HIGGINS, Joe (SP)	6,496	+120 6,616		+270 6,886	+74 6,960
*LAWLOR, Liam (FF)	4,241	+30 4,271		+89 4,360	+27 4,387
*LENIHAN, Brian Joseph (FF)	6,842	+77 6,919		+57 6,976	+52 7,028
LYONS, Seán (Ind)	585	−585 —			
McCANN, John (SF)	2,004	+31 2,035		+211 2,246	+11 2,257
Mac GIOLLA, Tomás (WP)	1,135	+22 1,157		−1,157 —	
MALONE, Ciara (Ind)	36	−36 —			
MORRISSEY, Tom (PD)	3,050	+83 3,133		+35 3,168	+73 3,241
NON-TRANSFERABLE		41		63	20

5th Count	6th Count	7th Count	8th Count	9th Count
Transfer of **Gogarty's** Votes	Transfer of **McCann's** Votes	Transfer of **Hanrahan's** Votes	Transfer of **Morrissey's** Votes	Transfer of **Lenihan's** Surplus
+422 5,851	+226 6,077	+109 6,186	+616 6,802	+50 6,852
+328 6,663	+101 6,764	+178 6,942	+703 7,645	+53 7,698
−2,011 —				
+155 2,457	+107 2,564	−2,564 —		
+325 7,285	+809 8,094	— —	— —	— —
+110 4,497	+341 4,838	+836 5,674	+1,697 7,371	+426 7,797
+181 7,209	+279 7,488	+1,056 8,544	— —	−529 8,015
+91 2,348	−2,348 —			
+198 3,439	+94 3,533	+234 3,767	−3,767 —	
201	391	151	751	—

Dublin West

Elected

Joe Higgins (SP)	6th Count
Brian Joseph Lenihan (FF)*	7th Count
Liam Lawlor (FF)*	9th Count
Austin Currie (FG)*	9th Count

Voting by Party

1st Preference	Number	%	% 1992
Fianna Fáil	13,299	33.19	31.31
Fine Gael	6,788	16.94	14.37
Labour	4,853	12.11	22.60
Prog Democrats	3,050	7.61	4.03
Green Party	1,732	4.32	2.44
Sinn Féin	2,004	5.00	2.78
Socialist Party	6,496	16.21	—
Workers' Party	1,135	2.83	7.34
Others	717	1.79	15.13

Statistics

Population	89,383	
Electorate	66,419	
Total Poll	40,297	60.67
Spoiled Votes	223	0.55
Valid Poll	40,074	60.34
Seats	4	
Quota	8,015	
Candidates	14	

Seats

FF	2
FG	1
SP	1
SP gain from Lab	

The constituency of Dublin West is slightly smaller than in the 1992 General Election, having gained an area with a population of 13,847 from the constituency of Dublin North and having lost an area with a population of 16,494 to the constituency of Dublin Central.

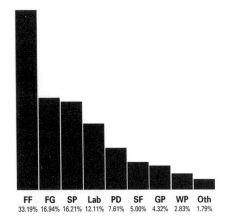

FF	FG	SP	Lab	PD	SF	GP	WP	Oth
33.19%	16.94%	16.21%	12.11%	7.61%	5.00%	4.32%	2.83%	1.79%

Joe Higgins (SP)

Home Address
155 Briarwood Close, Mulhuddart, Dublin 15
Telephone
Home (01) 820 1753
Birth Place/Date
Dingle, Co Kerry. May 1949
Education
Christian Brothers' School, Dingle. University College, Dublin (BA, HDipEd)
Occupation
Full-time public representative. Formerly second-level teacher

Joe Higgins is a new Dáil deputy. He contested the 1992 general election in Dublin West, and a by-election in the constituency in 1996 as a Militant Labour candidate.

He was elected to Dublin County Council in 1991 and is now a member of Fingal County Council.

Chairman of the Federation of Dublin Anti-Water Charges Campaigns. Member of Blakestown and Mountview Addiction Support Group; Member of Environmental Committee of Huntstown Development Group.

Brian Joseph Lenihan (FF)

Home Address
Longwood, Somerton Road, Strawberry Beds, Dublin 20
Constituency Office
Laurel Business Centre, Castleknock, Dublin 15
Telephone
Home (01) 821 4058; *Office* (01) 822 0970; *Fax* (01) 822 0972
Birth Place/Date
Dublin. May 1959
Married
Patricia Ryan. 1 son, 1 daughter
Education
Belvedere College, Dublin; Trinity College, Dublin; Cambridge University; King's Inns (BA [Mod], LLB)
Occupation
Public representative. Senior Counsel

Brian Lenihan has been a Dáil deputy since April 1996, when he won a by-election in Dublin West caused by the death of his father, Brian Lenihan, who had been a Dáil deputy for the constituency since 1977.

He served on the Criminal Injuries Compensation Board 1992-95, and the Garda Complaints Appeals Board 1992-96. He served as honorary secretary, Incorporated Council of Law Reporting and as chairman, Make a Wish Foundation of Ireland.

He is a son of Brian Lenihan, a former Tánaiste, former Minister for Foreign Affairs, Minister for Agriculture, Minister for Defence, Minister for Forestry and Fisheries, Minister for Transport and Power, Minister for Education, Minister for Justice, a Dáil deputy for Roscommon-Leitrim 1961-73 and for Dublin West 1977-95. He is a brother of Conor Lenihan, Dáil deputy for Dublin South-West since 1997, and a nephew of Mary O'Rourke, Minister for Public Enterprise, deputy Leader of Fianna Fáil and a Dáil deputy since 1982. Grandson of Patrick Lenihan, Dáil deputy 1965-70.

Liam Lawlor (FF)

Home Address
Somerton House, Lucan, Co Dublin
Telephone
Constituency Office (01) 628 0507;
Fax (01) 624 1842
Birth Place/Date
Dublin. October 1945
Married
Hazel Barber. 3 sons, 1 daughter
Education
Synge Street CBS, Dublin; College of
Technology, Bolton Street, Dublin
(Engineering Diploma)
Occupation
Full-time public representative. Formerly
managing director of refrigeration engineering
company

Liam Lawlor was first elected to the Dáil for the
then 3-seat constituency of Dublin West in
1977. He was an unsuccessful candidate in
the 5-seat constituency of Dublin West in
1981. He regained his seat in February 1982,
but again lost it in November 1982. Re-elected
in February 1987 and subsequent elections.

Fianna Fáil spokesperson on Arts, Culture and
Heritage 1995-97. Convenor, Dáil Committee
for Enterprise and Economic Strategy 1993-
95. Chairman, Oireachtas Joint Committee on
Commercial State-Sponsored Bodies 1987-89.

Member, Dublin County Council 1979-91
(vice-chairman 1985/86); former chairman,
Eastern Region Development Organisation.
Member, Trilateral Commission.

Former member, Boards of Management of
Lucan Vocational School, Coolmine Community
School and Collinstown Park Community School.

Former member, National Engineering and
Electrical Trade Union.

He played hurling for Dublin senior teams and
Leinster Railway Cup teams.

Austin Currie (FG)

Home Addresses
Tullydraw, Ballyowen Lane, Lucan, Co Dublin;
Dungannon, Co Tyrone
Telephone
Home (01) 626 5047
Birth Place/Date
Coalisland, Co Tyrone. October 1939
Married
Annita Lynch. 2 sons, 3 daughters
Education
St Patrick's Academy, Dungannon, Co Tyrone;
Queen's University, Belfast (BA); Research
Fellow, Trinity College, Dublin, 1976
Occupation
Public representative. Formerly teacher

Austin Currie was Minister of State at the
Department of Health with special responsibility
for all aspects relating to Child Care and
Children's Policy, and Minister of State at the
Department of Education and Minister of State
at the Department of Justice 1994-97.

He was first elected to the Dáil in 1989.
He was the Fine Gael candidate in the
Presidential Election of 1990. Fine Gael
spokesperson on Energy since 1997; on
Housing and Urban Renewal 1993-94. Front
bench spokesperson on Communications
1990-93. Member of the British-Irish
Parliamentary Body, 1991-94.

Elected to the Stormont Parliament as Nationalist
member for East Tyrone at a by-election in
1964 and was, at 24, the youngest member
ever elected to Stormont and continued to be
a member until prorogued. Chief organiser,
first civil rights march, Coalisland 1968. With
5 other opposition members of the Stormont
Parliament, he formed the SDLP in October
1971.

Member of the Northern Ireland Assembly
1973-75 and participated in the Sunningdale
Conference. Minister of Housing, Local
Government and Planning in the Northern
Ireland Executive, January-May 1974.

Member, Northern Ireland Constitutional
Convention 1975; Northern Ireland Assembly
in 1982.

Member, New Ireland Forum 1983.

'What Have I Done?' Joe Higgins, the newly-elected socialist TD for Dublin West, arrives at the Dáil with his supporters.

Seats 5 Quota 9,043	1st Count	2nd Count Transfer of **Barrett's** Surplus	3rd Count Transfer of **Stokes's, Allshire–Tyrrell's, Abum's, Tyaransen's** and **Madigan's** Votes	4th Count Transfer of **Casey's** Votes	5th Count Transfer of **MacDowell's** Votes	6th Count Transfer of **Andrews's** Surplus	7th Count Transfer of **Keogh's** Votes
ABUM, Jog Monster Raving Looney (Ind)	288	— 288	−288 —				
ALLSHIRE–TYRRELL, Hazel (Ind)	53	— 53	−53 —				
*****ANDREWS**, David (FF)	8,933	+7 8,940	+255 9,195	— 	— 	−152 9,043	
BARNES, Monica (FG)	7,576	+125 7,701	+244 7,945	+200 8,145	+633 8,778	+23 8,801	+1,056 9,857
*****BARRETT**, Seán (FG)	9223	−180 9,043					
*****BHREATHNACH**, Niamh (Lab)	4,698	+21 4,719	+157 4,876	+71 4,947	+553 5,500	+9 5,509	+337 5,846
CASEY, Gerard (CSP)	2,000	+2 2,002	+91 2,093	−2,093 —			
*****GILMORE**, Éamon (DL)	7,534	+17 7,551	+268 7,819	+181 8,000	+949 8,949	+18 8,967	+414 9,381
HANAFIN, Mary (FF)	5,079	+1 5,080	+165 5,245	+953 6,198	+393 6,591	+77 6,668	+2,916 9,584
*****KEOGH**, Helen (PD)	4,636	+4 4,640	+160 4,800	+175 4,975	+425 5,400	+25 5,425	−5,425 —
MacDOWELL, Vincent (GP)	2,762	+2 2,764	+375 3,139	+315 3,454	−3,454 —		
MADIGAN, Paddy (Ind)	1,082	+1 1,083	−1,083 —				
STOKES, Rory (Ind)	41	— 41	−41 —				
TYARANSEN, Olaf Paul (Ind)	348	— 348	−348 —				
NON-TRANSFERABLE		—	98	198	501	—	702

Dún Laoghaire

Elected

Seán Barrett (FG)*	1st Count
David Andrews (FF)*	3rd Count
Monica Barnes (FG)	7th Count
Mary Hanafin (FF)	7th Count
Éamon Gilmore (DL)*	7th Count

Voting by Party

1st Preference	Number	%	% 1992
Fianna Fáil	14,012	25.83	31.18
Fine Gael	16,799	30.96	21.55
Labour	4,698	8.66	16.97
Prog Democrats	4,636	8.55	10.94
Green Party	2,762	5.09	3.00
Sinn Féin	—	—	1.35
Democratic Left	7,534	13.89	11.87
Christian Solidarity	2,000	3.69	—
Workers' Party	—	—	0.19
Others	1,812	3.34	2.95

Statistics

Population	111,223	
Electorate	87,994	
Total Poll	54,646	62.10
Spoiled Votes	393	0.72
Valid Poll	54,253	61.66
Seats	5	
Quota	9,043	
Candidates	14	

Seats

FF	2
FG	2
DL	1

FF and FG gains from Lab and PD

The constituency of Dún Laoghaire is somewhat smaller than in the 1992 General Election, having lost an area with a population of 3,539 to the constituency of Dublin South and an area with a population of 584 to the constituency of Dublin South-East.

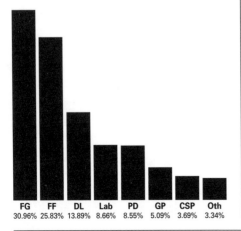

FG	FF	DL	Lab	PD	GP	CSP	Oth
30.96%	25.83%	13.89%	8.66%	8.55%	5.09%	3.69%	3.34%

Seán Barrett (FG)

Home Address
Avondale, Ballinclea Road, Killiney, Co Dublin
Telephone
Home (01) 285 2077
Birth Place/Date
Dublin. August 1944
Married
Sheila Hyde. 2 sons, 3 daughters
Education
Christian Brothers' College, Monkstown Park, Co Dublin; Presentation College, Glasthule, Co Dublin
Occupation
Public representative and insurance broker (FLIA)

Seán Barrett was Minister for Defence and Minister for the Marine 1995-97; Minister of State at the Department of the Taoiseach and Minister of State at the Department of Defence and Government Chief Whip 1994-95; Minister of State at the Department of the Taoiseach and at the Department of Defence, and Government Chief Whip December 1982-February 1986; Minister of State at the Department of Education with special responsibility for Sport, and Leader of the House with responsibility for Dáil Reform February 1986-March 1987. Fine Gael Whip since 1997; front bench spokesperson on Defence and Marine 1993-94; Environment 1994; Industry and Commerce 1989-91; Justice 1987-89. Assistant Government Whip 1981-82. Fine Gael Chief Whip March-November 1982. He was first elected to the Dáil in 1981. He was a candidate in the 1977 general election.

Member, Dublin County Council 1974-82 (chairman 1981/82, vice-chairman 1980/81), and 1991-94. Vocational Education Committee 1974-82.

Member, Board of Management of Cabinteely School since 1975 (chairman 1977 and 1980).

David Andrews (FF)

Home Address
102 Avoca Park, Blackrock, Co Dublin
Business Address
Department of Foreign Affairs, St Stephen's Green, Dublin 2
Telephone
Business (01) 478 0822; *Home* (01) 283 5755
Birth Place/Date
Dublin. March 1935
Married
Annette Cusack. 2 sons, 3 daughters
Education
Mount St Joseph's Cistercian College, Roscrea, Co Tipperary; University College, Dublin; King's Inns, Dublin (BCL, BL)
Occupation
Government Minister. Senior Counsel

David Andrews was appointed Minister for Foreign Affairs in October 1997. He was Minister for Defence June-October 1997. Minister for Defence and Minister for the Marine 1993-94. Minister for Foreign Affairs 1992-93. He was Parliamentary Secretary to the Taoiseach 1970-73; Minister of State at the Department of Foreign Affairs July 1977-December 1979. Minister of State at the Department of Justice 1978-79. Government Chief Whip 1970-73; front bench spokesman on Justice and Social Welfare 1973-77; Tourism and Trade 1995-97. He has represented the constituency of Dún Laoghaire since 1965.

He served as a member, Committee on the Constitution 1967; New Ireland Forum; Consultative Assembly of the Council of Europe; British-Irish Parliamentary Body 1991-92.

He is patron and former president of the University College, Dublin, Association Football Club. President of Leinster Senior League. Patron and life member, Football Association of Ireland. He played rugby for Galwegians RFC and Palmerston RFC and represented Connacht at inter-provincial level, and he played soccer for UCD. Member, Leopardstown Lions Club.

He is a brother of Niall Andrews, MEP for Dublin and former Dáil deputy.

Monica Barnes (FG)

Home Address
5 Arnold Park, Glenageary, Co Dublin
Telephone
Home (01) 285 3751
Birth Place/Date
Carrickmacross, Co Monaghan. February 1936
Married
Bob Barnes. 1 son, 2 daughters
Education
St Louis Convent, Carrickmacross; Oranges' Academy, Belfast
Occupation
Full-time public representative. Formerly administrator, lecturer

Monica Barnes was previously a Dáil deputy November 1982-92. Senator, Labour Panel 1981-November 1982. She served as Fine Gael opposition spokesperson on Women's Affairs in the Dáil and as Chairperson, Oireachtas Committee on Women's Rights. She contested the European elections of 1979 and 1994 in the Leinster constituency and was a Fine Gael general election candidate in 1981, February 1982 and 1992. Fine Gael spokesperson on Law Reform and Assistant Whip in the Seanad, April-November 1982.

Member, Women's Representative Committee, 1974-78; Irish Association of Civil Liberty; Irish Anti-Apartheid Movement; Campaign for Nuclear Disarmament (CND); Employment Equality Agency 1977-82; Femscan Committee; National Forum on Cancer Services.

Founder member, Council for the Status of Women, 1973 (Administrator 1978-81). Life member, Business and Professional Women's Club, Dún Laoghaire. Vice-chairperson, Women's Political Association, 1973/74. Vice-president, Women's Federation, European People's Party. First woman vice-president, Fine Gael, 1980/81.

Mary Hanafin (FF)

Home Address
7 Oaklands Drive, Rathgar, Dublin 6
Constituency Office
7 Newtown Park, Blackrock, Co Dublin
Telephone
Constituency Office (01) 283 6533; *Fax* (01) 283 6533
Birth Place/Date
Thurles, Co Tipperary. June 1959
Married
Éamon Leahy
Education
Presentation Convent, Thurles; St Patrick's College, Maynooth; Dublin Institute of Technology (BA, HDipEd, Diploma in Legal Studies)
Occupation
Full-time public representative. Formerly secondary school teacher

Mary Hanafin is a new Dáil deputy. She was a candidate in Dublin South-East constituency in the 1989 General Election. She was a member of Dublin City Council 1985-91 and of the City of Dublin Vocational Education Committee 1985-91.

Member of the Senate of the National University of Ireland since 1988. Joint Honorary Treasurer of Fianna Fáil since 1993. Stagiaire scholarship to European Parliament. Robert Schuman silver medal for services towards European unity.

She is a daughter of Desmond Hanafin, Senator 1969-93, and since 1997.

Éamon Gilmore (DL)

Home Address
1 Corbawn Close, Shankill, Co Dublin
Telephone
Home (01) 282 1363; *Business* (01) 618 4037, *Fax* (01) 618 4161
Birth Place/Date
Galway. April 1955
Married
Carol Hanney. 2 sons, 1 daughter
Education
Garbally College, Ballinasloe, Co Galway; University College, Galway (BA)
Occupation
Full-time public representative. Formerly trade union official

Éamon Gilmore was Minister of State at the Department of the Marine, with special responsibility for Port Development, Pollution and Nuclear Hazards 1994-97. He was first elected to the Dáil in 1989 as a Workers' Party deputy. During the lifetime of the 26th Dáil, 6 of the 7 Workers' Party deputies formed a new party, which was later called Democratic Left. He contested the Dáil general elections in 1987 and November 1982 for the Workers' Party. Democratic Left spokesperson on Education, Environment, Justice, Transport, Energy and Communications 1993-94. Democratic Left spokesperson on the Environment, Marine, Agriculture and Public Enterprise since 1997.

Member, Dublin County Council 1985-95 (chairman, Dún Laoghaire-Rathdown Area Committee 1992/93); Dún Laoghaire Borough Corporation 1985-95; Dún Laoghaire Vocational Education Committee 1985-95.

President, UCG Students' Union 1974/75; president, Union of Students in Ireland 1976-78.

Irish Transport and General Workers' Union (now SIPTU) since 1978 (acting branch secretary, Galway, 1978-79; branch secretary, Tralee 1980-81; secretary, professional and managerial branches 1981-89).

Member, CND; Greenpeace; Irish Council Against Blood Sports.

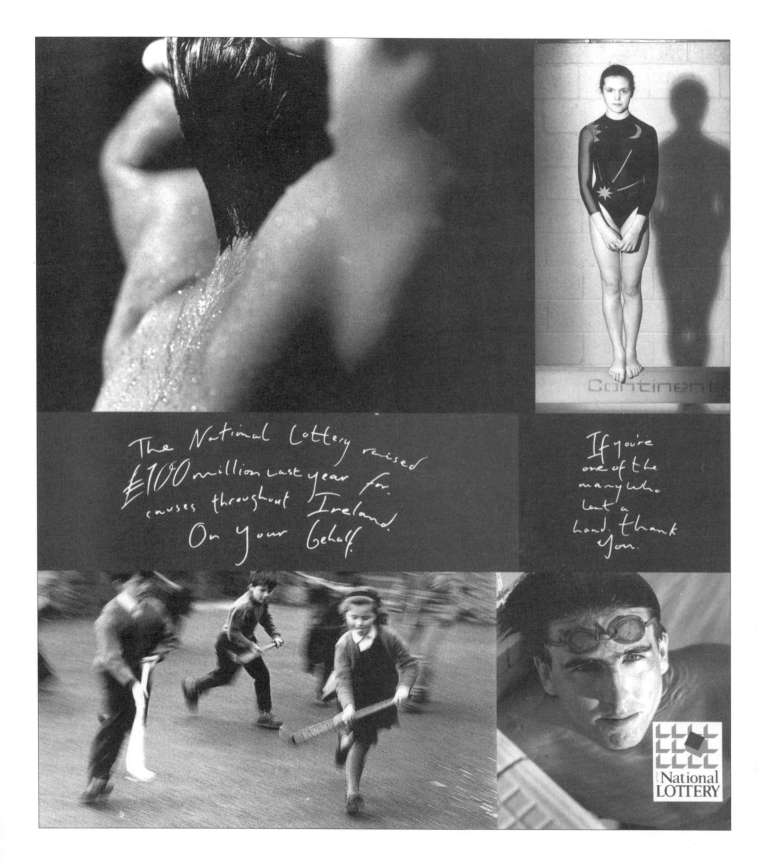

The National Lottery raised £100 million last year for causes throughout Ireland. On your behalf.

If you're one of the many who lent a hand, thank you.

National LOTTERY

Seats 4 Quota 8,584	1st Count	2nd Count Transfer of **Campbell's, Ganly's** and **Hynes's** Votes	3rd Count Transfer of **Finnegan's** Votes	4th Count Transfer of **Burke's** (Joe) Votes	5th Count Transfer of **Keaveney's** Votes
BURKE, Joe (PD)	3,182	+121 3,303	+352 3,655	−3,655 —	
BURKE, Ulick (FG)	6,931	+505 7,436	+55 7,491	+253 7,744	+826 8,570
CALLANAN, Joe (FF)	6,221	+382 6,603	+326 6,929	+492 7,421	+211 7,632
CAMPBELL, Paul (NLP)	98	−98 —			
*****CONNAUGHTON**, Paul (FG)	6,445	+175 6,620	+189 6,809	+521 7,330	+1,496 8,826
FINNEGAN, Pat (FF)	2,670	+40 2,710	−2,710 —		
GANLY, Sheila Mary (Ind)	705	−705 —			
HYNES, Pat (Ind)	1,298	−1,298 —			
KEAVENEY, Colm (Lab)	3,400	+204 3,604	+304 3,908	+1,041 4,949	−4,949 —
*****KITT**, Michael P. (FF)	5,436	+198 5,634	+1,128 6,762	+761 7,523	+932 8,455
*****TREACY**, Noel (FF)	6,531	+323 6,854	+295 7,149	+375 7,524	+446 7,970
NON-TRANSFERABLE		153	61	212	1,038

Elected

Paul Connaughton (FG)*	5th Count
Ulick Burke (FG)	5th Count
Michael P. Kitt (FF)*	5th Count
Noel Treacy (FF)*	5th Count

Voting by Party

1st Preference	Number	%	% 1992
Fianna Fáil	20,858	48.60	48.48
Fine Gael	13,376	31.17	31.66
Labour	3,400	7.92	5.46
Prog Democrats	3,182	7.41	13.35
Sinn Féin	—	—	1.05
Natural Law Party	98	0.23	—
Others	2,003	4.67	—

Statistics

Population	80,113	
Electorate	61,075	
Total Poll	43,368	71.01
Spoiled Votes	451	1.04
Valid Poll	42,917	70.27
Seats	4	
Quota	8,584	
Candidates	11	

Seats

FF	2
FG	2

FG gain additional seat

The constituency of Galway East has gained a seat since the 1992 General Election. The population has increased by 20,999, taken from the old Mayo constituencies and the constituency of Galway West.

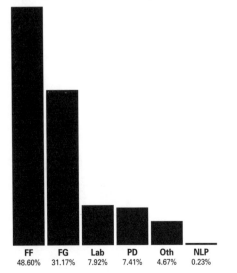

FF	FG	Lab	PD	Oth	NLP
48.60%	31.17%	7.92%	7.41%	4.67%	0.23%

Paul Connaughton (FG)

Home Address
Mount Bellew, Ballinasloe, Co Galway
Telephone
Home (0905) 79249
Birth Place/Date
Mount Bellew. June 1944
Married
Bernadette Keating. 2 sons, 5 daughters
Education
St Mary's Secondary School, Ballygar, Co Galway; St Jarlath's Vocational School, Mount Bellew; Mount Bellew Agricultural College; Athenry Agricultural College, Co Galway; IMI Management Course
Occupation
Public representative, farmer. Formerly general manager, Tuam Livestock Mart

Paul Connaughton was Minister of State at the Department of Agriculture with special responsibility for Land Structure and Development 1982-87. He was first elected to the Dáil in 1981. He contested the 1977 Dáil general election as a Fine Gael candidate in Galway East and a by-election in the old Galway North-East constituency in 1975. Senator, Agricultural Panel, 1977-81. Fine Gael spokesperson on Agriculture - Food since 1997; on Energy and Western Development 1993-94 and Energy, Agriculture and Rural Development 1994. He has served as Fine Gael front bench spokesperson on Agriculture, Social Welfare, Regional Development, Defence, and deputy spokesperson on Tourism.

Member, Galway County Council 1979-85 and since 1991; Galway County Committee of Agriculture 1979-85.

Member, Macra na Feirme; Irish Farmers' Association; Mount Bellew Town Development Association; Tuam Chamber of Commerce; Gaelic Athletic Association.

Ulick Burke (FG)

Home Address
Eagle Hill, Abbey, Loughrea, Co Galway
Constituency Office
Main Street, Loughrea
Telephone
Home (0509) 45218; *Mobile* (086) 811 0556
Birth Place/Date
Loughrea. November 1943
Married
Maeve Naughton. 5 sons, 2 daughters
Education
St Molaise's College, Portumna, Co Galway; University College, Galway (BA, HDipEd)
Occupation
Full-time public representative. Formerly secondary teacher at St Joseph's College, Garbally, Ballinasloe, Co Galway

Ulick Burke is a new Dáil deputy. He was a Senator 1981-82 and 1983-87.

Member, Galway County Council since 1974; Galway Vocational Education Committee since 1974 (former chairman). Former member, Western Health Board; Central Executive Committee of ASTI.

Galway East constituency, previously a 3-seater, had an extra seat and major boundary changes for the 1997 general election.

Michael P. Kitt (FF)

Home Address
Castleblakeney, Ballinasloe, Co Galway
Telephone
Home (0905) 78148; *Office* (0905) 78148;
Mobile (088) 254 4345; *Fax* (0905) 78148
Birth Place/Date
Tuam, Co Galway. May 1950
Married
Catherine Mannion. 3 sons, 1 daughter
Education
St Jarlath's College, Tuam; University College,
Galway; St Patrick's Teachers' Training
College, Drumcondra, Dublin; University
College, Dublin (BA, HDipEd)
Occupation
Full-time public representative. Formerly
primary teacher

Michael Kitt was Minister of State at the
Department of the Taoiseach November
1991-February 1992. He was first elected to
the Dáil in a by-election in March 1975 in the
old constituency of Galway North-East, caused
by the death of his father, Michael Kitt. He
lost his seat in the subsequent general election
in March 1977 but was re-elected in 1981 for
the new constituency of Galway East. Senator,
Administrative Panel 1977-81. Spokesperson
on Emigration issues and Third World issues
1995-97.

Member, Galway County Council 1975-91
(chairman 1985/86); Galway County
Vocational Education Committee 1975-79;
Galway County Committee of Agriculture
1975-85; Vice-chairman, Galway-Mayo
Regional Development Organisation 1985/86.
Member, Western Health Board 1992.

Member, Irish National Teachers'
Organisation; Caltra Gaelic Athletic
Association; Comhaltas Ceoltóirí Éireann.

He is a son of Michael F. Kitt, Dáil deputy for
Galway constituencies 1948-51, 1957-75 and
Parliamentary Secretary to the Minister for the
Gaeltacht 1970-73. Brother of Tom Kitt, Dáil
deputy for Dublin South since 1987, and
Minister of State.

Noel Treacy (FF)

Home Address
Gurteen, Ballinasloe, Co Galway
Business Address
Department of Enterprise, Trade and Employment,
Kildare Street, Dublin 2, and Department of
Education, Marlborough Street, Dublin 1
Telephone
Home (0905) 77094; *Business* (01) 661 4444;
(01) 873 4700
Birth Place/Date
Ballinasloe. December 1952
Married
Mary Cloonan. 4 daughters
Education
St Joseph's College, Garbally Park, Ballinasloe
Occupation
Minister of State. Formerly auctioneer

Noel Treacy was appointed Minister of State at
the Department of Enterprise, Trade and
Employment and at the Department of
Education, with special responsibility for Science
and Technology, in October 1997. He was
Minister of State at the Departments of the
Taoiseach, Finance, and Transport, Energy and
Communications, with special responsibility
for Energy 1993-94. He was Minister of State
at the Department of Finance with special
responsibility for the Office of Public Works and
the Central Development Committee 1992-93.
Minister of State at the Department of Health
1989-91. He was previously Minister of State
at the Department of Finance 1987-89 with
responsibility for the Office of Public Works,
and Minister of State at the Department of the
Taoiseach June 1988-89 with responsibility for
Heritage Affairs. He was first elected to the Dáil
in May 1982 in a by-election. Fianna Fáil deputy
spokesman on Defence 1983-87.

Member, Galway County Council 1985-91
(chairman 1986/87); Galway County Vocational
Education Committee 1985-91.

Member, Macra na Feirme since 1968 and
former chairman of County Executive. Former
member, Macra na Tuaithe and Muintir na
Tíre. Member, Institute of Professional
Auctioneers and Valuers; Irish Livestock
Auctioneers' Association.

Galway West

Seats 5 Quota 8,036	1st Count	2nd Count Transfer of **Fahey's** Surplus	3rd Count Transfer of **Ó Cuív's** Surplus	4th Count Transfer of **Ní Dhomhnaill's** and **Ming's** Votes	5th Count Transfer of **Downes's** Votes
A, Ming (Ind)	548	+5 553	+1 554	−554 —	
BÁINÍN Ó FOIGHIL, Pól (FG)	1,807	+19 1,826	+10 1,836	+77 1,913	+48 1,961
COX, Margaret (FF)	2,941	+442 3,383	+67 3,450	+47 3,497	+163 3,660
*CUÍV, Éamon Ó (FF)	8,250	— —	−214 8,036		
DOWNES, Liam (NP)	959	+8 967	+2 969	+24 993	−993 —
EGAN, Mike (SF)	1,209	+26 1,235	+5 1,240	+81 1,321	+52 1,373
FAHEY, Frank (FF)	9,321	−1,285 8,036			
FITZPATRICK, Pat (GP)	1,660	+15 1,675	+2 1,677	+190 1,867	+110 1,977
*HIGGINS, Michael D. (Lab)	4,856	+86 4,942	+10 4,952	+124 5,076	+69 5,145
*McCORMACK, Pádraic (FG)	7,221	+114 7,335	+16 7,351	+41 7,392	+128 7,520
*MOLLOY, Robert (PD)	5,914	+302 6,216	+41 6,257	+73 6,330	+246 6,576
Ní DHOMHNAILL, Maria (NLP)	205	+2 207	+1 208	−208 —	
O'MALLEY, Thomas (FG)	1,682	+17 1,699	+2 1,701	+28 1,729	+33 1,762
Ó NEACHTAIN, Seán (FF)	1,639	+249 1,888	+57 1,945	+52 1,997	+67 2,064
NON-TRANSFERABLE		—	—	25	77

6th Count	7th Count	8th Count	9th Count	10th Count	11th Count
Transfer of **Egan's** Votes	Transfer of **O'Malley's** Votes	Transfer of **McCormack's** Surplus	Transfer of **Ó Neachtain's** Votes	Transfer of **Fitzpatrick's** Votes	Transfer of **Ó Foighil's** Votes
+48 2,009	+276 2,285	+301 2,586	+236 2,822	+228 3,050	−3,050 —
+245 3,905	+64 3,969	+9 3,978	+961 4,939	+318 5,257	+248 5,505
−1,373 —					
+318 2,295	+69 2,364	+12 2,376	+58 2,434	−2,434 —	
+234 5,379	+275 5,654	+105 5,759	+149 5,908	+1,230 7,138	+1,318 8,456
+81 7,601	+894 8,495	−459 8,036			
+127 6,703	+137 6,840	+27 6,867	+519 7,386	+286 7,672	+545 8,217
+16 1,778	−1,778 —				
+139 2,203	+27 2,230	+5 2,235	−2,235 —		
165	36	—	312	372	939

Galway West

Elected

Frank Fahey (FF)	1st Count
Éamon Ó Cuív (FF)*	1st Count
Pádraic McCormack (FG)*	7th Count
Michael D. Higgins (Lab)*	11th Count
Robert Molloy (PD)*	11th Count

Voting by Party

1st Preference	Number	%	% 1992
Fianna Fáil	22,151	45.94	43.77
Fine Gael	10,710	22.21	16.92
Labour	4,856	10.07	17.68
Prog Democrats	5,914	12.27	13.39
Green Party	1,660	3.44	—
Sinn Féin	1,209	2.51	0.69
Democratic Left	—	—	0.78
National Party	959	1.99	—
Natural Law Party	205	0.43	—
Others	548	1.14	6.76

Statistics

Population	100,251	
Electorate	78,064	
Total Poll	48,612	62.27
Spoiled Votes	400	0.82
Valid Poll	48,212	61.76
Seats	5	
Quota	8,036	
Candidates	14	

Seats

FF	2
FG	1
Lab	1
PD	1
No change	

The constituency of Galway West is somewhat smaller than in the 1992 General Election, having suffered a net loss of population of 13,064, which comprises losses to the constituency of Galway East, offset by gains from the old constituencies of Mayo.

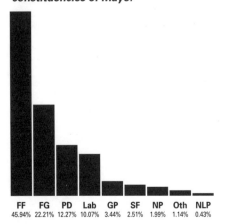

FF	FG	PD	Lab	GP	SF	NP	Oth	NLP
45.94%	22.21%	12.27%	10.07%	3.44%	2.51%	1.99%	1.14%	0.43%

Frank Fahey (FF)

Home Address
4 Corrig Ban, Menlo, Co Galway
Business Address
Department of Health and Children, Hawkins House, Hawkins Street, Dublin 2
Telephone
Business (01) 671 4711
Birth Place/Date
Dublin. June 1951
Married
Ethelle Griffin. 2 sons, 1 daughter
Education
St Mary's College, Galway; Our Lady's College, Gort; University College, Galway (BA, HDipEd)
Occupation
Minister of State. Formerly secondary school teacher

Frank Fahey was appointed Minister of State at the Department of Health and Children, with special responsibility for children in July 1997. He was Minister of State at the Department of Education with special responsibility for Youth and Sport 1987-92 and also at the Department of Tourism, Transport and Communications, with special responsibility for Sports Tourism. He was first elected to the Dáil in February 1982 and continued to 1992 when he lost his seat. Senator, Labour Panel, 1993-97.

He was Fianna Fáil deputy spokesman on Youth Affairs and Sport 1982-87 in the Dáil.

Former member, Galway County Council; Galway County Vocational Education Committee; Western Health Board; Galway-Mayo Regional Development Organisation.

Éamon Ó Cuív (FF)

Home Address
Corr na Móna, Co na Gaillimhe
Constituency Office
3 Plás Victoria, Gaillimh
Business Address
Department of Arts, Heritage, Gaeltacht and the Islands, Mespil Road, Dublin 4
Telephone
Home (092) 48021; *Office* (091) 562846; *Fax* (091) 562844; *Business* (01) 667 0788
Birth Place/Date
Dublin. June 1950
Married
Áine Ní Choncheanainn. 3 sons, 1 daughter
Education
Oatlands College, Mount Merrion, Dublin; University College, Dublin (BSc)
Occupation
Minister of State. Formerly co-operative manager

Éamon Ó Cuív was appointed Minister of State at the Department of Arts, Heritage, Gaeltacht and the Islands, with special responsibility for the Gaeltacht and the Islands, in July 1997. He was party spokesperson for Rural Development and the Islands 1995-97. He has been a Dáil deputy since 1992. He was a Senator, Cultural and Educational Panel, 1989-92.

Member, Galway County Council 1991-97, and of a number of subsidiary committees.

He was manager of a Gaeltacht co-operative involved in agricultural services, agriculture, timber milling, tourism and cultural and social development.

Éamon Ó Cuív is grandson of Éamon de Valera, President 1959-73, Taoiseach 1937-48, 1951-54, 1957-59; President of Executive Council of Irish Free State 1932-37; President, first Dáil 1919-21; President, second Dáil 1921-January 1922.

He is a nephew of Major Vivion de Valera, Dáil deputy for Dublin north city and central city constituencies 1945-81.

Pádraic McCormack (FG)

Home Address
3 Renmore Park, Galway
Constituency Office
114 Bohermore, Galway
Telephone
Home (091) 753992; *Office* (091) 568686
Birth Place/Date
Longford. May 1942
Married
Eilish King. 2 sons, 2 daughters
Education
Ballymahon Secondary School; Multyfarnham Agricultural College (Dip Agr Sci)
Occupation
Full-time public representative. Formerly auctioneer and company director

Pádraic McCormack has been a Dáil deputy since 1989. He contested the elections of 1977, 1981 and February 1982. Senator, Agricultural Panel, 1987-89. Fine Gael spokesperson on Food and Rural Development 1993-94, on Housing, Local Government, Urban Renewal and Reforms 1994; on Mentally Handicapped 1989-93. Convenor, Select Committee on Finance and General Affairs 1995-97.

Member of Galway County Council since 1974; Galway City Council since 1985 when he became the first Fine Gael councillor elected on the same day to a county and a county borough council, and is at present the only councillor in Ireland to be a member of both a county council and a county borough council. Mayor of Galway 1992/93; member of Galway Harbour Board since 1979 (chairman 1990); General Council of County Councils 1979-87 (vice-chairman 1984/85)

Member, board of Galway Leisureland since 1986.

Member, Gaelic Athletic Association.

Michael D. Higgins (Lab)

Home Address
Letteragh, Circular Road, Galway
Telephone
Home (091) 524513
Birth Place/Date
Limerick. April 1941
Married
Sabina Coyne. 3 sons, 1 daughter
Education
St Flannan's College, Ennis, Co Clare; University College, Galway; Indiana University; Manchester University (BA, BComm, MA [Indiana])
Occupation
Public representative. University lecturer

Michael D. Higgins was Minister for Arts, Culture and the Gaeltacht January 1993-November 1994 and December 1994-97. He was first elected to the Dáil in 1981. He lost his seat in the general election of November 1982, and regained it in 1987. Senator, NUI constituency 1982-87 and Taoiseach's Nominee, 1973-77. Labour Party candidate in Galway West in the general elections of 1969, 1973 and 1977 and also contested the European Parliament elections in the Connacht-Ulster constituency in 1979 and 1985.

Labour Party spokesperson on Education, Gaeltacht and the Islands since 1997; on Foreign Affairs, Gaeltacht, 1989; Education, the Gaeltacht and Overseas Development, 1987-89. Member, Oireachtas Joint Committee on the Irish Language 1987. Women's Rights Committee, Oireachtas Joint Committee on the Secondary Legislation of the European Communities.

Member, Galway City Council 1985-93. Alderman, Galway Borough Council 1974-85 (Mayor of Galway, 1982/83 and 1991/92). Member, Galway County Council 1974-85; Western Health Board; Governing Body, University College, Galway.

Chairman of the Labour Party 1978-87. First recipient of the MacBride International Peace Prize, 1992.

Author of two collections of poems, *The Betrayal*, 1990, and *The Season of Fire*, 1993, and contributor to many political and philosophical journals.

Robert Molloy (PD)

Home Address
St Mary's, Rockbarton, Salthill, Galway
Business Address
Department of the Environment and Local Government, Custom House, Dublin 1
Telephone
Home (091) 521765; *Business* (01) 679 3377; *Fax* (01) 878 6676; *Constituency Office* (01) 677 6077
Birth Place/Date
Galway. July 1936
Married
Phyllis Barry. 2 sons, 2 daughters
Education
St Ignatius' College, Galway; University College, Galway (BComm)
Occupation
Minister of State. Formerly company director

Bobby Molloy was appointed Minister of State to the Government and Minister of State at the Department of the Environment and Local Government in June 1997. As Minister of State to the Government he has the right to attend Cabinet meetings but not to vote. At the Department of Environment and Local Government he has special responsibility for Housing and Urban Renewal. He was Minister for Energy 1989-92. Minister for Defence 1977-79. Minister for Local Government 1970-73; Parliamentary Secretary to the Minister for Education 1969-70. Fianna Fáil spokesman on Local Government 1973-75; on Posts and Telegraphs 1975; on Environment 1982-86.

He had been a Fianna Fáil deputy for Galway West from 1965 to 1986 when he joined the Progressive Democrats.

Progressive Democrat spokesperson on Agriculture and Gaeltacht 1993-97; on Transport, Energy and Communications, Tourism and Trade and Gaeltacht 1994-97.

Former member of the Council of Europe.

Member, Galway County Council 1967-70, 1974-77 and 1985-91; Galway Borough Council 1967-70 (Mayor 1968/69); Galway City Council 1985-91; Western Health Board 1967-70; Galway Harbour Board (chairman 1974-77 and 1985-90).

Kerry North

Seats 3 Quota 8,945	1st Count	2nd Count Transfer of **Spring's** Surplus	3rd Count Transfer of **Deenihan's** Surplus	4th Count Transfer of **O'Connell's** and **McEllistrim's** Votes
*DEENIHAN, Jimmy (FG)	8,689	+1,022 9,711	−766 8,945	
FERRIS, Martin (SF)	5,691	+312 6,003	+258 6,261	+1,033 7,294
*FOLEY, Denis (FF)	5,376	+231 5,607	+275 5,882	+3,837 9,719
McELLISTRIM, Thomas (FF)	4,036	+137 4,173	+104 4,277	−4,277 —
O'CONNELL, Ciarán (NP)	1,288	+52 1,340	+129 1,469	−1,469 —
*SPRING, Dick (Lab)	10,699	−1,754 8,945		
NON-TRANSFERABLE		—	—	876

Elected

Dick Spring (Lab)*	1st Count
Jimmy Deenihan (FG)*	2nd Count
Denis Foley (FF)*	4th Count

Voting by Party

1st Preference	Number	%	% 1992
Fianna Fáil	9,412	26.31	36.47
Fine Gael	8,689	24.29	23.93
Labour	10,699	29.90	33.93
Sinn Féin	5,691	15.91	2.36
National Party	1,288	3.60	—
Others	—	—	3.31

Statistics

Population	61,467	
Electorate	51,348	
Total Poll	36,063	70.23
Spoiled Votes	284	0.79
Valid Poll	35,779	69.68
Seats	3	
Quota	8,945	
Candidates	6	

Seats

FF	1
FG	1
Lab	1
No change	

The constituency of Kerry North is unchanged since the 1992 General Election.

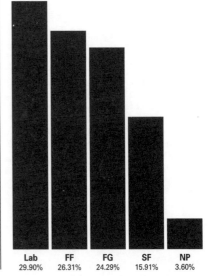

Lab	FF	FG	SF	NP
29.90%	26.31%	24.29%	15.91%	3.60%

Dick Spring (Lab)

Home Address
Cloonanorig, Tralee, Co Kerry
Telephone
Home (066) 25337
Birth Place/Date
Tralee. August 1950
Married
Kristi Hutcheson. 2 sons, 1 daughter
Education
Christian Brothers' School, Tralee; Mount St Joseph's College, Roscrea, Co Tipperary; Trinity College, Dublin; King's Inns, Dublin (BA, BL)
Occupation
Leader of the Labour Party. Formerly Barrister-at-Law

Dick Spring was Tánaiste and Minister for Foreign Affairs January 1993-November 1994 and December 1994-97. He was Tánaiste 1982-87. He was Minister for Energy 1983-87; Minister for the Environment 1982-83. He was Minister of State at the Department of Justice with special responsibility for Law Reform June 1981-February 1982. He was first elected to the Dáil in 1981.

Co-chairman, British-Irish Intergovernment Conference 1993-97.

Leader of the Labour Party since 1982 and spokesperson on Industry and Northern Ireland, 1987-92; on Foreign Affairs and Northern Ireland since 1997. Member, New Ireland Forum; British-Irish Parliamentary Body 1991-92. Member of Government negotiating team on Anglo-Irish Agreement, 1985.

Member, Kerry County Council 1979-82 and 1991-93; Tralee Urban District Council 1979-81; Tralee and Fenit Harbour Commissioners 1979-81.

Dick Spring won 3 caps with the Irish rugby team and played inter-county football and hurling with Kerry.

He is a son of Dan Spring, Labour Dáil deputy for Kerry North 1943-81 and Parliamentary Secretary to the Minister for Local Government 1956-57.

Jimmy Deenihan (FG)

Home Address
Finuge, Lixnaw, Co Kerry
Telephone
Home (068) 40235 and 40154
Birth Place/Date
Listowel, Co Kerry. September 1952
Married
Mary Dowling
Education
St Michael's College, Listowel; National College of Physical Education, Limerick (BEd)
Occupation
Full-time public representative. Formerly teacher

Jimmy Deenihan was Minister of State at the Department of Agriculture, Food and Forestry with special responsibility for Rural Development, the LEADER programme, and monitoring the activities of An Bord Bia and the food industry 1994-97. He has been a Dáil deputy since 1987. He was a Senator, Taoiseach's Nominee 1982-87. He was a candidate in the general election of November 1982.

Fine Gael spokesperson on the Office of Public Works since 1997; front bench spokesperson on Tourism and Trade 1993-94. Spokesperson on Youth and Sports 1988-93, and in Seanad Éireann 1982-87.

Member, Kerry County Council 1985-94; Kerry County Vocational Education Committee; Library Committee 1985-94.

Member, Gaelic Athletic Association. He won All-Ireland football medals with Kerry in 1975, 1978, 1979, 1980 and 1981 and was captain of the 1981 team. He also won four National League medals and five Railway Cup medals. GAA All-Star Award 1981.

Denis Foley (FF)

Home Address
St Joseph's, 2 Staughtons Row, Tralee, Co Kerry
Telephone
Home (066) 21174; *Fax* (066) 21254
Birth Place/Date
Tralee. May 1934
Married
Hannah O'Halloran. 1 son, 3 daughters
Education
Christian Brothers' School, Tralee; St Mary's Secondary School, Tralee; Central Technical School, Tralee
Occupation
Public representative. Formerly rate collector

Denis Foley was first elected to the Dáil in 1981, lost his seat in the 1989 general election, and regained it in 1992. Senator, Industrial and Commercial Panel 1989-92.

Member, Dáil Committee of Public Accounts since 1981 (chairman 1982-87 and 1994-97).

Member, Kerry County Council since 1979 (chairman 1983/84 and 1993/94); Regional Development Organisation since 1979 (chairman 1983/84 and 1986/87); Tralee Vocational Education Committee 1979-85; Kerry County Library Committee since 1979 (chairman 1984); Kerry County Fisheries Committee since 1991.

Member, Tralee and Fenit Harbour Commissioners since 1991. Director, Cork and Kerry Tourism since 1980 (chairman 1987/88). Chairman, Tralee Tourism Co Ltd 1990-97. Chairman, Tralee Development Association 1976-79. President, Tralee Junior Chamber 1971-72; Amateur Basketball Association of Ireland 1972-74. Director, Cork-Swansea Ferry Company Ltd 1985-93.

Jackie Healy-Rae, the poll-topper in South Kerry, outside Leinster House.

Seats 3 Quota 8,875	1st Count	2nd Count Transfer of **Gleeson's** Votes	3rd Count Transfer of **Cronin's** Votes	4th Count Transfer of **Kelly's** Votes	5th Count Transfer of **O'Leary's** Votes	6th Count Transfer of **O'Donoghue's** Surplus	7th Count Transfer of **O'Connor's** Votes
CRONIN, P.J. (Ind)	1,557	+160 1,717	−1,717 —				
GLEESON, Michael (SKIA)	1,388	−1,388 —					
HEALY–RAE, Jackie (Ind)	7,220	+343 7,563	+568 8,131	+187 8,318	+845 9,163	— —	— —
KELLY, Jim (FG)	1,847	+81 1,928	+132 2,060	−2,060 —			
Mac GEARAILT, Breandán (Ind)	4,172	+93 4,265	+137 4,402	+145 4,547	+139 4,686	+646 5,332	+643 5,975
*MOYNIHAN–CRONIN, Breeda (Lab)	4,988	+277 5,265	+285 5,550	+348 5,898	+352 6,250	+456 6,706	+3,254 9,960
O'CONNOR, Aidan (FG)	3,041	+163 3,204	+149 3,353	+1,225 4,578	+151 4,729	+175 4,904	−4,904 —
*O'DONOGHUE, John (FF)	7,204	+76 7,280	+128 7,408	+79 7,487	+2,859 10,346	−1,471 8,875	
O'LEARY, Brian (FF)	4,079	+169 4,248	+216 4,464	+29 4,493	−4,493 —		
NON-TRANSFERABLE		26	102	47	147	194	1,007

Kerry South

Elected

Voting by Party

1st Preference	Number	%	% 1992
Fianna Fáil	11,283	31.79	45.87
Fine Gael	4,888	13.77	19.89
Labour	4,988	14.05	24.05
Sinn Féin	—	—	1.06
Others	14,337	40.39	9.13

Statistics

Population	60,427	
Electorate	48,164	
Total Poll	35,799	74.33
Spoiled Votes	303	0.85
Valid Poll	35,496	73.70
Seats	3	
Quota	8,875	
Candidates	9	

Seats

FF	1
Lab	1
Ind	1
Ind gain from FF	

The constituency of Kerry South is unchanged since the 1992 General Election.

Oth	FF	Lab	FG
40.39%	31.79%	14.05%	13.77%

John O'Donoghue (FF)

Home Address
Garranearagh, Cahirciveen, Co Kerry
Business Address
Department of Justice, Equality and Law Reform, St Stephen's Green, Dublin 2
Telephone
Home (066) 72413/72631; *Business* (01) 602 8202
Birth Place/Date
Cahirciveen. May 1956
Married
Kate Ann Murphy. 2 sons, 1 daughter
Education
CBS, Cahirciveen; University College, Cork; Incorporated Law Society of Ireland (BCL, LLB), Dublin
Occupation
Government Minister. Formerly solicitor

John O'Donoghue was appointed Minister for Justice, Equality and Law Reform in June 1997. He was Minister of State at the Department of Finance, with special responsibility for the Office of Public Works, November 1991-February 1992. He was first elected to the Dáil in 1987.

He was Fianna Fáil front bench spokesperson on Justice 1995-97.

Member, Oireachtas Joint Committee on the Irish Language 1987-89; Oireachtas Joint Committee on the Secondary Legislation of the European Communities 1989-91; Special Dáil Committees on Judicial Separation, Child Care, Foreign Adoptions, Solicitors Bill (chairman). Member, British-Irish Parliamentary Body 1993-97. He served as chairman of Oireachtas Drugs Sub-Committee.

Member, Kerry County Council 1985-91 (chairman 1990/91); Southern Health Board and the Psychiatric Services Committee 1982-97 (chairman 1992/93); Kerry County Committee of Agriculture 1985-88; Kerry County Fisheries Committee 1989-91 (chairman); Kerry County Library Committee 1991-97.

Member, St Mary's Gaelic Athletic Association Club and Cahirciveen Social Services Committee.

Jackie Healy-Rae (Ind)

Home Address
Main Street, Kilgarvan, Co Kerry
Business Address
Main Street, Kilgarvan
Telephone
Home (064) 85315; *Constituency Office* (064) 37376; *Fax* (064) 37375
Birth Place/Date
Kilgarvan. March 1931
Marital Status
Separated. 4 sons, 2 daughters
Occupation
Full-time public representative. Formerly farmer, publican, plant-hire business

Jackie Healy-Rae is a new Dáil deputy. He contested the election as an independent after failing to get a nomination as a candidate from his then party, Fianna Fáil.

Fianna Fáil member of Kerry County Council 1974-97, and since then as an independent. Chairman of County Council 1995/96. He has served for many years on the Southern Health Board (chairman 1981/82).

Chairman for 7 years of Comhaltas Ceoltóirí Chiarraí.

Breeda Moynihan-Cronin (Lab)

Home Address
10 Muckross Grove, Killarney, Co Kerry
Telephone
Home (064) 34993; *Fax* (064) 34993
Birth Place/Date
Killarney. March 1953
Married
Daniel C. Cronin
Education
St Bridgid's Secondary School, Killarney; Sion
Hill College, Dublin; Skerry's College, Cork
Occupation
Full-time public representative. Formerly bank
official

Breeda Moynihan-Cronin has been a Dáil
deputy since 1992. During the 27th Dáil she
served on the Joint Oireachtas Committee on
Women's Rights and the Joint Oireachtas
Committee on the Family. Party spokesperson
on Equality and Law Reform since 1997.

Member, Kerry County Council since 1991;
County Kerry Vocational Education Committee
since 1991; Kerry Historical Monuments
Committee since 1991.

She was involved in amateur dramatics and
won many awards. She helped form the Ivy
Leaf Theatre Company in Castleisland and
was instrumental in setting up the Ivy Leaf
Centre there.

She is daughter of Michael Moynihan, Dáil
deputy for Kerry South 1981-87 and 1989-92.

Seats 3 Quota 7,850	1st Count	2nd Count Transfer of **English's** Votes	3rd Count Transfer of **French's** Votes	4th Count Transfer of **Conway's** Votes	5th Count Transfer of **Murphy's** Votes
CONWAY, Timmy (PD)	2,101	+151 2,252	+99 2,351	−2,351 —	
***DURKAN**, Bernard (FG)	6,653	+151 6,804	+1,128 7,932	— —	— —
ENGLISH, Seán (GP)	1,403	−1,403 —			
FRENCH, Mary (FG)	1,569	+150 1,719	−1,719 —		
KELLY, Paul (FF)	4,039	+121 4,160	+37 4,197	+682 4,879	+703 5,582
***McCREEVY**, Charlie (FF)	6,905	+150 7,055	+97 7,152	+1,004 8,156	— —
MURPHY, Catherine (DL)	2,762	+305 3,067	+137 3,204	+188 3,392	−3,392 —
***STAGG**, Emmet (Lab)	5,964	+291 6,255	+190 6,445	+276 6,721	+2,231 8,952
NON-TRANSFERABLE		84	31	201	458

Kildare North

Elected

Bernard Durkan (FG)*	3rd Count
Charlie McCreevy (FF)*	4th Count
Emmet Stagg (Lab)*	5th Count

Voting by Party

1st Preference	Number	%	% 1992†
Fianna Fáil	10,944	34.86	33.48
Fine Gael	8,222	26.19	22.44
Labour	5,964	19.00	26.82
Prog Democrats	2,101	6.69	7.00
Green Party	1,403	4.47	2.11
Sinn Féin	—	—	1.43
Democratic Left	2,762	8.80	3.20
Others	—	—	3.52

Statistics

Population	61,970	
Electorate	52,388	
Total Poll	31,691	60.49
Spoiled Votes	295	0.93
Valid Poll	31,396	59.93
Seats	3	
Quota	7,850	
Candidates	8	

Seats

FF	1
FG	1
Lab	1

† 1992 percentages are for the old Kildare constituency

Kildare North is a new constituency.

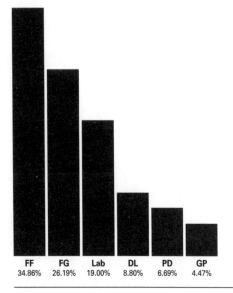

FF	FG	Lab	DL	PD	GP
34.86%	26.19%	19.00%	8.80%	6.69%	4.47%

Bernard Durkan (FG)

Home Address
Timard, Maynooth, Co Kildare
Telephone
Home (01) 628 6063/628 5215
Birth Place/Date
Killasser, Co Mayo. March 1945
Married
Hillary Spence. 2 sons
Education
St John's, Carramore, Co Mayo
Occupation
Full-time public representative. Formerly agricultural contractor

Bernard Durkan was Minister of State at the Department of Social Welfare, with special responsibility for Information and Customer Services and the Integration of the Tax and Social Welfare Codes, 1994-97. He was first elected to the Dáil in 1981. He was unsuccessful in the February 1982 general election but regained his seat in the November 1982 general election. Senator, April-November 1982, Agricultural Panel.

Fine Gael spokesperson on Overseas Development Assistance and Human Rights since 1997; on Health 1994; spokesperson on the Office of Tánaiste and on the National Development Plan 1993-94; on the Insurance Industry 1991-92; on Trade and Marketing 1989-91; on the Food Industry 1987-89. Assistant Whip 1986-87.

Member, Kildare County Council since 1976 (chairman 1986/87); Eastern Health Board since 1979; Kildare Local Health Committee, 1976-86. He has served on the Eastern Regional Development Organisation and various Dáil Committees, including Public Accounts and Foreign Affairs.

Charlie McCreevy (FF)

Home Address
Celbridge, Co Kildare
Constituency Office
Hillview House, Kilcullen Road, Naas, Co Kildare
Business Address
Department of Finance, Upper Merrion Street, Dublin 2
Telephone
Constituency Office (045) 876816;
Fax (045) 876092; *Business* (01) 676 7571;
Fax (01) 676 1951
Birth Place/Date
Sallins, Co Kildare. September 1949
Marital status
Separated. 4 sons, 3 daughters
Education
Naas CBS; Franciscan College, Gormanston, Co Meath; University College, Dublin (BComm, FCA)
Occupation
Government Minister. Formerly chartered accountant

Charlie McCreevy was appointed Minister for Finance in June 1997. He was Minister for Tourism and Trade 1993-94. He was Minister for Social Welfare February 1992-January 1993. He was first elected to the Dáil in 1977 for the then 3-seat constituency of Kildare.

Party front bench spokesperson on Finance 1995-97.

Member, Kildare County Council 1979-85. Member of various Oireachtas committees; Kill Club Gaelic Athletic Association; Institute of Chartered Accountants.

Emmet Stagg (Lab)

Home Address
736 Lodge Park, Straffan, Co Kildare
Telephone
Home (01) 627 2149
Birth Place/Date
Mayo. October 1944
Married
Mary Morris. 1 son, 1 daughter
Education
Ballinrobe CBS; College of Technology, Kevin
Street, Dublin; member, Institute of Medical
Laboratory Sciences
Occupation
Full-tme public representative. Formerly
medical laboratory technologist

Emmet Stagg was Minister of State at the
Department of the Environment, with special
responsibility for Housing and Urban Renewal
1993-94; Minister of State at the Department
of Transport, Energy and Communications,
with special responsibility for Nuclear Safety,
Renewable Energy, Gas and Oil Industry, Air
Safety, Road Haulage and Bus Regulation
1994-97. He was first elected to the Dáil in
1987. He was a candidate in the 1981 general
election.

Labour Party spokesperson on Public
Enterprise since 1997; on Social Welfare
1989-92; on Agriculture 1987-89. Vice-
chairman of the Labour Party 1987-89.

Member, Kildare County Council 1978-93
(chairperson 1981/82); Kildare County
Vocational Education Committee 1985-93;
Eastern Health Board 1978-85; Kildare County
Library Committee 1975-89.

Member, SIPTU.

Member, Gaelic Athletic Association and
president of Celbridge Soccer Club. President,
Maynooth Soccer Club.

At the count: Seán Haughey TD (right) with brothers Conor and Ciaran.

Seats 3
Quota 7,203

	1st Count	2nd Count	3rd Count	4th Count	5th Count
		Transfer of **Browne's** and **Walsh's** Votes	Transfer of **Hendy's** Votes	Transfer of **Dardis's** Votes	Transfer of **Power's** Surplus
BROWNE, Francis J. (Ind)	618	−618 —			
DARDIS, John (PD)	3,895	+143 4,038	+76 4,114	−4,114 —	
***DUKES**, Alan (FG)	6,260	+166 6,426	+993 7,419	— —	— —
HENDY, Rainsford F. (FG)	1,371	+28 1,399	−1,399 —		
Ó FEARGHAIL, Seán (FF)	4,503	+247 4,750	+45 4,795	+1,112 5,907	+694 6,601
***POWER**, Seán (FF)	5,665	+383 6,048	+76 6,124	+1,942 8,066	−863 7,203
WALL, Jack (Lab)	5,834	+243 6,077	+174 6,251	+619 6,870	+169 7,039
WALSH, Christy (FF)	662	−662 —			
NON-TRANSFERABLE		70	35	441	—

Kildare South

Elected

Alan Dukes (FG)*	3rd Count
Seán Power (FF)*	4th Count
Jack Wall (Lab)	5th Count

Voting by Party

1st Preference	Number	%	% 1992†
Fianna Fáil	10,830	37.59	33.48
Fine Gael	7,631	26.49	22.44
Labour	5,834	20.25	26.82
Prog Democrats	3,895	13.52	7.00
Green Party	—	—	2.11
Sinn Féin	—	—	1.43
Democratic Left	—	—	3.20
Others	618	2.15	3.52

Statistics

Population	60,686	
Electorate	47,852	
Total Poll	29,173	60.97
Spoiled Votes	365	1.25
Valid Poll	28,808	60.20
Seats	3	
Quota	7,203	
Candidates	8	

Seats

FF	1
FG	1
Lab	1

† 1992 percentages are for the old Kildare constituency.

Kildare South is a new constituency.

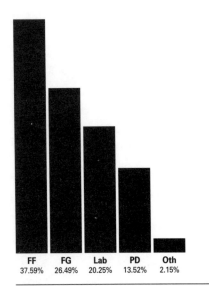

FF	FG	Lab	PD	Oth
37.59%	26.49%	20.25%	13.52%	2.15%

Alan Dukes (FG)

Home Address
Tully West, Kildare
Telephone
Home (045) 521912
Birth Place/Date
Drimnagh, Dublin. April 1945
Married
Fionnuala Corcoran. 2 daughters
Education
Coláiste Mhuire, Parnell Square, Dublin; University College, Dublin (BA, MA)
Occupation
Full-time public representative. Formerly economist

Alan Dukes was Minister for Transport, Energy and Communications December 1996-June 1997.

He was Minister for Justice February 1986-March 1987; Minister for Finance December 1982-February 1986; Minister for Agriculture July 1981-March 1982. He was first elected to the Dáil in 1981.

He was Leader of Fine Gael 1987-90. Chairman, Joint Committee on Foreign Affairs 1995-96. Front bench spokesperson on the Environment and Local Government since 1997; on Agriculture 1993-94; Environment 1992-93; Agriculture March-December 1982.

Member of the Council of State 1988-90. Adjunct Professor of Public Administration and Management, University of Limerick 1991-96.

President, Irish Council of the European Movement 1987-91. Chairman, Irish Council of the European Movement 1996 and since 1997. Vice-president, European People's Party 1987-96. Vice-president, International European Movement 1991-96.

Governor, European Investment Bank, December 1982-February 1986.

Chief economist of the Irish Farmers' Association, 1969-72; director, Irish Farmers' Association Brussels Office, 1973-76. Member of Cabinet of Commissioner Richard Burke, EEC Commission, 1977-80.

Seán Power (FF)

Home Address
Caragh, Naas, Co Kildare
Business Address
Cill Dara House, Main Street, Newbridge, Co Kildare
Telephone
(045) 432289; *Fax* (045) 435380
Birth Place/Date
Caragh, Naas. October 1960
Married
Deirdre Malone. 3 sons
Education
Naas CBS
Occupation
Public representative. Bookmaker

Seán Power was first elected to the Dáil in 1989.

During the 27th Dáil he served on the Select Committee on Legislation and Security, Committee on Procedure and Privileges; Committee of Selection. Fianna Fáil Assistant Chief Whip.

Member, Raheen and Éire Óg Gaelic Football Club.

Son of Paddy Power, Dáil deputy for Kildare 1969-89, Minister for Defence March-December 1982, Minister for Fisheries and Forestry 1979-81 and member, European Parliament 1977-79.

Jack Wall (Lab)

Home Address
Castlemitchell, Athy, Co Kildare
Telephone
Home/Office (0507) 31495; *Mobile* (088)
257 0275; *Fax* (0507) 31798
Birth Place/Date
Castledermot, Co Kildare. July 1945
Married
Anne Byrne. 2 sons, 2 daughters
Education
Castledermot Vocational School; Kevin Street
College of Technology, Dublin
Occupation
Full-time public representative. Formerly
electrician

Jack Wall is a new Dáil deputy. He was the
only new Labour deputy to be elected to the
28th Dáil. Senator, Taoiseach's Nominee,
1993-97. Labour Party spokesperson on
Tourism, Sport and Recreation since 1997.
Party spokesperson in the Seanad on Social
Welfare and a member of the Oireachtas
Committees on Small Businesses and State-
Sponsored Bodies.

Member, Athy Urban District Council since
1993 (chairman 1994/95).

Chairman, Kildare GAA County Board since
1989. Director, Athy Credit Union.

Comedy Store: Proinsias De Rossa and Brendan O'Carroll.

Seats 5 Quota 9,679	1st Count	2nd Count Transfer of **Cowen's** Surplus	3rd Count Transfer of **Seery's,** **McCormack's,** **Fennelly's** and **McNamee's** Votes	4th Count Transfer of **Honan's** Votes	5th Count Transfer of **Killally's** Votes
*COWEN, Brian (FF)	10,865	−1,186 9,679			
ENRIGHT, Thomas W. (FG)	8,375	+103 8,478	+282 8,760	+432 9,192	+366 9,558
FENNELLY, Seán (Ind)	516	+9 525	−525 —		
*FLANAGAN, Charles (FG)	8,104	+28 8,132	+252 8,384	+611 8,995	+271 9,266
FLEMING, Seán (FF)	5,481	+329 5,810	+350 6,160	+744 6,904	+3,463 10,367
*GALLAGHER, Pat (Lab)	6,741	+106 6,847	+254 7,101	+441 7,542	+511 8,053
HONAN, Cathy (PD)	3,778	+87 3,865	+225 4,090	−4,090 —	
KILLALLY, Gerard (FF)	4,328	+379 4,707	+192 4,899	+537 5,436	−5,436 —
McCORMACK, Joe (Ind)	378	+1 379	−379 —		
McNAMEE, Peter (NP)	1,099	+6 1,105	−1,105 —		
MOLONEY, John (FF)	8,271	+135 8,406	+296 8,702	+1,098 9,800	—
SEERY, Paddy (NLP)	134	+3 137	−137 —		
NON-TRANSFERABLE		—	295	227	825

Laois-Offaly

Elected

Brian Cowen (FF)*	1st Count
John Moloney (FF)	4th Count
Seán Fleming (FF)	5th Count
Thomas W. Enright (FG)	5th Count
Charles Flanagan (FG)*	5th Count

Voting by Party

1st Preference	Number	%	% 1992
Fianna Fáil	28,945	49.85	51.82
Fine Gael	16,479	28.38	23.82
Labour	6,741	11.61	12.98
Prog Democrats	3,778	6.51	6.63
Sinn Féin	—	—	1.24
National Party	1,099	1.89	—
Natural Law Party	134	0.23	—
Others	894	1.54	3.51

Statistics

Population	110,808	
Electorate	84,358	
Total Poll	58,612	69.48
Spoiled Votes	542	0.92
Valid Poll	58,070	68.84
Seats	5	
Quota	9,679	
Candidates	12	

Seats

FF	3
FG	2

FG gain from Lab

The constituency of Laois-Offaly is unchanged since the 1992 General Election.

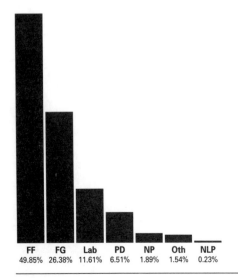

FF	FG	Lab	PD	NP	Oth	NLP
49.85%	26.38%	11.61%	6.51%	1.89%	1.54%	0.23%

Brian Cowen (FF)

Home Address
Ballard, Tullamore, Co Offaly
Business Address
Department of Health and Children, Hawkins House, Dublin 2
Telephone
Home (0506) 52047; *Business* (01) 671 1026
Birth Place/Date
Tullamore. January 1960
Married
Mary Molloy. 1 daughter
Education
Ardscoil Naomh Ciarán, Clara, Co Offaly; Cistercian College, Roscrea, Co Tipperary; University College, Dublin (BCL); Incorporated Law Society of Ireland, Dublin
Occupation
Government Minister. Formerly solicitor

Brian Cowen was appointed Minister for Health and Children in June 1997. He was Minister for Transport, Energy and Communications 1993-94; Minister for Labour February 1992-January 1993. He was elected to the Dáil in a by-election in June 1984 caused by the death of his father, Bernard Cowen. That was the first occasion on which he had contested an election for public office.

Party front bench spokesperson on Agriculture, Food and Forestry 1995-97 and on Health 1997.

Member, Offaly County Council 1984-92; Offaly County Vocational Education Committee 1989-92; British-Irish Parliamentary Body, 1991-92.

President, Clara Gaelic Athletic Association Club.

He is a son of the late Bernard Cowen, Fianna Fáil Dáil deputy for Laois-Offaly 1969-73 and 1977-84, Senator 1973-77 and Minister of State at the Department of Agriculture March-December 1982.

John Moloney (FF)

Home Address
27 Patrick Street, Mountmellick, Co Laois
Constituency Office
26 Patrick Street, Mountmellick
Telephone
Home/Office (0502) 24391; *Mobile* (087) 262 5395
Birth Place/Date
Port Laoise, Co Laois. June 1953
Married
Patricia McEvoy. 2 sons, 1 daughter
Education
Patrician Brothers' College, Ballyfin, Co Laois
Occupation
Full-time public representative. Formerly air traffic controller, publican and undertaker

John Moloney is a new Dáil deputy. He was a candidate in the 1992 general election.

Member, Laois County Council since 1981 (chairman 1989/90). Member, Mountmellick Town Commissioners since 1985 (chairman 1996/97). Member, Midland Health Board; Laois County Enterprise Board; Laois Rural Development Board. Chairman, Mountmellick Community Employment Scheme; Mountmellick Tidy Towns Committee; Kyletelisha Environmental Group.

John Moloney represents the third generation of his family to serve on Laois County Council.

Seán Fleming (FF)

Home Address
Castletown, Port Laoise, Co Laois
Telephone
Home (0502) 32692
Birth Place/Date
Castletown, Co Laois. February 1958
Married
Mary O'Gorman. 1 son
Education
Salesian College, Ballinakill; University College, Dublin (BComm, Chartered Accountant, Fellow of the Institute of Chartered Accountants in Ireland)
Occupation
Full-time public representative. Formerly Financial Director of Fianna Fáil at national level

Seán Fleming is a new Dáil deputy. This was the first time he contested a general election.

The Laois-Offaly constituency was exceptional in the 1997 General Election in that two of the outgoing three Fianna Fáil deputies (Ger Connolly and Liam Hyland) did not seek re-election.

Although Counties Laois and Offaly have been together in the one constituency since the foundation of the State, and frequently returned three Fianna Fáil deputies, this is the first occasion that two of the three came from Co Laois.

Thomas W. Enright (FG)

Home Address
John's Mall, Birr, Co Offaly
Business Address
John's Place, Birr
Telephone
Home (0509) 20839; *Mobile* (088) 258 1553; *Fax* (0509) 20802
Birth Place/Date
Shinrone, Co Offaly. July 1940
Married
Rita Mary Hanniffy. 1 son, 4 daughters
Education
Cistercian College, Roscrea, Co Tipperary; University College, Dublin; Law School of the Incorporated Law Society of Ireland
Occupation
Solicitor, public representative

Tom Enright was previously a Dáil deputy 1969-92. Senator, Administrative Panel 1993-97.

Fine Gael spokesperson on Tourism 1977-79; on Consumer Affairs 1979-81; on the Public Service June-November 1982; on the Office of Public Works 1987-89.

Chairman, Fine Gael Parliamentary Party 1989-92.

Member, Foreign Affairs Committee 1994-97.

Member, Offaly County Council since 1967; Offaly County Vocational Education Committee 1967-85; Offaly County Committee of Agriculture 1967-85; Offaly Health Committee since 1985; Midland Regional Development Organisation 1974-85 (chairman 1979-85).

Member, Birr Chamber of Commerce; Birr Golf Club; Birr Gaelic Athletic Association.

Charles Flanagan (FG)

Home Address
Glenlahan, Stradbally Road, Port Laoise, Co Laois
Business Address
Lismard Court, Port Laoise, Co Laois
Telephone
Home (0502) 60707; *Business* (0502) 20232/ 21468; *Fax* (0502) 60519
Birth Place/Date
Dublin. November 1956
Married
Mary McCormack. 1 daughter
Education
Coláiste na Rinne, Waterford; Knockbeg College, Carlow; University College, Dublin (BA); Law School of the Incorporated Law Society
Occupation
Public representative. Solicitor

Charlie Flanagan has been a Dáil deputy since 1987. Fine Gael spokesperson on Criminal Law Reform, Northern Ireland since 1997; Party leader on British-Irish Parliamentary body since 1997; front bench spokesperson on Health 1993-94; on Transport and Tourism 1992-93; Fine Gael Chief Whip 1990-92; party spokesperson on Law Reform 1988-90; Assistant Whip of the Fine Gael Parliamentary Party 1987-88.

Chairman, Select Committee on Legislation and Security 1995-97. Vice-chairman, Joint Committee on Women's Rights 1995-97.

Member, Laois County Council; former member, Mountmellick Town Commissioners; member, Midland Health Board.

Founder-member of Young Fine Gael.

He is son of the late Oliver J. Flanagan, Dáil deputy for Laois-Offaly 1943-87, and member of Laois County Council 1942-87, Minister for Defence 1976-77, Parliamentary Secretary to the Minister for Local Government 1975-76, and to the Minister for Agriculture and Fisheries 1954-57.

Limerick East

Seats 5 Quota 8,284	1st Count	2nd Count Transfer of **O'Dea's** Surplus	3rd Count Transfer of **Noonan's** Surplus	4th Count Transfer of **Riordan's, Hannan's** and **Sheppard's** Votes	5th Count Transfer of **Bennis's** Votes
BENNIS, Nora (NP)	1,533	+77 1,610	+27 1,637	+93 1,730	−1,730 —
CREIGHTON, Edmond (PD)	1,817	+142 1,959	+29 1,988	+33 2,021	+129 2,150
HANNAN, Noel Raymond (Ind)	195	+22 217	+5 222	−222 —	
JACKMAN, Mary (FG)	3,084	+125 3,209	+999 4,208	+119 4,327	+272 4,599
***KEMMY**, Jim (Lab)	2,702	+231 2,933	+220 3,153	+176 3,329	+110 3,439
***NOONAN**, Michael (FG)	10,092	— —	−1,806 8,284		
***O'DEA**, Willie (FF)	12,581	−4,297 8,284			
***O'MALLEY**, Desmond J. (PD)	4,358	+478 4,836	+145 4,981	+82 5,063	+215 5,278
O'SULLIVAN, Jan (Lab)	1,866	+118 1,984	+131 2,115	+177 2,292	+61 2,353
POWER, Peter (FF)	2,362	+978 3,340	+53 3,393	+90 3,483	+301 3,784
RIORDAN, Denis (Ind)	108	+4 112	+2 114	−114 —	
RYAN, John (DL)	3,403	+279 3,682	+27 3,809	+185 3,994	+98 4,092
SHEPPARD, Eric (GP)	802	+41 843	+15 858	−858 —	
WADE, Eddie (FF)	4,798	+1,802 6,600	+55 6,655	+113 6,768	+266 7,034
NON-TRANSFERABLE		—	—	126	278

Limerick East

6th Count	7th Count	8th Count	9th Count	10th Count	11th Count
Transfer of **Creighton's** Votes	Transfer of **O'Sullivan's** Votes	Transfer of **Power's** Votes	Transfer of **Wade's** Surplus	Transfer of **O'Malley's** Surplus	Transfer of **Ryan's** Votes
−2,150 —					
+156 4,755	+351 5,106	+224 5,330	+129 5,459	+60 5,519	+980 6,499
+70 3,509	+1,116 4,625	+250 4,875	+128 5,003	+44 5,047	+2,126 7,173
+1,283 6,561	+153 6,714	+764 7,478	+941 8,419	−135 8,284	
+30 2,383	−2,383 —				
+119 3,903	+90 3,993	−3,993 —			
+37 4,129	+433 4,562	+194 4,756	+117 4,873	+31 4,904	−4,904 —
+326 7,360	+91 7,451	+2,181 9,632	−1,348 8,284		
129	149	380	33	—	1,798

Limerick East

Elected

Willie O'Dea (FF)*	1st Count
Michael Noonan (FG)*	1st Count
Eddie Wade (FF)	8th Count
Desmond J. O'Malley (PD)*	9th Count
Jim Kemmy (Lab)*	11th Count

Voting by Party

1st Preference	Number	%	% 1992
Fianna Fáil	19,741	39.72	30.25
Fine Gael	13,176	26.51	15.61
Labour	4,568	9.19	23.48
Prog Democrats	6,175	12.42	26.14
Green Party	802	1.61	—
Sinn Féin	—	—	0.83
Democratic Left	3,403	6.85	1.73
National Party	1,533	3.08	—
Others	303	0.61	1.97

Statistics

Population	103,441	
Electorate	76,705	
Total Poll	50,049	65.25
Spoiled Votes	348	0.70
Valid Poll	49,701	64.79
Seats	5	
Quota	8,284	
Candidates	14	

Seats

FF	2
FG	1
Lab	1
PD	1
FF gain from PD	

The constituency of Limerick East is unchanged since the 1992 General Election.

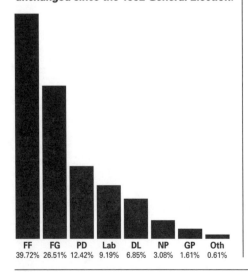

FF	FG	PD	Lab	DL	NP	GP	Oth
39.72%	26.51%	12.42%	9.19%	6.85%	3.08%	1.61%	0.61%

Willie O'Dea (FF)

Home Address
9 Naughton Place, Henry Street, Limerick
Constituency Office
2 Glenview Gardens, Farranshore, Limerick
Business Address
Department of Education, Science and Technology, Marlborough Street, Dublin 1
Telephone
Home (061) 54488; *Business* (01) 873 4700
Birth Place/Date
Limerick. November 1952
Married
Geraldine Kennedy
Education
Patrician Brothers' College, Ballyfin, Co Laois; University College, Dublin; King's Inns, Dublin; Institute of Certified Accountants (BCL, LLM, BL, Certified Accountant)
Occupation
Minister of State. Formerly accountant

Willie O'Dea was appointed Minister of State at the Department of Education, Science and Technology, with special responsibility for Adult Education, Youth Affairs and School Transport in July 1997. He was Minister of State at the Departments of Justice and Health 1993-94; Minister of State at the Department of Justice February 1992-January 1993. He was first elected a Dáil deputy in February 1982.

Willie O'Dea was an unsuccessful candidate in the general election of 1981.

Michael Noonan (FG)

Home Address
18 Gouldavoher Estate, Father Russell Road, Limerick
Telephone
Home (061) 229350
Birth Place/Date
Limerick. May 1943
Married
Florence Knightly. 3 sons, 2 daughters
Education
St Patrick's Secondary School, Glin, Co Limerick; St Patrick's Teachers' Training College, Drumcondra, Dublin; University College, Dublin (BA, HDipEd)
Occupation
Full-time public representative. Formerly teacher

Michael Noonan was Minister for Health 1994-97; Minister for Justice December 1982-February 1986; Minister for Industry and Commerce February 1986-March 1987; Minister for Energy January-March 1987. He was first elected to the Dáil in 1981. The 1981 general election was the first election in which he was a candidate for a Dáil seat.

Fine Gael front bench spokesperson on Finance since 1997; on Transport, Energy and Communications 1993-94; on Finance 1987-93; on Education 1982.

Member, Limerick County Council 1974-82 and 1991-94; Mid-Western Health Board 1974-82 and 1991-94.

Member, Association of Secondary Teachers of Ireland.

Eddie Wade (FF)

Home Address
Cahernorry, Drombanna, Co Limerick
Constituency Office
Caherconlish, Co Limerick
Telephone
Home (061) 351467
Birth Place/Date
Limerick. June 1948
Education
Technical Institute, Limerick
Occupation
Full-time public representative. Formerly salesman

Eddie Wade is a new Dáil deputy. He was a candidate for Limerick East in the 1989 and 1992 general elections.

He has served as a member of Limerick County Council since 1979 and as chairman of the Council on 3 occasions. He has also served on the County Limerick Vocational Education Committee, Mid-Western Health Board, and Mid-West Development Advisory Group for European Funding.

He has been an officer for 20 years with East Limerick Divisional Board of the GAA. Vice-chairman, Limerick County Board of GAA, and a selector with county teams in all grades.

Desmond J. O'Malley (PD)

Home Address
11 Cecil Street, Limerick
Telephone
Business (01) 618 3333
Birth Place/Date
Limerick. February 1939
Married
Patricia McAleer. 2 sons, 4 daughters
Education
Crescent College, Limerick; University College, Dublin; Incorporated Law Society of Ireland (BCL)
Occupation
Full-time public representative. Formerly solicitor

Des O'Malley was Minister for Industry and Commerce from July 1989 to November 1992, when he resigned. He was Minister for Trade, Commerce and Tourism March-October 1982. Minister for Industry, Commerce and Tourism December 1979-June 1981; Minister for Industry, Commerce and Energy November 1977-December 1979. Minister for Industry and Commerce July-November 1977; Minister for Justice 1970-73. Parliamentary Secretary to the Taoiseach and to the Minister for Defence and Government Chief Whip 1969-70. Progressive Democrats spokesperson on Foreign Affairs and Northern Ireland 1993-97. Member, numerous Dáil Committees.

He had been a Fianna Fáil deputy from 1968 when he won a by-election in Limerick East caused by the death of his uncle, until he lost the party whip in May 1984. He was expelled from the Fianna Fáil party in February 1985.

Des O'Malley founded the Progressive Democrats on 21 December 1985, and became the first Party Leader. Resigned as Leader, October 1993.

Member, Limerick City Council 1974-77. He is a nephew of the late Donogh O'Malley, Fianna Fáil Dáil deputy for Limerick East 1954-68, Parliamentary Secretary 1961-65, Minister for Health 1965-66, and Minister for Education 1966-68.

Jim Kemmy (Lab)

Jim Kemmy, Dáil deputy 1981-82 and from 1987, died on 25 September 1997 following a short illness.

He was first elected to the Dáil as an Independent in 1981 and held his seat until November 1982. He was re-elected in 1987 for the Democratic Socialist Party. In 1991 he re-joined the Labour Party.

He was chairperson of the Labour Party from 1993 and vice-chairperson 1991-92.

He was a member of Limerick City Council from 1974, Alderman from 1979, and Mayor 1991-92. He was chairman of the Historic Monuments Advisory Committee of Limerick City Council and of the Art Gallery Committee. He was President of the Delegate Board of the Mechanics' Institute, Limerick from 1970. He was a founder member in 1982 and President of the Democratic Socialist Party. He was a member of the Labour Party 1963-72.

He was secretary of the Limerick branch of the Brick and Stonelayers Trade Union from 1960 and Limerick Building Trades Group from 1968.

He was a member of the Irish Labour History Society and the Old Limerick Society; editor of the *Limerick Socialist* 1972-81 and of the *Old Limerick Journal* from 1979. He was editor of *The Limerick Anthology* (1996) and *The Limerick Compendium* (1997), and joint author of *Limerick in Old Picture Postcards* (1977).

Jim Kemmy was a stonemason by profession.

Bertie Ahern following his election as Taoiseach.

Seats 3
Quota 8,404

	1st Count	2nd Count	3rd Count	4th Count	5th Count	6th Count	7th Count
		Transfer of **Mac Domhnaill's** Votes	Transfer of **McDonnell's** Votes	Transfer of **Kelly's** Votes	Transfer of **Gallahue's** Votes	Transfer of **Clifford's** Votes	Transfer of **Collins's** Surplus
BRENNAN, Michael (Ind)	3,661	+34 3,695	+195 3,890	+177 4,067	+879 4,946	+528 5,474	+1,109 6,583
CLIFFORD, John (FF)	3,921	+32 3,953	+302 4,255	+82 4,337	+600 4,937	−4,937 —	
COLLINS, Michael (FF)	6,985	+44 7,029	+328 7,357	+162 7,519	+717 8,236	+3,456 11,692	−3,288 8,404
*FINUCANE, Michael (FG)	5,476	+47 5,523	+156 5,679	+491 6,170	+503 6,673	+250 6,923	+407 7,330
GALLAHUE, John (Ind)	3,355	+58 3,413	+108 3,521	+168 3,689	−3,689 —		
KELLY, Mary (Lab)	1,418	+60 1,478	+106 1,584	−1,584 —			
Mac DOMHNAILL, Mike (Ind)	366	−366 —					
McDONNELL, Jeanette (PD)	1,406	+38 1,444	−1,444 —				
NEVILLE, Dan (FG)	7,026	+36 7,062	+203 7,265	+407 7,672	+581 8,253	+348 8,601	— —
NON-TRANSFERABLE		17	46	97	409	355	1,772

Limerick West

Elected

Michael Collins (FF)	6th Count
Dan Neville (FG)	6th Count
Michael Finucane (FG)*	7th Count

Voting by Party

1st Preference	Number	%	% 1992
Fianna Fáil	10,906	32.44	47.41
Fine Gael	12,502	37.19	30.87
Labour	1,418	4.22	10.83
Prog Democrats	1,406	4.18	7.36
Sinn Féin	—	—	1.09
Others	7,382	21.96	2.43

Statistics

Population	61,359	
Electorate	47,859	
Total Poll	33,979	71.00
Spoiled Votes	365	1.07
Valid Poll	33,614	70.24
Seats	3	
Quota	8,404	
Candidates	9	

Seats

FF	1
FG	2

FG gain from FF

The constituency of Limerick West is unchanged since the 1992 General Election.

FG	FF	Oth	Lab	SF
37.19%	32.44%	21.96%	4.22%	4.18%

Michael Collins (FF)

Home Address
White Oaks, Red House Hill, Patrickswell, Co Limerick
Constituency Office
Convent Terrace, Abbeyfeale, Co Limerick
Business Address
Railway Hotel, Parnell Street, Limerick
Telephone
Home (061) 355081; *Constituency Office* (068) 31126; *Mobile* (087) 235 6012; *Fax* (061) 419762; *Business* (061) 413653
Birth Place/Date
Abbeyfeale, Co Limerick. November 1940
Married
Una Farrell. 1 son, 2 daughters
Education
St Munchin's College, Limerick
Occupation
Full-time public representative. Hotel company director

Michael Collins is a new Dáil deputy. This was the first occasion on which he contested a general election.

Member, Limerick County Council since 1979 (chairman 1990/91).

He is a brother of Gerry Collins, Dáil deputy for Limerick West 1967-97, member of the European Parliament since 1994 and a former Minister for Foreign Affairs, Minister for Justice and Minister for Posts and Telegraphs.

He is a son of James J. Collins, Dáil deputy for Limerick West 1948-67.

Dan Neville (FG)

Home Address
Kiltannan, Croagh, Co Limerick
Telephone
Home/Constituency Office (061) 396351; *Mobile* (086) 243 5536; *Fax* (061) 396351
Birth Place/Date
Croagh. December 1946
Married
Goretti O'Callaghan. 2 sons, 2 daughters
Education
Adare CBS, Co Limerick; University of Limerick, School of Management Studies; University College, Cork (Industrial Engineering, Personnel Management, Social Science)
Occupation
Full-time public representative. Formerly personnel manager

Dan Neville is a new Dáil deputy. Fine Gael spokesperson on Children since 1997. He was a Senator, Labour Panel, 1989-97. Deputy Leader of Fine Gael in the Seanad and spokesperson on Justice and Law Reform 1992-97. He was a candidate in Limerick West in the general elections of 1987 and 1992.

Member, Limerick County Council since 1985; Mid-Western Health Board since 1991; Association of Health Boards since 1991; General Council of County Councils since 1991.

Michael Finucane (FG)

Home Address
Ardnacrohy, Newcastle West, Co Limerick
Constituency Office
North Quay, Newcastle West
Telephone
Home & Business (069) 62742; *Mobile* (087)
260 3840; *Fax* (069) 61946
Birth Place/Date
Limerick. February 1943
Married
Hannah Hartnett. 1 son, 2 daughters
Education
St Senan's Secondary School, Foynes, Co
Limerick (Dip Ind Eng)
Occupation
Full-time public representative. Formerly
shipping agency manager, recruitment and
training consultant

Michael Finucane was first elected to the Dáil
in 1989 in Limerick West and has represented
the constituency since.

Fine Gael front bench spokesperson on the
Marine and Natural Resources since 1997.
Assistant Whip 1995-97. Spokesperson on
Commerce and Technology 1993-94; on
Taxation 1989-92. Chairman, Fine Gael
Finance and General Affairs Committee
1993-97.

Member, Limerick County Council since 1985;
Mid-Western Health Board since 1995;
County Enterprise Board; Foynes Harbour
Trustees since 1985.

There is only one political issue in Ireland.

The Sunday Times *is* the Sunday Papers for Ireland

Seats 4 Quota 9,457	1st Count	2nd Count Transfer of **Sheerin's** and **Gaffney's** Votes	3rd Count Transfer of **Sexton's** Votes	4th Count Transfer of **Leyden's** Votes	5th Count Transfer of **Foxe's** Votes	6th Count Transfer of **Reynolds's** Surplus	7th Count Transfer of **Connor's** Votes	8th Count Transfer of **Naughten's** Surplus
BELTON, Louis J. (FG)	5,696	+104 5,800	+499 6,299	+57 6,356	+158 6,514	+185 6,699	+616 7,315	+2,317 9,632
*CONNOR, John (FG)	5,104	+238 5,342	+46 5,388	+171 5,559	+651 6,210	+3 6,213	−6,213 —	
*DOHERTY, Seán (FF)	5,768	+282 6,050	+141 6,191	+1,255 7,446	+1,080 8,526	+117 8,643	+1,050 9,693	— —
FINNERAN, Michael (FF)	4,414	+43 4,457	+88 4,545	+978 5,523	+837 6,360	+67 6,427	+227 6,654	+334 6,988
*FOXE, Tom (Ind)	4,082	+198 4,280	+185 4,465	+535 5,000	−5,000 —			
GAFFNEY, Marian (Lab)	699	−699 —						
LEYDEN, Terry (FF)	3,308	+74 3,382	+131 3,513	−3,513 —				
NAUGHTEN, Denis (FG)	6,652	+149 6,801	+116 6,917	+374 7,291	+1,749 9,040	+18 9,058	+3,810 12,868	−3,411 9,457
*REYNOLDS, Albert (FF)	8,742	+51 8,793	+1,054 9,847	— —	— —	−390 9,457		
SEXTON, Mae (PD)	2,289	+57 2,346	−2,346 —					
SHEERIN, Brian (Ind)	526	−526 —						
NON-TRANSFERABLE		29	86	143	525	—	510	760

Longford-Roscommon

Elected

Albert Reynolds (FF)*	3rd Count
Denis Naughten (FG)	7th Count
Seán Doherty (FF)*	7th Count
Louis J. Belton (FG)	8th Count

Voting by Party

1st Preference	Number	%	% 1992
Fianna Fáil	22,232	47.02	52.28
Fine Gael	17,452	36.91	29.92
Labour	699	1.48	1.31
Prog Democrats	2,289	4.84	—
Green Party	—	—	0.23
Sinn Féin	—	—	0.35
Others	4,608	9.75	15.90

Statistics

Population	82,193	
Electorate	63,942	
Total Poll	47,843	74.82
Spoiled Votes	563	1.18
Valid Poll	47,280	73.94
Seats	4	
Quota	9,457	
Candidates	11	

Seats

FF	2
FG	2
FG gain from Ind	

The constituency of Longford-Roscommon is unchanged since the 1992 General Election.

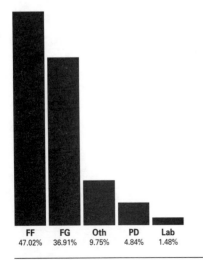

FF	FG	Oth	PD	Lab
47.02%	36.91%	9.75%	4.84%	1.48%

Albert Reynolds (FF)

Home Address
Mount Carmel House, Dublin Road, Longford
Constituency Office
Church Street, Longford
Telephone
(043) 45070
Birth Place/Date
Rooskey, Co Roscommon. November 1932
Married
Kathleen Coen. 2 sons, 5 daughters
Education
Summerhill College, Sligo
Occupation
Public representative, company director

Albert Reynolds was Taoiseach 1992-94. He first became Taoiseach on 11 February 1992, on the resignation of Charles J. Haughey. He led the Fianna Fáil/Progressive Democrats Coalition Government until November 1992. He again became Taoiseach, of a Fianna Fáil/Labour Coalition, on 12 January 1993 and continued until 15 December 1994 when he resigned without a dissolution of the Dáil. He was acting Taoiseach November 1992-January 1993.

He was Minister for Foreign Affairs, in addition to being Taoiseach, November-December 1994; Minister for Finance November 1988-November 1991; Minister for Industry and Commerce March 1987-November 1988; Minister for Industry and Energy March-December 1982; Minister for Posts and Telegraphs and Minister for Transport 1979-81. He was first elected to the Dáil in 1977.

Leader and president of Fianna Fáil 1992-94 and vice-president 1983-92.

Fianna Fáil spokesman on Energy 1985-87; on Industry and Employment 1983-85.

Member, Longford County Council 1974-79; Longford County Committee of Agriculture 1974-79; Longford Health Committee 1974-79.

President, Longford Chamber of Commerce 1974-78.

Denis Naughten (FG)

Home Address
Ardkeenan, Drum, Athlone, Co Roscommon
Constituency Office
Abbey Street, Roscommon
Telephone
Home (0902) 37100; *Constituency Office* (0903) 27557; *Fax* (0903) 27556
Birth Place/Date
Drum, Athlone. June 1973
Education
St Aloysius College, Athlone; University College, Dublin; University College, Cork (BSc)
Occupation
Full-time public representative. Formerly research scientist

Denis Naughten is a new Dáil deputy, and the youngest member of the 28th Dáil. This was the first general election he contested. Senator, Agricultural Panel, 1997. Fine Gael spokesperson on Adult Education, Youth Affairs and School Transport since 1997.

Member, Roscommon County Council since 1997; Western Health Board since 1997; Association of Health Boards since 1997.

He is a son of the late Liam Naughten, Dáil deputy February 1982-89; Senator, Agricultural Panel 1981-February 1982 and 1989-96, Leas-Chathaoirleach of the Seanad 1989-95 and Cathaoirleach 1995-96.

Seán Doherty (FF)

Home Address
Cootehall, Boyle, Co Roscommon
Telephone
Home (079) 67005
Birth Place/Date
Roscommon. June 1944
Married
Maura Nangle. 4 daughters
Education
Presentation Brothers, Carrick-on-Shannon;
University College, Dublin; King's Inns, Dublin
Occupation
Public representative. Company director

Seán Doherty was Minister for Justice March-December 1982. He was Minister of State at the Department of Justice 1979-81. He was first elected to the Dáil in 1977 for Roscommon-Leitrim constituency. He was re-elected in 1981 for Roscommon constituency and continued to represent that constituency until he lost his seat in the general election of 1989. Senator, Administrative Panel, 1989-92 and Cathaoirleach of the Seanad November 1989-January 1992, and *ex-officio* member of the Council of State. He was an unsuccessful candidate in Connacht-Ulster constituency in the European Parliament elections in 1989.

Member, Roscommon County Council 1973-91. He served as chairman of the Western Health Board; chairman and director of Midland Regional Tourism Organisation, and Director of Ireland West. Member, Roscommon Archaeological and Historical Society.

Louis J. Belton (FG)

Home Address
Kenagh, Co Longford
Constituency Office
Dublin Street, Longford
Telephone
Home (043) 22245; *Constituency Office* (043) 48499; *Fax* (043) 48499
Birth Place/Date
Longford. November 1943
Education
St Mel's College, Longford
Occupation
Full-time public representative. Formerly building society employee

Louis J. Belton was previously a Dáil deputy for Longford-Westmeath 1989-92, when he was the first Longford-based Fine Gael deputy since General Seán Mac Eoin in 1965. He was a candidate in the new constituency of Longford-Roscommon in the general election of 1992. Senator, Administrative Panel 1992-97 and spokesperson on Defence and the Marine.

Member, Longford County Council since 1979; Longford ACOT 1979-87; Midland Regional Development Organisation 1979-87; General Council of County Councils since 1985.

Member, Ballymahon Show Society; Ballymahon Drama Society; Kenagh Gaelic Athletic Association (former player); Longford Rugby Football Club (former player).

He is the sixth member of the Belton family to be a member of the Dáil.

Louth

Seats 4 Quota 9,002	1st Count	2nd Count Transfer of **Ahern's** Surplus	3rd Count Transfer of **Taaffe's** and **Doyle's** Votes	4th Count Transfer of **Salter's** Votes	5th Count Transfer of **Healy's** Votes
*AHERN, Dermot (FF)	10,192	−1,190 9,002			
*BELL, Michael (Lab)	4,725	+46 4,771	+58 4,829	+22 4,851	+107 4,958
BRENNAN, Terry (FG)	3,723	+53 3,776	+31 3,807	+33 3,840	+11 3,851
DOYLE, Brian (Ind)	475	+16 491	−491 —		
GODFREY, Frank (Ind)	1,037	+8 1,045	+22 1,067	+51 1,118	+49 1,167
GREHAN, Mary (PD)	2,395	+141 2,536	+56 2,592	+89 2,681	+13 2,694
HANRATTY, Owen (SF)	2,760	+56 2,816	+74 2,890	+44 2,934	+492 3,426
HEALY, Maeve (SF)	891	+8 899	+17 916	+13 929	−929 —
*KIRK, Séamus (FF)	5,667	+667 6,334	+47 6,381	+163 6,544	+50 6,594
McCANN, Neil (GP)	1,403	+25 1,428	+103 1,531	+105 1,636	+49 1,685
*McGAHON, Brendan (FG)	4,346	+83 4,429	+75 4,504	+80 4,584	+13 4,597
O'BRIEN CAMPBELL, Maria (FF)	2,151	+64 2,215	+6 2,221	+24 2,245	+50 2,295
O'DOWD, Fergus (FG)	4,486	+13 4,499	+7 4,506	+32 4,538	+60 4,598
SALTER, Michael G. (Ind)	686	+9 695	+30 725	−725 —	
TAAFFE, Dessie (Ind)	71	+1 72	−72 —		
NON-TRANSFERABLE			37	69	35

6th Count	7th Count	8th Count	9th Count	10th Count	11th Count	12th Count
Transfer of **Godfrey's** Votes	Transfer of **McCann's** Votes	Transfer of **O'Brien Campbell's** Votes	Transfer of **Grehan's** Votes	Transfer of **Hannratty's** Votes	Transfer of **Brennan's** Votes	Transfer of **Kirk's** Surplus
+278 5,236	+282 5,518	+387 5,905	+325 6,230	+525 6,755	+561 7,316	+114 7,430
+24 3,875	+160 4,035	+15 4,050	+257 4,307	+281 4,588	−4,588 —	
−1,167 —						
+66 2,760	+281 3,041	+215 3,256	−3,256 —			
+39 3,465	+137 3,602	+56 3,658	+155 3,813	−3,813 —		
+103 6,697	+184 6,881	+1,279 8,160	+1,239 9,399	— —	— —	−397 9,002
+77 1,762	−1,762 —					
+41 4,638	+221 4,859	+8 4,867	+489 5,356	+512 5,868	+2,207 8,075	+187 8,262
+179 2,474	+59 2,533	−2,533 —				
+269 4,867	+199 5,066	+371 5,437	+267 5,704	+167 5,871	+1,082 6,953	+96 7,049
91	239	202	524	2,328	738	

Louth

Elected

Dermot Ahern (FF)*	1st Count
Séamus Kirk (FF)*	9th Count
Brendan McGahon (FG)*	12th Count
Michael Bell (Lab)*	12th Count

Voting by Party

1st Preference	Number	%	% 1992
Fianna Fáil	18,010	40.02	41.77
Fine Gael	12,555	27.90	24.92
Labour	4,725	10.50	22.10
Prog Democrats	2,395	5.32	—
Green Party	1,403	3.12	—
Sinn Féin	3,651	8.11	3.92
Workers' Party	—	—	0.57
Others	2,269	5.04	6.71

Statistics

Population	90,724	
Electorate	71,086	
Total Poll	45,611	64.16
Spoiled Votes	603	1.32
Valid Poll	45,008	63.31
Seats	4	
Quota	9,002	
Candidates	15	

Seats

FF	2
FG	1
Lab	1
No change	

The constituency of Louth is unchanged since the 1992 General Election.

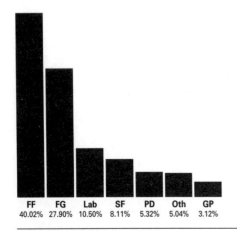

FF	FG	Lab	SF	PD	Oth	GP
40.02%	27.90%	10.50%	8.11%	5.32%	5.04%	3.12%

Dermot Ahern (FF)

Home Address
Hill Cottage, The Crescent, Blackrock, Co Louth
Business Address
Department of Social, Community and Family Affairs, Áras Mhic Dhiarmada, Store Street, Dublin 1
Telephone
Home (042) 21473; *Business* (01) 874 8844; *Fax* (01) 704 3869; *Constituency Office* (042) 39609/29023; *Fax* (042) 29016
Birth Place/Date
Drogheda. February 1955
Married
Maeve Coleman. 2 daughters
Education
Marist College, Dundalk, Co Louth; University College, Dublin; Incorporated Law Society of Ireland (BCL)
Occupation
Government Minister. Formerly solicitor

Dermot Ahern was appointed Minister for Social, Community and Family Affairs in June 1997. He was Minister of State at the Department of the Taoiseach with special responsibility as Government Chief Whip, and Minister of State at the Department of Defence November 1991-February 1992. He has been a member of the Dáil since February 1987. Assistant Government Whip 1988-91.

Fianna Fáil Chief Whip, Leader of the House in opposition and in charge of Parliamentary Strategy and Legislative Proposals in the House 1995-97.

Member, British-Irish Parliamentary Body 1991-97 (co-chairman 1993-95).

Member, Louth County Council 1979-91.

Séamus Kirk (FF)

Home Address
Rathiddy, Knockbridge, Dundalk, Co Louth
Telephone
Home (042) 31032
Birth Place/Date
Drumkeith. April 1945
Married
Mary McGeough. 3 sons, 1 daughter
Education
Dundalk CBS
Occupation
Full-time public representative. Farmer

Séamus Kirk was Minister of State at the Department of Agriculture and Food with special responsibility for Horticulture March 1987-February 1992. He was first elected to the Dáil in November 1982. Fianna Fáil spokesman on Horticulture 1983-87.

Member, Committee on Co-operation with Developing Countries 1982-87; Committee on State-Sponsored bodies 1992-97.

Member, Forum for Peace and Reconciliation 1994-96.

Member, Louth County Council 1974-85; Louth County Health Committee 1974-85; Louth County Committee of Agriculture 1974-85; East Border Region Committee 1974-85.

Member, Gaelic Athletic Association since 1958. Member, Tidy Towns Committee.

Brendan McGahon (FG)

Home Address
Annaverna, Ravensdale, Dundalk, Co Louth
Telephone
Home (042) 32620
Birth Place/Date
Dundalk. November 1936
Married
Celine Lundy. 2 sons, 3 daughters
Education
St Mary's College, Dundalk
Occupation
Public representative. Newspaper distributor

Brendan McGahon has been a Dáil deputy since November 1982. Member, Committee of Public Accounts since 1983 (acting chairman 1992/93). He was an unsuccessful Dáil candidate in the general elections of 1981 and February 1982.

Member, Dundalk Urban District Council since 1979; Louth County Council since 1979; Dundalk Harbour Board 1979-85; Louth County Vocational Education Committee 1979-85.

Played football for Dundalk FC in the League of Ireland. Also played rugby with Dundalk RFC.

Michael Bell (Lab)

Home Address
122 Newfield Estate, Drogheda, Co Louth
Business Address
Connolly Hall, Palace Street, Drogheda
Telephone
(041) 38573; *Fax* (041) 42048
Birth Place/Date
Drogheda. October 1936
Married
Betty Plunkett. 2 sons, 3 daughters
Education
St Laurence's College, Drogheda
Occupation
Full-time public representative. Formerly trade union national official

Michael Bell has been a Dáil deputy since November 1982. He was an unsuccessful Dáil candidate in 1981 and February 1982.

Chairman, Select Committee on Enterprise and Economic Strategy and Chairman, Select Committee of Members' Interests of Dáil Éireann, during the 27th Dáil.

Chairman, Labour Parliamentary Party. Party spokesperson on Social Welfare 1987-89 and since 1997; Industry and Commerce 1989-90; Justice 1991; Social Welfare 1992.

Member, Louth County Council since 1974; Drogheda Corporation since 1974; North-Eastern Health Board 1982-85; Drogheda Harbour Commissioners (former chairman).

Former director, Institute for Industrial Research and Standards.

Former General Secretary IS&LWU. Former National Group Secretary ITGWU. Member ICTU 1965-82.

'Would you like to swap places?' Michael Noonan greets Commissioner Pádraig Flynn and Mrs Flynn at Leinster House.

Seats 5 Quota 10,310	1st Count	2nd Count Transfer of **Cullen's** and **Sherry's** Votes	3rd Count Transfer of **Crowley's** Votes	4th Count Transfer of **Finn's** Votes	5th Count Transfer of **Ginty's** Votes	6th Count Transfer of **Caffrey's** Votes	7th Count Transfer of **Morley's** Votes	8th Count Transfer of **Higgins's** Surplus
CAFFREY, Ernie (FG)	4,579	+29 4,608	+65 4,673	+28 4,701	+706 5,407	−5,407 —		
COOPER–FLYNN, Beverley (FF)	8,353	+65 8,418	+93 8,511	+142 8,653	+113 8,766	+178 8,944	+2,143 11,087	— —
CROWLEY, Ann (GP)	938	+84 1,022	−1,022 —					
CULLEN, Cormac Connie (Ind)	119	−119 —						
FINN, Richard (Ind)	1,683	+46 1,729	+71 1,800	−1,800 —				
GINTY, Gerry (Ind)	1,656	+186 1,842	+99 1,941	+138 2,079	−2,079 —			
*****HIGGINS**, Jim (FG)	6,945	+61 7,006	+63 7,069	+602 7,671	+130 7,801	+2,173 9,974	+1,189 11,163	−853 10,310
*****HUGHES**, Séamus (FF)	6,791	+68 6,859	+94 6,953	+55 7,008	+84 7,092	+59 7,151	+1,018 8,169	+226 8,395
*****KENNY**, Enda (FG)	8,568	+58 8,626	+171 8,797	+192 8,989	+94 9,083	+1,127 10,210	+218 10,428	— —
*****MOFFATT**, Tom (FF)	5,735	+30 5,765	+36 5,801	+19 5,820	+564 6,384	+1,477 7,861	+1,592 9,453	+223 9,676
*****MORLEY**, P.J. (FF)	5,692	+103 5,795	+52 5,847	+531 6,378	+80 6,458	+39 6,497	−6,497 —	
*****RING**, Michael (FG)	10,066	+77 10,143	+207 10,350	—	—	—	—	—
SHERRY, Ciarán (NP)	733	−733 —						
NON-TRANSFERABLE		45	71	93	308	354	337	404

Mayo

Elected

Voting by Party

1st Preference	Number	%	% 1992†
Fianna Fáil	26,571	42.95	50.34
Fine Gael	30,158	48.75	41.91
Green Party	938	1.52	—
National Party	733	1.18	—
Others	3,458	5.59	7.75

Statistics

Population	110,713	
Electorate	87,719	
Total Poll	62,472	71.22
Spoiled Votes	614	0.98
Valid Poll	61,858	70.52
Seats	5	
Quota	10,310	
Candidates	13	

Seats

FF	2
FG	3

† 1992 percentages are for the total of the old constituencies of Mayo East and Mayo West.

Mayo is a new constituency and comprises the administrative county of Mayo. The population is 7,935 less than the combination of the old constituencies of Mayo East and Mayo West.

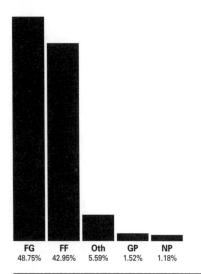

FG 48.75%   FF 42.95%   Oth 5.59%   GP 1.52%   NP 1.18%

Michael Ring (FG)

Home Address
The Paddock, Westport, Co Mayo
Constituency Office
Quay Street, Westport
Telephone
Home (098) 25734; *Constituency Office* (098) 27012; *Fax* (098) 27644
Birth Place/Date
Westport. December 1953
Married
Anne Fitzgerald. 1 son, 2 daughters
Education
Westport Vocational School
Occupation
Full-time public representative. Auctioneer

Michael Ring has been a Dáil deputy since June 1994, when he won a by-election in the old constituency of Mayo West caused by the resignation of Deputy Pádraig Flynn (FF) to become a European Commissioner. Fine Gael spokesperson Agriculture - Livestock Breeding and Horticulture since 1997.

Member, Mayo County Council since 1991, and of a number of its subsidiary committees; Westport Urban District Council since 1979 (chairman 1982/83 and 1988/89).

In a revision of the constituencies, the two Mayo 3-seaters of Mayo East and Mayo West were amalgamated into one 5-seater. This resulted in 6 outgoing Dáil deputies in the contest for the 5 seats in the 1997 general election.

Jim Higgins (FG)

Home Address
Devlis, Ballyhaunis, Co Mayo
Telephone
Home (0907) 30052; *Business* (01) 661 0735
Birth Place/Date
Ballyhaunis. May 1945
Married
Marian Hannan. 4 daughters
Education
St Jarlath's College, Tuam, Co Galway; University College, Galway (BA, HDipEd)
Occupation
Full-time public representative. Formerly community school teacher

Jim Higgins was Minister of State at the department of Finance February-May 1995; Minister of State at the Department of the Taoiseach and Department of Defence and Government Chief Whip May 1995-97. He has been a Dáil deputy since 1987. He was a candidate in the general elections of June 1981 and February and November 1982. Fine Gael front bench spokesperson on Justice, Equality and Law Reform since 1997; on Education 1990-94. Chief Whip 1988-90.

He was a Senator, Labour Panel 1983-87, and Taoiseach's Nominee June 1981-February 1982. Chairman, Fine Gael Parliamentary Party 1994-95.

Member, Mayo County Council 1979-95 and former vice-chairman; former vice-chairman Mayo County Vocational Education Committee.

Former member, Junior Chamber, Ireland; Western Care of the Mentally Handicapped Association; Gaelic Athletic Association.

Captain, Junior Chamber Ireland Debating Championship, 1978. Twice Junior Chamber Ireland Best Individual Speaker (1978 and 1979). Captain, International Tripartite Debating Team.

Beverley Cooper-Flynn (FF)

Home Address
2 The Manor Village, Westport Road, Castlebar, Co Mayo
Constituency Office
Newtown, Castlebar, Co Mayo
Telephone
Home (094) 26800; *Mobile* (087) 256 0229; *Constituency Office* (094) 27035
Birth Place/Date
Tuam, Co Galway. June 1966
Married
John Cooper
Education
St Joseph's Secondary School, Castlebar; University College, Dublin (BComm), IPM, ACII
Occupation
Full-time public representative. Formerly bank manager

Beverley Cooper-Flynn is a new Dáil deputy. She was a candidate in the Mayo West by-election in June 1994.

Member of Mayo County Council since September 1996.

She is a daughter of Pádraig Flynn, Fianna Fáil Dáil deputy for Mayo West 1977-93, a former Minister for Justice, for Industry and Commerce, for the Environment, for Trade, Commerce and Tourism and for the Gaeltacht. Since January 1993 he has been a European Commissioner.

Enda Kenny (FG)

Home Address
Tucker Street, Castlebar, Co Mayo
Business Address
Tucker Street, Castlebar
Telephone
(094) 25600
Birth Place/Date
Castlebar. April 1951
Married
Fionnuala O'Kelly. 2 sons, 1 daughter
Education
St Gerald's Secondary School, Castlebar; St Patrick's Teachers' Training College, Drumcondra, Dublin; University College, Galway
Occupation
Full-time public representative. Formerly national school teacher

Enda Kenny was Minister for Tourism and Trade 1994-97. He was Minister of State at the Department of Education and at the Department of Labour with special responsibility for Youth Affairs, February 1986-March 1987. He was first elected to the Dáil in November 1975. Front bench spokesperson on Arts, Heritage , Gaeltacht and the Islands since 1997. Fine Gael Chief Whip 1992-94 and front bench spokesperson on Regional Development 1994. Front bench spokesperson on the Gaeltacht 1987-88 and in 1982; on Western Development 1982; on Youth Affairs and Sport 1977-80. Chairman, Fine Gael Economic Affairs Committee 1991-92. Member, New Ireland Forum. British-Irish Parliamentary Body 1991-92.

Member, Mayo County Council 1975-95; former chairman, Mayo Vocational Education Committee; West Mayo Vocational Education Committee; Western Health Board.

He is the son of the late Henry Kenny, Dáil deputy for Mayo South 1954-69, and for Mayo West 1969-75, and Parliamentary Secretary to the Minister for Finance 1973-75.

Tom Moffatt (FF)

Home Address
Castle Road, Ballina, Co Mayo
Constituency Office
Tolan (Bridge) Street, Ballina
Business Address
Department of Health and Children, Hawkins House, Hawkins Street, Dublin 2
Telephone
Home (096) 22868/71588; *Constituency Office* (096) 71588; *Fax* (096) 71646; *Business* (01) 671 4711
Birth Place/Date
Ballina. January 1940
Married
Patricia Cashman. 2 sons, 3 daughters
Education
St Muredach's College, Ballina; All Hallows College, Dublin; University College, Galway (MB, BCh, BAO, DCH, DRCOG (RCSI))
Occupation
Minister of State. Medical doctor (GP)

Dr Tom Moffatt was appointed Minister of State at the Department of Health and Children, with special responsibility for Food Safety and Older People, in July 1997. He has been a Dáil deputy since 1992. The 1992 general election was the first occasion on which he ran for public office. He won the Fianna Fáil seat left vacant by the resignation of Seán Calleary, former Minister of State and Dáil deputy for Mayo East 1973-92. Member, British-Irish Parliamentary Body 1993-97.

Party spokesperson on Mental Health 1995-97.

Member, Irish Medical Organisation; Irish College of General Practitioners; Irish Sports Medical Association.

Holder of Mayo, Galway and Connacht athletic titles. Played Gaelic football at club and university levels and has since been active with the game as an administrator and medical officer.

Meath

Seats 5 Quota 9,449	1st Count	2nd Count Transfer of **Bruton's** Surplus	3rd Count Transfer of **Tallon's, O'Connell's,** and **Farrelly's** (Pauline) Votes	4th Count Transfer of **Gorman's** Votes
BRADY, Johnny (FF)	7,372	+51 7,423	+55 7,478	+28 7,506
***BRUTON**, John (FG)	13,037	−3,588 9,449		
CURRAN, Brian (CSP)	1,031	+24 1,055	+15 1,070	+19 1,089
***DEMPSEY**, Noel (FF)	8,701	+269 8,970	+39 9,009	+96 9,105
FARRELLY, John V. (FG)	5,348	+1,819 7,167	+123 7,290	+95 7,385
FARRELLY, Pauline (Ind)	564	+43 607	−607 —	
***FITZGERALD**, Brian (Lab)	3,695	+453 4,148	+60 4,208	+200 4,408
GORMAN, Christy (DL)	798	+50 848	+23 871	−871 —
HOLLOWAY, James (FG)	2,548	+554 3,102	+104 3,206	+153 3,359
KELLY, Tom (Ind)	1,305	+41 1,346	+29 1,375	+16 1,391
KELLY McCORMACK, Anne (GP)	1,103	+42 1,145	+76 1,221	+51 1,272
O'CONNELL, Jackie (Ind)	152	+5 157	−157 —	
OWENS, Ronnie (PD)	1,344	+35 1,379	+38 1,417	+24 1,441
REILLY, Joe (SF)	2,000	+20 2,020	+21 2,041	+125 2,166
TALLON, Jim (Ind)	24	+1 25	−25 —	
***WALLACE**, Mary (FF)	7,669	+181 7,850	+167 8,017	+35 8,052
NON-TRANSFERABLE		—	39	29

5th Count	6th Count	7th Count	8th Count	9th Count	10th Count
Transfer of **Curran's** Votes	Transfer of **Kelly McCormack's** Votes	Transfer of **Kelly's** Votes	Transfer of **Owens's** Votes	Transfer of **Reilly's** Votes	Transfer of **Holloway's** Votes
+148 7,654	+57 7,711	+40 7,751	+401 8,152	+794 8,946	+233 9,179
−1,089 —					
+148 9,253	+124 9,377	+141 9,518	— —	— —	— —
+134 7,519	+135 7,654	+276 7,930	+192 8,122	+217 8,339	+2,553 10,892
+53 4,461	+233 4,694	+229 4,923	+60 4,983	+284 5,267	+603 5,870
+102 3,461	+114 3,575	+88 3,663	+138 3,801	+291 4,092	−4,092 —
+52 1,443	+105 1,548	−1,548 —			
+80 1,352	−1,352 —				
+52 1,493	+117 1,610	+90 1,700	−1,700 —		
+62 2,228	+116 2,344	+80 2,424	+61 2,485	−2,485 —	
+149 8,201	+186 8,387	+387 8,774	+678 9,452	— —	— —
109	165	217	170	899	703

Meath

Elected

John Bruton (FG)*	1st Count
Noel Dempsey (FF)*	7th Count
Mary Wallace (FF)*	8th Count
John V. Farrelly (FG)	10th Count
Johnny Brady (FF)	10th Count

Voting by Party

1st Preference	Number	%	% 1992
Fianna Fáil	23,742	41.88	45.08
Fine Gael	20,933	36.92	26.48
Labour	3,695	6.52	17.55
Prog Democrats	1,344	2.37	2.22
Green Party	1,103	1.95	1.27
Sinn Féin	2,000	3.53	1.25
Democratic Left	798	1.41	1.58
Christian Solidarity	1,031	1.82	—
Others	2,045	3.61	4.56

Statistics

Population	105,370	
Electorate	90,125	
Total Poll	57,265	63.54
Spoiled Votes	574	1.00
Valid Poll	56,691	62.90
Seats	5	
Quota	9,449	
Candidates	16	

Seats

FF	3
FG	2

FG gain from Lab

The constituency of Meath is unchanged since the 1992 General Election.

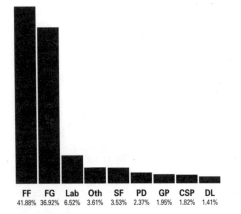

FF	FG	Lab	Oth	SF	PD	GP	CSP	DL
41.88%	36.92%	6.52%	3.61%	3.53%	2.37%	1.95%	1.82%	1.41%

John Bruton (FG)

Home Address
Cornelstown, Dunboyne, Co Meath
Telephone
Office (01) 618 3117, 618 3107
Birth Place/Date
Dublin. May 1947
Married
Finola Gill. 1 son, 3 daughters
Education
St Dominic's College, Cabra, Dublin;
Clongowes Wood College, Co Kildare; UCD;
King's Inns, Dublin (BA, BL)
Occupation
Leader of Fine Gael

John Bruton was Taoiseach from December 1994 to June 1997, leading a 3-party Coalition Government of Fine Gael, Labour and Democratic Left.

He was Minister for Finance, February 1986-March 1987; Minister for the Public Service January-March 1987; Minister for Industry, Trade, Commerce and Tourism, December 1983-February 1986; Minister for Industry and Energy 1982-83; Minister for Finance June 1981-March 1982. Leader of the House 1982-86 with responsibility for implementing reforms in the Dáil. Parliamentary Secretary to the Minister for Education 1973-77 and to the Minister for Industry and Commerce 1975-77.

Leader of Fine Gael since 1990 and Party spokesperson on Northern Ireland; Deputy Leader of Fine Gael 1987-90. Front bench spokesperson on Education 1989-90; on Industry and Commerce 1987-89; on Finance January-June 1981 and in 1982; on Agriculture 1972-73 and 1977-January 1981. He was first elected to the Dáil in 1969, becoming the youngest member of the 19th Dáil.

Member, Parliamentary Assembly, Council of Europe 1989-90.

Publications: *Reform of the Dáil*, 1980; *A Better Way to Plan the Nation*, 1981; 'Real Issues or Mock Battles', *Furrow*, 1986.

Brother of Richard Bruton, Dáil deputy for Dublin North-Central since February 1982.

Noel Dempsey (FF)

Home Address
Newtown, Trim, Co Meath
Business Address
Department of the Environment and Local Government, Custom House, Dublin 1
Telephone
Home/Constituency Office (046) 31146;
Business (01) 679 3377; Fax (046) 36643,
(01) 874 2710
Birth Place/Date
Trim. January 1953
Married
Bernadette Rattigan. 2 sons, 2 daughters
Education
St Michael's CBS, Trim; University College, Dublin; St Patrick's College, Maynooth (BA, HDipEd); Diploma in Career Guidance; Diploma in Youth Leadership
Occupation
Government Minister. Formerly career guidance counsellor

Noel Dempsey was appointed Minister for the Environment and Local Government in June 1997. He was Minister of State at the Department of the Taoiseach with special responsibility as Government Chief Whip, and at the Department of Finance with special responsibility for the Office of Public Works, and at the Department of Defence 1993-94. He was Minister of State at the Departments of the Taoiseach and Defence (Chief Whip) February 1992-January 1993. He has been a Dáil deputy since 1987.

Party front bench spokesperson on the Environment 1995-97. Party convenor on Forum for Peace and Reconciliation.

Member, Meath County Council 1977-92 (chairman 1986/87); Trim Urban District Council (chairman 1981/82, 1985/86 and 1991/92); Meath Vocational Education Committee; Library Committee; Director of Dublin and Eastern Regional Tourism Organisation.

Former national secretary, Local Authority Members' Association.

Mary Wallace (FF)

Home Address
Fairyhouse Road, Ratoath, Co Meath
Business Address
Department of Justice, Equality and Law
Reform, 43-49 Mespil Road, Dublin 4
Telephone
Home/Office (01) 825 6259; *Business* (01) 667
0344; *Fax* (01) 825 6848, (01) 667 0369
Birth Place/Date
Dublin. June 1959
Married
Declan Gannon. 1 son
Education
Loreto Convent, Balbriggan, Co Dublin; Loreto
Convent, North Great George's Street, Dublin;
Rathmines College of Commerce, Dublin (Dip
Hospital & Health Services Administration)
Occupation
Minister of State. Formerly personnel
executive

Mary Wallace was appointed Minister of State
at the Department of Justice, Equality and
Law Reform, with special responsibility for
Equality and Disabilities, in July 1997. She has
been a Dáil deputy since 1989. She contested
the 1987 Dáil general election. Senator,
Administrative Panel, 1987-89. Fianna Fáil
spokesperson for people with disabilities and
carers 1995-97.

Chairperson, Oireachtas Joint Committee on
Women's Rights 1995-97 (vice-chairperson
1989-92).

Chairperson of Fianna Fáil National Women's
Committee 1992-94.

Member, Meath County Council 1982-97
when she was co-opted to the seat of her
father, Tom Wallace; North-Eastern Health
Board 1985-89; member, Meath Vocational
Education Committee 1991-95; Meath County
Committee of Agriculture 1982-87
(chairperson 1986/87); Blanchardstown
Hospital 1977-87.

John V. Farrelly (FG)

Home Address
Hurdlestown, Kells, Co Meath
Business Address
Nobber, Co Meath
Telephone
Home (046) 41290; *Business* (046) 29099
Birth Place/Date
Kilmainhamwood, Co Meath. November 1954
Married
Gwen Murphy. 2 daughters
Education
St Finian's College, Mullingar, Co Westmeath;
Warrenstown Agricultural College, Co Meath
Occupation
Full-time public representative. Formerly
auctioneer and farmer

John Farrelly was previously a Dáil deputy
1981-92. Senator, Agricultural Panel 1992-97.
Fine Gael front bench spokesperson on
Tourism 1991-92.

Member, Meath County Council since
February 1975 when he was co-opted to fill
the vacancy caused by the death of his father,
Denis Farrelly (chairman 1991/92).

He has served as member, Meath County
Committee of Agriculture (vice-chairman);
General Council of County Councils; North-
Eastern Health Board; ACOT (chairman Meath
Committee, 1979).

Member, Irish Farmers' Association; Gaelic
Athletic Association.

He is son of Denis Farrelly, Dáil deputy for
Meath 1961-69 and later a senator.

Johnny Brady (FF)

Home Address
Springville, Kilskyre, Kells, Co Meath
Telephone
Home (046) 40852
Birth Place/Date
Meath. January 1948
Married
Kathleen Clarke. 1 son
Education
Kells Vocational School.
Occupation
Full-time public representative. Farmer

Johnny Brady is a new Dáil deputy. This was
the first time he contested a general election.

He has been a member of Meath County
Council since 1974 (chairman 1995/96).
Former member of Meath County Committee
of Agriculture and of the North-Eastern Health
Board.

He served as chairman of Meath Juvenile
GAA Hurling Board for six years and with local
youth organisations.

John Bruton at his 50th birthday party.

Seats 4 Quota 9,034	1st Count	2nd Count Transfer of **Gillan's, Lawlor's** and **Lacken's** Votes	3rd Count Transfer of **McManus's** Votes	4th Count Transfer of **Leonard's** Votes	5th Count Transfer of **Forde's** Votes	6th Count Transfer of **Brennan's** Surplus
*BREE, Declan (Lab)	4,905	+183 5,088	+1,018 6,106	+608 6,714	+733 7,447	+522 7,969
*BRENNAN, Matt (FF)	6,461	+302 6,763	+290 7,053	+279 7,332	+3,181 10,513	−1,479 9,034
*ELLIS, John (FF)	7,051	+244 7,295	+626 7,921	+68 7,989	+1,082 9,071	— —
FORDE, Margaret G. (FF)	4,738	+567 5,305	+413 5,718	+402 6,120	−6,120 —	
GILLAN, Simeon (NLP)	154	−154 —				
LACKEN, John (CSP)	1,359	−1,359 —				
LAWLOR, Jim (PD)	745	−745 —				
LEONARD, Joe (FG)	4,016	+217 4,233	+120 4,353	−4,353 —		
McMANUS, Seán (SF)	3,208	+148 3,356	−3,356 —			
PERRY, John (FG)	5,786	+211 5,997	+143 6,140	+1,898 8,038	+402 8,440	+434 8,874
REYNOLDS, Gerard (FG)	6,743	+237 6,980	+247 7,227	+937 8,164	+301 8,465	+223 8,688
NON-TRANSFERABLE		149	499	161	421	300

Sligo-Leitrim

Elected

Matt Brennan (FF)*	5th Count
John Ellis (FF)*	5th Count
John Perry (FG)	6th Count
Gerard Reynolds (FG)	6th Count

Voting by Party

1st Preference	Number	%	% 1992
Fianna Fáil	18,250	40.41	45.61
Fine Gael	16,545	36.63	30.35
Labour	4,905	10.86	17.15
Prog Democrats	745	1.65	—
Sinn Féin	3,208	7.10	3.07
Christian Solidarity	1,359	3.01	—
Others	154	0.34	3.82

Statistics

Population	80,057	
Electorate	64,770	
Total Poll	45,618	70.43
Spoiled Votes	452	0.99
Valid Poll	45,166	69.73
Seats	4	
Quota	9,034	
Candidates	11	

Seats

FF	2
FG	2
FG gain from Lab	

The constituency of Sligo-Leitrim is unchanged since the 1992 General Election.

FF	FG	Lab	SF	CSP	PD	Oth
40.41%	36.63%	10.86%	7.10%	3.01%	1.65%	0.34%

Matt Brennan (FF)

Home Address
Ragoora, Cloonacool, Tubbercurry, Co Sligo
Telephone
Home (071) 85136; *Mobile* (086) 819 7919; *Fax* (071) 85337
Birth Place/Date
Cloonacool. October 1936
Married
Mary Vesey. 1 son, 1 daughter
Education
Vocational School, Tubbercurry; Theodore Roosevelt High School, Bronx, New York
Occupation
Full-time public representative. Formerly Vocational Education Committee instructor

Matt Brennan has been a Dáil deputy since February 1982. He was an unsuccessful candidate in the general election of June 1981. Member, Parliamentary Assembly, Council of Europe since 1992.

Member, Sligo County Council since 1974; member, Sligo Vocational Education Committee. Member, Tubbercurry Community Care. Former member, Junior Chamber, Tubbercurry.

Member, Gaelic Athletic Association.

Matt Brennan is a nephew of the late Dr Martin Brennan, Fianna Fáil Dáil deputy for Sligo-Leitrim 1938-48.

John Ellis (FF)

Home Address
Fenagh, Co Leitrim
Telephone
Home (078) 44252; *Fax* (078) 44017; *Mobile* (086) 259 4978
Birth Place/Date
Fenagh. May 1952
Married
Patricia Donnelly. 2 sons, 1 daughter
Education
St Felim's College, Ballinamore, Co Leitrim
Occupation
Full-time public representative. Farmer

John Ellis has been a member of the Dáil since 1987 and he was previously a Dáil deputy June 1981-November 1982. Senator 1977-81, and 1983-87, Agricultural Panel. He contested Dáil general elections in Roscommon-Leitrim in 1977 and Sligo-Leitrim in November 1982.

Chairman, Dáil Select Committee on Finance and General Affairs 1993-94. Member, Public Accounts Committee 1993-97. Member, British-Irish Parliamentary Body 1993-97.

Member, Oireachtas Joint Committee on the Secondary Legislation of the European Communities 1989-93 (chairman, Agricultural Sub-committee).

Executive member, Inter-Parliamentary Union.

Member, Leitrim County Council since 1974 (chairman 1986/87); General Council of County Councils 1979-91; General Council of Committees of Agriculture 1979-88.

Member, Midland and Western Livestock Improvement Society.

Member, Gaelic Athletic Association.

John Perry (FG)

Home Address
Teeling Street, Ballymote, Co Sligo
Constituency Offices
Teeling Street, Ballymote; Westward Town
Centre, Sligo
Telephone
Home (071) 83372; *Constituency Office*
(071) 89333/51011; *Mobile* (087) 245 9407;
Fax (071) 83349
Birth Place/Date
Ballymote. August 1956
Married
Marie Mulvey
Education
Corran College, Ballymote
Occupation
Public representative, businessman

John Perry is a new Dáil deputy. This was the
first time he contested a general election.
Fine Gael spokesperson on Science,
Technology, Small Business and Enterprise,
Border Counties since 1997.

He is chairman of Ballymote Community
Enterprise, the first economic community
enterprise established in Sligo to create long-
term employment. Chairman of Ballymote
Cattle and Horse Show and a member of
community and development committees and
organisations.

Winner of the *Irish Quality Business* award in
1991 and 1992. Recipient of Sligo *Person of
the Year* award, 1993.

Gerard Reynolds (FG)

Home Address
Main Street, Ballinamore, Co Leitrim
Telephone
(078) 44016
Birth Place/Date
Dublin. April 1961
Education
St Joseph's College, Ballinasloe; New York
University (BSc)
Occupation
Public representative, businessman

Gerard Reynolds was previously a Dáil deputy
1989-92. Senator, Industrial and Commercial
Panel 1987-89 and 1993-97. He was Fine Gael
spokesperson in the Dáil on Tourism and in
the Seanad on Industry, Commerce, Forestry
and on Health.

Member of Leitrim County Council since
1985; Leitrim Vocational Education
Committee.

Son of Pat Joe Reynolds, Parliamentary
Secretary to the Minister for Local
Government and to the Minister for the Public
Service 1976-77, Dáil deputy for Roscommon
1961-69 and for Roscommon-Leitrim 1973-77;
Senator, Administrative Panel, 1969-73;
Senator, Industrial and Commercial Panel,
1977-87 and Cathaoirleach 1983-87.

Grandson of Patrick Reynolds, Dáil deputy for
Sligo-Leitrim 1927-32 and Mary Reynolds, Dáil
deputy for the same constituency 1932-33
and 1937-61.

Dick Spring canvassing in Donaghmede Shopping Centre with outgoing Labour TDs in Dublin North-East, Tommy Broughan and Seán Kenny. Broughan made it back; Kenny missed out.

Seats 3 Quota 9,989	1st Count	2nd Count Transfer of **Lowry's** Surplus	3rd Count Transfer of **MacBain's** Votes	4th Count Transfer of **O'Kennedy's** Surplus	5th Count Transfer of **Carey's** Votes	6th Count Transfer of **Hennessy's** Votes	7th Count Transfer of **O'Meara's** Votes
BERKERY, Tom (FG)	4,521	+445 4,966	+26 4,992	+22 5,014	+198 5,212	+273 5,485	+3,138 8,623
CAREY, Margaret (NP)	1,295	+137 1,432	+16 1,448	+16 1,464	−1,464 —		
HENNESSY, Joe (PD)	1,390	+82 1,472	+10 1,482	+16 1,498	+237 1,735	−1,735 —	
***LOWRY**, Michael (Ind)	11,638	−1,649 9,989					
MacBAIN, Gillies (Ind)	88	+20 108	−108 —				
O'KENNEDY, Michael (FF)	9,895	+301 10,196	— —	−207 9,989			
O'MEARA, Kathleen (Lab)	4,126	+470 4,596	+26 4,622	+38 4,660	+232 4,892	+326 5,218	−5,218 —
***SMITH**, Michael (FF)	6,999	+194 7,193	+13 7,206	+115 7,321	+472 7,793	+883 8,676	+1,078 9,754
NON-TRANSFERABLE			17	—	325	253	1,002

Tipperary North

Elected

Michael Lowry (Ind)*	1st Count
Michael O'Kennedy (FF)	2nd Count
Michael Smith (FF)*	7th Count

Voting by Party

1st Preference	Number	%	% 1992
Fianna Fáil	16,894	42.29	47.98
Fine Gael	4,521	11.32	28.07
Labour	4,126	10.33	22.75
Prog Democrats	1,390	3.48	—
Sinn Féin	—	—	1.20
National Party	1,295	3.24	—
Others	11,726	29.35	—

Statistics

Population	67,233	
Electorate	53,888	
Total Poll	40,289	74.76
Spoiled Votes	337	0.84
Valid Poll	39,952	74.14
Seats	3	
Quota	9,989	
Candidates	8	

Seats

FF	2
Ind	1

FF and Ind gains from FG and Lab

The constituency of Tipperary North is somewhat larger than in the 1992 General Election, having gained an area with a population of 9,379 from the constituency of Tipperary South.

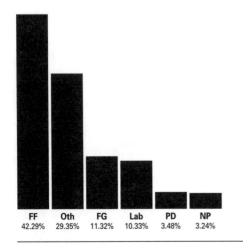

FF	Oth	FG	Lab	PD	NP
42.29%	29.35%	11.32%	10.33%	3.48%	3.24%

Michael Lowry (Ind)

Home Address
Glenreigh, Holycross, Thurles, Co Tipperary
Business Address
Abbey Road, Thurles
Telephone
Home (0504) 43182; *Business* (0504) 22022; *Fax* (0504) 23349
Birth Place/Date
Holycross. March 1954
Married
Catherine McGrath. 2 sons, 1 daughter
Education
Thurles CBS
Occupation
Public representative, company director

Michael Lowry was Minister for Transport, Energy and Communications 1994-November 1996 when he resigned. He has been a Dáil deputy since 1987, elected for Fine Gael in the general elections of 1987, 1989 and 1992 and as an independent in 1997. He resigned from the Fine Gael Parliamentary Party in 1997.

Chairman, Fine Gael Parliamentary Party 1993-94. Member of front bench 1993-94. Fine Gael Leader of the British-Irish Parliamentary Body 1994.

Previously Fine Gael Dáil spokesperson on Science and Technology, the Environment, Consumer Affairs and Marketing.

Member, Tipperary (North Riding) County Council 1979-95. He served on County Development Team, Mid-Western Health Board and Association of Health Boards in Ireland.

Chairman, Semple Stadium Management Committee. Former chairman, County Tipperary Gaelic Athletic Association Board and Mid-Tipperary GAA Board.

Michael O'Kennedy (FF)

Home Address
Gortlandroe, Nenagh, Co Tipperary
Telephone
Home (067) 31484
Birth Place/Date
Nenagh. February 1936
Married
Breda Heavey. 2 sons, 1 daughter
Education
St Flannan's College, Ennis, Co Clare; St Patrick's College, Maynooth; University College, Dublin; King's Inns, Dublin (MA, BL)
Occupation
Public representative. Senior Counsel

Michael O'Kennedy was Minister for Agriculture and Food 1987-February 1992. EEC Commissioner 1981-82. Minister for Foreign Affairs 1977-79. Minister for Finance 1979-81. Minister without Portfolio December 1972-January 1973. Minister for Transport and Power January-March 1973. Parliamentary Secretary to the Minister for Education 1970-72 with special responsibility for Youth and Sport. Dáil deputy for Tipperary North from 1969 until he resigned to become EEC Commissioner. Re-elected to the Dáil in the February 1982 general election (resigned as EEC Commissioner) and continued until 1992 when he lost his seat. Senator, Administrative Panel 1993-97. Senator and front bench spokesman 1965-69.

Fianna Fáil spokesman on Finance 1983-87; on Foreign Affairs 1973-77. Chairman, Inter-party Committee on the Implications of Irish Unity 1972-73. Member, All-Party Committee on Irish Relations 1973-77. Member, Committee on the Constitution, 1967. Member, Nenagh Urban District Council 1974-77 (chairman 1974/75).

Michael Smith (FF)

Home Address
Lismackin, Roscrea, Co Tipperary
Business Address
Department of Defence, Parkgate, Dublin 8
Telephone
Home (0505) 43157; *Business* (01) 804 2106
Birth Place/Date
Roscrea. November 1940
Married
Mary Therese Ryan. 1 son, 6 daughters
Education
Templemore CBS, Co Tipperary; University
College, Cork (DPA)
Occupation
Government Minister

Michael Smith was appointed Minister for
Defence in October 1997. He was Minister
of State at the Department of Education and
at the Department of Enterprise, Trade and
Employment, with special responsibility for
Science and Technology July-October 1997.
He was Minister for the Environment
February 1992-94. He was also Minister for
Education November-December 1994. He
was Minister of State at the Department of
Industry and Commerce, with special
responsibility for Science and Technology July
1989-November 1991. He was Minister for
Energy November 1988-July 1989; Minister
of State at the Department of Energy with
special responsibility for Forestry March 1987-
November 1988. Minister of State at the
Department of Agriculture December 1980-
June 1981. He was first elected to the Dáil in
1969 and represented Tipperary North until
1973 when he lost his seat to the Labour
Party. Regained the seat in 1977 at the
expense of Fine Gael. Lost his seat again in
the February 1982 election. He was a
candidate in the November 1982 election.
Senator, Agricultural Panel, 1982-83; Cultural
and Educational Panel 1983-87.

Former member, Tipperary North Riding
County Council (chairman 1986/87).

Member, Irish Farmers' Association since
1969; member, ITGWU (now SIPTU) 1967-69.

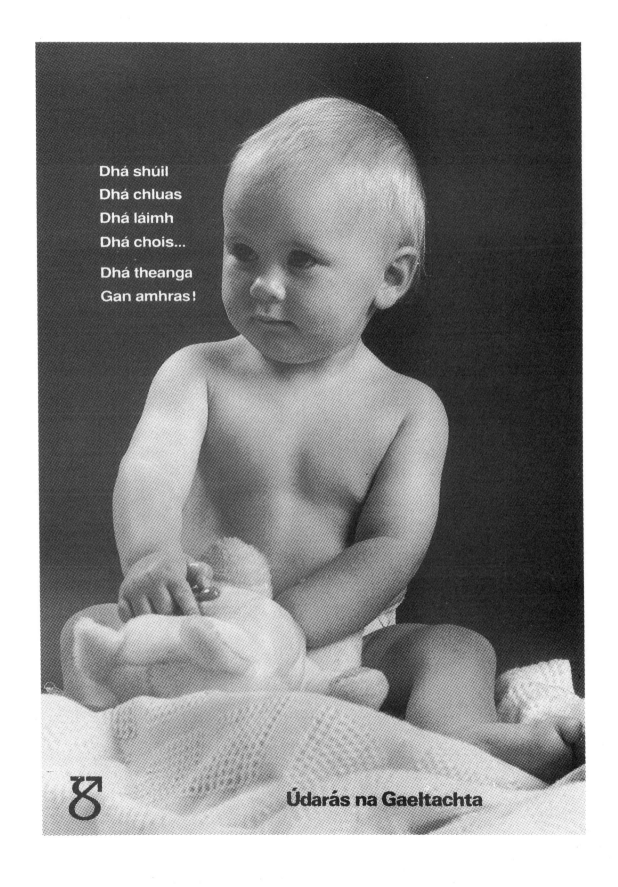

Dhá shúil
Dhá chluas
Dhá láimh
Dhá chois...

Dhá theanga
Gan amhras!

Údarás na Gaeltachta

Seats 3	1st Count	2nd Count	3rd Count	4th Count	5th Count
Quota 8,816		Transfer of **Davern's** Surplus	Transfer of **Harold-Barry's** Votes	Transfer of **Maguire's** Votes	Transfer of **Ahearn's** Surplus
*AHEARN, Theresa (FG)	8,494	+19 8,513	+604 9,117	— —	−301 8,816
*DAVERN, Noel (FF)	8,995	−179 8,816			
*FERRIS, Michael (Lab)	5,681	+12 5,693	+335 6,028	+1,783 7,811	+238 8,049
HAROLD-BARRY, John (NP)	2,125	+5 2,130	−2,130 —		
HEALY, Séamus (Ind)	5,814	+19 5,833	+335 6,168	+1,383 7,551	+63 7,614
MAGUIRE, Michael (FF)	4,151	+124 4,275	+645 4,920	−4,920 —	
NON-TRANSFERABLE		—	211	1,754	—

Tipperary South

Elected

Voting by Party

1st Preference	Number	%	% 1992
Fianna Fáil	13,146	37.28	38.22
Fine Gael	8,494	24.09	27.62
Labour	5,681	16.11	20.94
Sinn Féin	—		0.52
National Party	2,125	6.03	—
Others	5,814	16.49	12.70

Statistics

Population	67,091	
Electorate	51,925	
Total Poll	35,634	68.63
Spoiled Votes	374	1.05
Valid Poll	35,260	67.91
Seats	3	
Quota	8,816	
Candidates	6	

Seats

FF	1
FG	1
Lab	1

Seán Treacy (Ind), outgoing Ceann Comhairle, did not exercise his right to be returned automatically.

The constituency of Tipperary South has one less seat than in the 1992 General Election. It has also lost an area with a population of 9,379 to the constituency of Tipperary North and an area with a population of 1,063 to the constituency of Waterford.

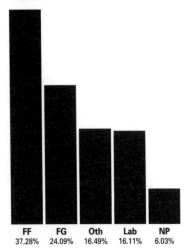

FF	FG	Oth	Lab	NP
37.28%	24.09%	16.49%	16.11%	6.03%

Noel Davern (FF)

Home Address
Tannersrath, Clonmel, Co Tipperary
Business Address
Department of Agriculture and Food, Kildare Street, Dublin 2
Telephone
Home (052) 22991; *Business* (01) 678 9227/ 607 2000; *Fax* (052) 29800/(01) 676 3947
Birth Place/Date
Cashel, Co Tipperary. December 1945
Married
Anne Marie Carroll. 2 sons, 1 daughter
Education
Cashel CBS; Franciscan College, Gormanston, Co Meath
Occupation
Minister of State

Noel Davern was appointed Minister of State at the Department of Agriculture and Food, with special responsibility for Livestock Breeding and Horticulture in July 1997. He was Minister for Education November 1991-February 1992. He was first elected to the Dáil in 1969, winning a seat previously held by his brother, Don Davern, Parliamentary Secretary to the Minister for Agriculture, who died while in office, 1968. He continued as a Dáil deputy until 1981 but did not contest the general election in that year. Re-elected to the Dáil in March 1987 and has been a Dáil deputy since.

Elected to the European Parliament 1979 and continued as a member until the 1984 Elections when he was an unsuccessful candidate.

Member, Tipperary (SR) County Council 1985-92; Vocational Education Committee; ACOT Committee; National Museum Advisory Committee.

He is a son of Michael Davern, Dáil deputy for Tipperary South 1948-65, and brother of Don Davern, Dáil deputy for the same constituency 1965-68.

Theresa Ahearn (FG)

Home Address
Ballindoney, Grange, Clonmel, Co Tipperary
Telephone
Home (052) 38142; *Fax* (052) 38368
Birth Place/Date
Golden, Co Tipperary. May 1951
Married
Liam Ahearn. 4 sons
Education
Presentation Convent, Cashel, Co Tipperary; University College, Dublin; St Patrick's College, Maynooth (BA, HDipEd)
Occupation
Full-time public representative. Formerly mathematics teacher, Central Technical Institute, Clonmel

Theresa Ahearn has been a Dáil deputy since 1989.

Fine Gael spokesperson on Equality and Disabilities since 1997; front bench spokesperson on Energy 1992-93 and on Labour 1992. Spokesperson on Women's Affairs and Chairperson of the Oireachtas Joint Committee on Women's Affairs 1993-95. During the 27th Dáil she also served on Foreign Affairs, Enterprise and Economic Strategy, Social Affairs and Small Businesses Committees.

Member of Tipperary (SR) County Council since 1983 (chairperson 1994/95); Tipperary (SR) County Committee of Agriculture 1983-85; South Tipperary Vocational Education Committee since 1985; Local Health Committee 1983-87; Alderman Clonmel Corporation since 1994.

Former member, Macra na Feirme. Member, Teachers' Union of Ireland since 1972. Member, Irish Farmers' Association.

Michael Ferris (Lab)

Home Address
Rosanna, Tipperary, Co Tipperary
Telephone
Home and Office (062) 52265;
Mobile (087) 254 0756; *Fax* (062) 52580
Birth Place/Date
Bansha, Co Tipperary. November 1931
Married
Ellen Kiely. 4 sons, 2 daughters
Education
Tipperary CBS; Tipperary VEC; Salesian
Agricultural College, Tipperary
Occupation
Full-time public representative. Formerly
director and secretary to veterinary practice

Michael Ferris was first elected to the Dáil in
1989. Labour Party Chief Whip and Assistant
Government Whip 1993. He has been party
spokesperson on Social Welfare, Health and
Agriculture. Spokesperson on Natural
Resources since 1997.

Senator, Agricultural Panel, 1981-89, and
1975-77. Leader, Labour Party Seanad Group,
Deputy Leader of the Seanad 1982-87.

In the 27th Dáil he served as Chairman of
Joint Committee on European Affairs 1995-97
and as a member of the Dáil Committee of
Selection, Committee on Procedure and
Privileges, Select Committee on Foreign
Affairs; Executive, Irish Parliamentary
Association; Joint Committee on Standing
Orders; Select Committee on Financial and
General Affairs. President, COSAC since 1996.

Vice-chairman, Labour Party 1979-86.

Member, Tipperary (SR) County Council since
1967 (chairman 1973/74 and 1981/82);
Tipperary UDC since 1985 (chairman 1987/88);
Tipperary VEC 1974-85; South-Eastern Health
Board 1973-85 (chairman 1974/75 and 1978/79);
Tipperary (SR) ACOT Committee (chairman
1969/70 and 1982/83); Local Health Committee
(chairman 1977/78). Chairman, General Council
of Agricultural Committees 1982/83.

Member, Bansha Agricultural Show Society
(chairman 1980/87 and President since 1995).

Waterford

Seats 4 Quota 8,960	1st Count	2nd Count Transfer of **Kennedy's** Votes	3rd Count Transfer of **Kelly's** Votes	4th Count Transfer of **McCann's** and **Waters's** Votes
BULBULIA, Katharine (PD)	2,896	+6 2,902	+21 2,923	+160 3,083
*CULLEN, Martin (FF)	5,353	+32 5,385	+32 5,417	+128 5,545
CUMMINS, Maurice (FG)	3,664	+6 3,670	+16 3,686	+155 3,841
*DEASY, Austin (FG)	7,335	+14 7,349	+28 7,377	+160 7,537
KELLY, Jimmy (SWP)	702	+6 708	−708 —	
*KENNEALLY, Brendan (FF)	5,971	+12 5,983	+37 6,020	+215 6,235
KENNEDY, Michael (NLP)	149	−149 —		
KIRWAN, Dermot (Ind)	2,946	+6 2,952	+34 2,986	+197 3,183
McCANN, Brendan (GP)	809	+12 821	+48 869	−869 —
O'REGAN, Martin (WP)	4,139	+8 4,147	+355 4,502	+187 4,689
*O'SHEA, Brian (Lab)	5,271	+10 5,281	+75 5,356	+232 5,588
WATERS, Declan (NP)	855	+8 863	+11 874	−874 —
WILKINSON, Ollie (FF)	4,707	+18 4,725	+19 4,744	+160 4,904
NON-TRANSFERABLE		11	32	149

Waterford

5th Count	6th Count	7th Count	8th Count	9th Count
Transfer of **Bulbulia's** Votes	Transfer of **Kirwan's** Votes	Transfer of **Cummins's** Votes	Transfer of **Deasy's** Surplus	Transfer of **Wilkinson's** Votes
−3,083 —				
+982 6,527	+372 6,899	+285 7,184	+146 7,330	+1,399 8,729
+283 4,124	+256 4,380	−4,380 —		
+411 7,948	+795 8,743	+2,534 11,277	−2,317 8,960	
+561 6,796	+421 7,217	+208 7,425	+139 7,564	+2,516 10,080
+173 3,356	−3,356 —			
+99 4,788	+361 5,149	+345 5,494	+198 5,692	+91 5,783
+240 5,828	+507 6,335	+789 7,124	+1,563 8,687	+586 9,273
+206 5,110	+308 5,418	+67 5,485	+77 5,562	−5,562 —
128	336	152	194	970

Waterford

Elected

Austin Deasy (FG)*	7th Count
Brendan Kenneally (FF)*	9th Count
Brian O'Shea (Lab)*	9th Count
Martin Cullen (FF)*	9th Count

Voting by Party

1st Preference	Number	%	% 1992
Fianna Fáil	16,031	35.79	28.39
Fine Gael	10,999	24.55	22.13
Labour	5,271	11.77	26.14
Prog Democrats	2,896	6.46	9.34
Green Party	809	1.81	—
Sinn Féin	—	—	1.19
Democratic Left	—	—	2.42
Workers' Party	4,139	9.24	6.98
Socialist Workers'	702	1.57	—
Natural Law Party	149	0.33	—
Others	3,801	8.48	3.43

Statistics

Population	90,072	
Electorate	69,789	
Total Poll	45,464	65.14
Spoiled Votes	667	1.47
Valid Poll	44,797	64.19
Seats	4	
Quota	8,960	
Candidates	13	

Seats

FF	2
FG	1
Lab	1
No change	

The constituency of Waterford is slightly larger than in the 1992 General Election, having gained an area with a population of 1,063 from the constituency of Tipperary South.

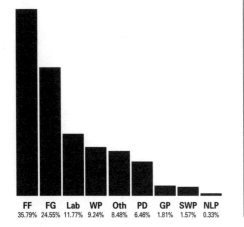

FF	FG	Lab	WP	Oth	PD	GP	SWP	NLP
35.79%	24.55%	11.77%	9.24%	8.48%	6.46%	1.81%	1.57%	0.33%

Austin Deasy (FG)

Home Address
Kilrush, Dungarvan, Co Waterford
Constituency Address
20 Grattan Street, Dungarvan, Co Waterford
Telephone
Home (058) 43003; *Fax* (058) 43003
Birth Place/Date
Dungarvan. August 1936
Married
Catherine Keating. 2 sons, 2 daughters
Education
Dungarvan CBS; University College, Cork (BSc, HDipEd)
Occupation
Full-time public representative. Formerly secondary school teacher

Austin Deasy was Minister for Agriculture 1982-87. He was first elected to the Dáil in 1977. He contested the Dáil general elections of 1969 and 1973. He was a Senator, Taoiseach's Nominee, 1973-77.

Fine Gael front bench spokesperson on the Marine 1992-93; on Agriculture 1991-92; on Tourism and Transport 1987-88; on Foreign Affairs 1982; on Fisheries 1977-79; on Transport 1979-81.

Member, Parliamentary Assembly of the Council of Europe 1993-97 and leader of Irish delegation on Council's Foreign Affairs Committee.

Member, Waterford County Council 1967-83 (chairman 1980/81); Waterford County Vocational Education Committee 1967-74; Dungarvan Urban District Council; former member, South-Eastern Health Board; Waterford Harbour Commissioners.

Member, Association of Secondary Teachers of Ireland since 1963.

Brendan Kenneally (FF)

Home Address
38 Viewmount Park, Dunmore Road, Waterford
Telephone
Home (051) 855964; *Fax* (051) 850597
Birth Place/Date
Waterford. April 1955
Married
Martina Crotty. 1 son, 2 daughters
Education
De La Salle College, Waterford; Waterford Institute of Technology
Occupation
Full-time public representative. Formerly accountant

Brendan Kenneally was Minister of State at the Department of Tourism, Transport and Communications February 1992-January 1993. He was first elected as a Dáil deputy in 1989.

Party deputy spokesperson on Equality and Law Reform 1994-97.

Member, Waterford Corporation 1985-92 (Mayor 1988/89); Waterford Local Health Committee 1985-87. Director, South-Eastern Airport Company 1985-92. Member, Waterford Youth Committee 1987-91. President, Waterford Area Basketball Board.

Brendan Kenneally is son of Billy Kenneally, Fianna Fáil Dáil deputy for Waterford 1965-February 1982, and grandson of William Kenneally, Fianna Fáil Dáil deputy for Waterford 1952-61.

Brian O'Shea (Lab)

Home Address
61 Sweetbriar Lane, Tramore, Co Waterford
Telephone
Home (051) 381913; *Fax* (051) 386427
Birth Place/Date
Waterford. December 1944
Married
Eileen Walsh. 2 sons, 4 daughters
Education
Mount Sion CBS, Waterford; St Patrick's
Teachers' Training College, Dublin
Occupation
Full-time public representative. Formerly
national school teacher

Brian O'Shea was Minister of State at the
Department of Agriculture, with special
responsibility for Food and Horticulture 1993-
94; Minister of State at the Department of
Health, with special responsibility for Mental
Handicap, Health Promotion, Food Safety and
Public Health 1994-97. He was first elected to
the Dáil in 1989. He contested the Dáil
general elections of 1987, November and
February 1982 in Waterford.

Senator, Industrial and Commercial Panel,
1987-89. Labour Party spokesperson on
Defence since 1997; on Education 1989-92;
Seanad spokesperson on Education 1987-89.

Member, Waterford County Council 1985-93;
Waterford City Council 1985-93; Tramore Town
Commissioners 1979-93.

Former Chairman, South-Eastern Airport
Company; former president of Waterford
Council of Trade Unions; former president of
Tramore Community Care Organisation;
former chairman of Waterford City Branch of
INTO.

Martin Cullen (FF)

Home Address
Abbey House, Abbey Road, Ferrybank,
Waterford
Business Address
Office of Public Works, St Stephen's Green,
Dublin 2
Telephone
Home (051) 851112; *Business* (01) 661 3111;
Fax (01) 661 2531; *Constituency Office* (051)
851112; *Fax* (051) 851543
Birth Place/Date
Waterford. November 1954
Married
Dorthe Larsen. 3 sons, 1 daughter
Education
Waterpark College, Waterford; Waterford
Regional Technical College (member,
Marketing Institute of Ireland)
Occupation
Minister of State. Formerly chief executive of
the Federation of Transport Operators

Martin Cullen was appointed Minister of State at
the Department of Finance, with special
responsibility for the Office of Public Works in
July 1997. He was first elected to the Dáil as a
Progressive Democrat deputy in 1987, lost his
seat in the General Election of 1989 and regained
it in 1992. During the 27th Dáil he resigned from
the Progressive Democrats and joined Fianna
Fáil. Senator, Taoiseach's Nominee, 1989-92.
Progressive Democrat spokesperson on
Enterprise and Employment 1993; Industry and
Commerce 1988-89; Tourism, Transport and
Communications 1987-88.

Member, Waterford City Council 1991-97
(Mayor 1993/94; his father and grandfather
were both former Mayors of Waterford);
Waterford Vocational Education Committee
since 1991-97. Former director, Waterford
Economic Development Board and South-East
Regional Tourism Organisation.

Founder member, Waterford Round Table
1979 (chairman 1984/85). Area chairman
Round Table Ireland 1985we/86.

Westmeath

Seats 3 Quota 8,197	1st Count	2nd Count Transfer of **Cooney's** and **Murray's** Votes	3rd Count Transfer of **Glynn's** Votes	4th Count Transfer of **Whelan's** Votes
ABBOTT, Henry (FF)	4,706	+220 4,926	+1,904 6,830	+252 7,082
COONEY, Benny (Ind)	175	−175 —		
GLYNN, Camillus (FF)	3,005	+193 3,198	−3,198 —	
*McGRATH, Paul (FG)	5,218	+170 5,388	+301 5,689	+2,760 8,449
MURRAY, Danny (NP)	1,118	−1,118 —		
*O'ROURKE, Mary (FF)	7,262	+192 7,454	+779 8,233	—
*PENROSE, Willie (Lab)	8,037	+234 8,271	— —	— —
WHELAN, Joe (FG)	3,266	+95 3,361	+47 3,408	−3,408 —
NON-TRANSFERABLE		189	167	396

Elected

Willie Penrose (Lab)*	2nd Count
Mary O'Rourke (FF)*	3rd Count
Paul McGrath (FG)*	4th Count

Voting by Party

1st Preference	Number	%	% 1992
Fianna Fáil	14,973	45.67	45.58
Fine Gael	8,484	25.88	26.69
Labour	8,037	24.51	20.13
Sinn Féin	—	—	1.05
Others	1,293	3.94	6.54

Statistics

Population	61,880	
Electorate	49,007	
Total Poll	33,084	67.51
Spoiled Votes	297	0.90
Valid Poll	32,787	66.90
Seats	3	
Quota	8,197	
Candidates	8	

Seats

FF	1
FG	1
Lab	1
No change	

The constituency of Westmeath is unchanged since the 1992 General Election.

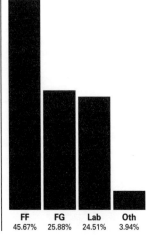

FF	FG	Lab	Oth
45.67%	25.88%	24.51%	3.94%

Willie Penrose (Lab)

Home Address
Ballintue, Ballynacargy, Co Westmeath
Constituency Office
Convent Lane, Bishopgate Street, Mullingar,
Co Westmeath
Telephone
Home (044) 73264; *Constituency Office*
(044) 43987; *Fax* (044) 43966
Birth Place/Date
Westmeath. August 1956
Married
Anne Fitzsimons. 3 daughters
Education
St Mary's CBS, Mullingar; Multyfarnham
Agricultural College, Co Westmeath;
University College, Dublin (BAgrSc, MAgrSc
[Economics]); King's Inns, Dublin (Diploma in
Legal Studies, Barrister-at-Law)
Occupation
Public representative. Barrister-at-Law

Willie Penrose has been a Dáil deputy since
1992. Labour Party spokesperson on
Agriculture and Rural Development 1992-97;
on Agriculture since 1997.

Member, Westmeath County Council since
1984 and the Council's Planning and
Environmental Committee, Agricultural
Committee and Coiste Gaeilge.

Member, Ballynacargy GAA club; Cullion
Hurling Club; GAA County Board Committee
on Cusack Park, Mullingar Development.
Member, Royal Canal Development Group.

The 3-seat constituency of Westmeath,
comprising the county of Westmeath plus
that part of Athlone west of the Shannon in
County Roscommon, was a totally new
constituency for the general election of 1992.
From 1923 to 1992 (except for 1935-47)
Westmeath was joined to Longford to form 1
constituency.

Mary O'Rourke (FF)

Home Address
Aisling, Arcadia, Athlone, Co Westmeath
Business Address
Department of Public Enterprise, 44 Kildare
Street, Dublin 2
Telephone
Home (0902) 75065/72313; *Business* (01)
661 0318/604 1074; *Fax* (01) 604 1183
Birth Place/Date
Athlone. May 1937
Married
Enda O'Rourke. 2 sons
Education
St Peter's, Athlone; Loreto Convent, Bray,
Co Wicklow; University College, Dublin;
Maynooth College (BA, HDipEd)
Occupation
Government Minister. Formerly secondary
school teacher

Mary O'Rourke was appointed Minister for
Public Enterprise in June 1997. She was
Minister of State at the Department of
Enterprise and Employment, with special
responsibility for Labour Affairs 1993-94. She
was Minister of State at the Department of
Industry and Commerce (Trade and Marketing)
February 1992-January 1993; Minister for
Health November 1991-February 1992;
Minister for Education 1987-91.

Deputy Leader of Fianna Fáil. Front bench
spokesperson on Enterprise and Employment
1995-97.

She was first elected to the Dáil in November
1982 for the old constituency of Longford-
Westmeath, and represented that constituency
until the boundary revisions of 1992. Senator,
Industrial and Commercial Panel 1981-82 and
Cultural and Educational Panel, April-November
1982.

Member, Westmeath County Council 1979-87.
Member, Athlone UDC 1974-87 (chairperson
1980/81, 1984/85 and 1986/87).

Mary O'Rourke and her brother Brian Lenihan,
TD, were the first brother and sister to serve
together in Cabinet. She is a daughter of the
late P.J. Lenihan, Dáil deputy for Longford-
Westmeath 1965-70, and aunt of deputies
Brian and Conor Lenihan.

Paul McGrath (FG)

Home Address
Carna, Irishtown, Mullingar, Co Westmeath
Constituency Office
Mary Street, Mullingar
Telephone
Home/Office (044) 40746; *Mobile* (088)
250 9374; *Fax* (044) 40087
Birth Place/Date
Ballymore, Co Westmeath. February 1948
Married
Josephine Carney. 2 sons, 2 daughters
Education
St Finian's College, Mullingar; Trinity and All
Saints Colleges, Leeds
Occupation
Full-time public representative. Formerly
national school teacher

Paul McGrath was first elected to the Dáil in
1989 in the old constituency of Longford-
Westmeath and since 1992 has represented
Westmeath. Fine Gael spokesperson on
Public Works 1993-94 and front bench
spokesperson on Education 1994.

Chairperson, Joint Oireachtas Committee on
the Family 1995-97.

Member, Westmeath County Council since
1991. He has served as a member of
Mullingar Youth Club (chairman 1974-78);
Midland Regional Youth Council; National
Federation of Youth Clubs; Royal Canal
Employment Project; Mullingar Show
Committee; Mullingar Squash Club; Leinster
Squash Rackets Association; Mullingar
Shamrocks GFC; Mullingar Golf Club.

Brendan Howlin and Dick Spring relax in St Stephen's Green.

Seats 5 Quota 9,282	1st Count	2nd Count Transfer of **Yates's** Surplus	3rd Count Transfer of **O'Connor's** Votes	4th Count Transfer of **Percival's** Votes	5th Count Transfer of **Enright's** Votes	6th Count Transfer of **Howlin's** Surplus	7th Count Transfer of **Doyle's** Votes	8th Count Transfer of **D'Arcy's** Surplus
ASPLE, Denis (FF)	6,038	+32 6,070	+82 6,152	+129 6,281	+149 6,430	+26 6,456	+727 7,183	+775 7,958
*BROWNE, John (FF)	8,646	+98 8,744	+110 8,854	+140 8,994	+159 9,153	+23 9,176	+394 9,570	— —
*BYRNE, Hugh (FF)	7,003	+32 7,035	+49 7,084	+95 7,179	+125 7,304	+19 7,323	+397 7,720	+696 8,416
D'ARCY, Michael (FG)	6,561	+225 6,786	+90 6,876	+122 6,998	+258 7,256	+34 7,290	+3,756 11,046	−1,764 9,282
*DOYLE, Avril (FG)	4,896	+300 5,196	+55 5,251	+167 5,418	+750 6,168	+126 6,294	−6,294 —	
ENRIGHT, Michael (DL)	1,454	+30 1,484	+29 1,513	+285 1,798	−1,798 —			
*HOWLIN, Brendan (Lab)	9,510	— —	— —	— —	— —	−228 9,282		
O'CONNOR, Michael (Ind)	616	+6 622	−622 —					
PERCIVAL, Marie (GP)	938	+19 957	+148 1,105	−1,105 —				
*YATES, Ivan (FG)	10,024	−742 9,282						
NON-TRANSFERABLE			59	167	357	—	1,020	293

Wexford

Elected

Ivan Yates (FG)*	1st Count
Brendan Howlin (Lab)*	1st Count
Michael D'Arcy (FG)	7th Count
John Browne (FF)*	7th Count
Hugh Byrne (FF)*	8th Count

Voting by Party

1st Preference	Number	%	% 1992
Fianna Fáil	21,687	38.95	42.44
Fine Gael	21,481	38.58	34.47
Labour	9,510	17.08	19.82
Green Party	938	1.68	—
Sinn Féin	—	—	0.79
Democratic Left	1,454	2.61	1.53
Others	616	1.11	0.96

Statistics

Population	102,069	
Electorate	83,775	
Total Poll	56,364	67.28
Spoiled Votes	678	1.20
Valid Poll	55,686	66.47
Seats	5	
Quota	9,282	
Candidates	10	

Seats

FF	2
FG	2
Lab	1
No change	

The constituency of Wexford is unchanged since the 1992 General Election.

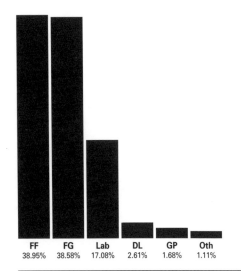

FF	FG	Lab	DL	GP	Oth
38.95%	38.58%	17.08%	2.61%	1.68%	1.11%

Ivan Yates (FG)

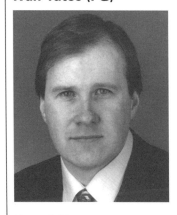

Home Address
Blackstoops, Enniscorthy, Co Wexford
Telephone
Home (054) 33793
Birth Place/Date
Dublin. October 1959
Married
Deirdre Boyd. 2 sons, 2 daughters
Education
St Columba's College, Rathfarnham, Co Dublin; Gurteen Agricultural College, Co Tipperary
Occupation
Public representative, farmer, businessman

Ivan Yates was Minister of Agriculture, Food and Forestry 1994-97. He was first elected to the Dáil in June 1981. He was the youngest member of the 22nd, 23rd and 24th Dálaí and youngest member of the Cabinet 1994-97.

Fine Gael front bench spokesperson on Public Enterprise, and responsible for Fine Gael Policy Development since 1997; spokesperson on Finance 1993-94; on Agriculture 1992-93; on Transport and Tourism 1990-92; on Health 1988-90; on Trade and Marketing 1987-88.

Chairman, Oireachtas Joint Committee on Small Businesses 1983-87.

Member, Enniscorthy Urban District Council 1979-95 (chairman 1989/90); Wexford County Council 1985-95. Former member, Wexford County Committee of Agriculture; Wexford Health Committee.

Former member, Irish Farmers' Association.

Brendan Howlin (Lab)

Home Address
Whiterock Hill, Wexford
Telephone
Home (053) 24036
Birth Place/Date
Wexford. May 1956
Education
Wexford CBS; St Patrick's Teachers' Training College, Drumcondra, Dublin
Occupation
Full-time public representative. Formerly national school teacher

Brendan Howlin was Minister for Health January 1993-November 1994; Minister for the Environment December 1994-97. He has been a Dáil deputy since 1987. He was a candidate in the general election held in November 1982. Senator, Taoiseach's Nominee, 1982-87.

Chief Whip, Labour Party, 1987-93 and since 1997. Party spokesperson on the Environment since 1997; on Health and Youth Affairs 1989-93. Spokesperson on Health and Women's Rights 1987-89. Spokesperson on Education in Seanad 1983-87.

Member, Wexford County Council 1985-93; Member, Wexford Borough Council 1981-93 (Alderman, 1985/93, Mayor 1986/87). Former member, Town of Wexford Vocational Education Committee.

Former chairman, Wexford Branch, INTO. Former vice-chairman, Wexford Council of Trade Unions.

Michael D'Arcy (FG)

Home Address
Annagh, Gorey, Co Wexford
Telephone
Home (055) 28177; *Office* (055) 22525
Birth Place/Date
Annagh, Gorey. March 1934
Married
Marie Collins. 2 sons, 2 daughters
Education
Gorey CBS
Occupation
Public representative, farmer

Michael D'Arcy was previously Dáil deputy for Wexford 1977-87, 1989-92. Senator, Agricultural Panel 1992-97.

Minister of State at the Department of Fisheries and Forestry and the Department of the Gaeltacht December 1982-February 1986, with special responsibility for Fisheries and Forestry. He was Minister of State at the Department of Agriculture, with special responsibility for Production and Marketing, June 1981-March 1982. He contested the constituency as a Fine Gael candidate in 1973 and 1987.

Member, Wexford County Council 1958-83 and since 1987 (chairman 1970/71 and 1982/83); Wexford County Committee of Agriculture 1958-81 (chairman 1965/66 and 1968/69); Wexford County Vocational Education Committee 1958-81 (chairman 1974-81).

Member, Irish Farmers' Association since 1958; Macra na Feirme 1950-67; Dublin District Milk Board 1965-76. Director, Agricultural Credit Corporation 1974-77.

John Browne (FF)

Home Address
Kilcannon, Enniscorthy, Co Wexford
Telephone
Home (054) 35046
Birth Place/Date
Marshalstown, Enniscorthy. August 1948
Married
Judy Doyle. 1 son, 3 daughters
Education
St Mary's CBS, Enniscorthy
Occupation
Full-time public representative. Formerly salesman

John Browne was Minister of State at the Department of the Environment, with special responsibility for Environmental Protection 1993-94. He was Minister of State at the Department of Agriculture and Food, with special responsibility for the Food Industry, February 1992-January 1993. He was first elected to the Dáil in November 1982 at his first attempt. He was Assistant Fianna Fáil Chief Whip 1982-87.

Member, Wexford County Council 1979-92; Enniscorthy Urban District Council 1979-92; Wexford County Health Committee 1979-92; Wexford County Vocational Education Committee 1979-92; Wexford Tourism Committee 1979-82.

Member, Gaelic Athletic Association, since 1965.

He is a nephew of Seán Browne, Fianna Fáil Dáil deputy for Wexford 1957-61, 1969-81 and February-November 1982, Leas-Cheann Comhairle of Dáil Éireann 1977-81, Seanad 1961-69.

Hugh Byrne (FF)

Home Address
Air Hill, Fethard, New Ross, Co Wexford
Business Address
Department of the Marine and Natural Resources, Leeson Lane, Dublin 2
Constituency Office
17 Quay Street, New Ross
Telephone
Home (051) 397125; *Constituency Office* (051) 425357; *Business* (01) 678 5444; *Mobile* (087) 258 5548; *Fax* (051) 397391 (H), (051) 425324 (C), (01) 661 0061 (B)
Birth Place/Date
Wexford. September 1943
Married
Mary Murphy. 3 sons, 4 daughters
Education
New Ross CBS; St Peter's College, Wexford
Occupation
Minister of State. Formerly auctioneer, farmer

Hugh Byrne was appointed Minister of State at the Department of the Marine and Natural Resources, with special responsibility for Aquaculture and Forestry in July 1997. He was first elected to the Dáil in 1981 and was a deputy for Wexford constituency until he lost his seat in the 1989 general election. He regained it in 1992. Senator, Taoiseach's Nominee, 1989-92. Spokesperson in Dáil 1982-87 and 1995-97 on Agriculture and in Seanad 1989-92 on Agriculture and Marine.

Member, Wexford County Council 1974-97 (chairman 1990/91). He has also served as a member of Wexford County Committee of Agriculture; General Council of Committees of Agriculture; New Ross Harbour Commissioners (chairman 1993-95); Macra na Feirme and Macra na Tuaithe National Councils and Executives. Chairman, Hook Heritage Trust, Duncannon Fort Trust.

He played inter-county football and hurling for Wexford and Kildare.

Wicklow

Seats 5 Quota 8,717	1st Count	2nd Count Transfer of **Keddy's** and **Perkins's** Votes	3rd Count Transfer of **Heaslip's** Votes	4th Count Transfer of **Collins's** Votes
COLLINS, Tim (Lab)	1,924	+148 2,072	+34 2,106	−2,106 —
***FOX**, Mildred (Ind)	5,590	+321 5,911	+267 6,178	+182 6,360
HEASLIP, Mary (PD)	1,726	+82 1,808	−1,808 —	
HONAN, Tom (FG)	2,021	+44 2,065	+52 2,117	+143 2,260
***JACOB**, Joe (FF)	6,150	+35 6,185	+351 6,536	+44 6,580
JONES, George (FG)	3,116	+102 3,218	+82 3,300	+205 3,505
***KAVANAGH**, Liam (Lab)	5,293	+71 5,364	+87 5,451	+773 6,224
KEDDY, Charlie (Ind)	316	−316 —		
KELLY, Nicky (Ind)	4,995	+183 5,178	+69 5,247	+52 5,299
LAWLOR, Michael D. (FF)	3,368	+55 3,423	+232 3,655	+48 3,703
***McMANUS**, Liz (DL)	5,226	+355 5,581	+141 5,722	+463 6,185
PERKINS, Alex (GP)	1,299	−1,299 —		
ROCHE, Dick (FF)	6,101	+99 6,200	+375 6,575	+97 6,672
TIMMINS, William (FG)	5,171	+54 5,225	+73 5,298	+66 5,364
NON-TRANSFERABLE		66	45	33

5th Count Transfer of **Honan's** Votes	6th Count Transfer of **Lawlor's** Votes	7th Count Transfer of **Jones's** Votes	8th Count Transfer of **Kelly's** Votes	9th Count Transfer of **Jacob's** Surplus
+117 6,477	+430 6,907	+437 7,344	+908 8,252	+96 8,348
−2,260 —				
+85 6,665	+1,327 7,992	+74 8,066	+931 8,997	−280 8,717
+727 4,232	+91 4,323	−4,323 —		
+197 6,421	+129 6,550	+442 6,992	+991 7,983	+88 8,071
+220 5,519	+114 5,633	+56 5,689	−5,689 —	
+28 3,731	−3,731 —			
+193 6,378	+305 6,683	+759 7,442	+1,056 8,498	+70 8,568
+43 6,715	+1,158 7,873	+283 8,156	+569 8,725	— —
+622 5,986	+79 6,065	+2,109 8,174	+326 8,500	+26 8,526
28	98	163	908	—

Wicklow

Voting by Party

1st Preference	Number	%	% 1992
Fianna Fáil	15,619	29.87	25.25
Fine Gael	10,308	19.71	17.71
Labour	7,217	13.80	22.82
Prog Democrats	1,726	3.30	2.63
Green Party	1,299	2.48	2.59
Sinn Féin	—	—	0.92
Democratic Left	5,226	9.99	10.62
Workers' Party	—	—	0.27
Others	10,901	20.84	17.18

Statistics

Population	100,815	
Electorate	80,458	
Total Poll	52,730	65.54
Spoiled Votes	434	0.82
Valid Poll	52,296	65.00
Seats	5	
Quota	8,717	
Candidates	14	

Seats

FF	2
FG	1
DL	1
Ind	1
FF gain from Lab	

The constituency of Wicklow is slightly larger than in the 1992 General Election, having gained an area with a population of 3,550 from the constituency of Carlow-Kilkenny.

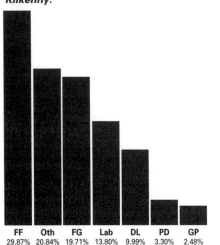

FF	Oth	FG	Lab	DL	PD	GP
29.87%	20.84%	19.71%	13.80%	9.99%	3.30%	2.48%

Joe Jacob (FF)

Home Address
Main Street, Rathdrum, Co Wicklow
Business Address
Department of Public Enterprise, 25 Clare Street, Dublin 2
Telephone
Home (0404) 46528; *Business*, (01) 670 7444; *Constituency Office* (0404) 46528; *Fax* (01) 604 1320 (B), (0404) 43026 (H)
Birth Place/Date
Kilrush, Co Clare. April 1939
Married
Patty Grant. 3 sons, 3 daughters
Education
De La Salle College, Wicklow; Terenure College, Dublin
Occupation
Minister of State, pub owner. Formerly distribution manager with Nítrigin Éireann Teoranta

Joe Jacob was appointed Minister of State at the Department of Public Enterprise, with special responsibility for Energy in July 1997. He was Leas-Cheann Comhairle of the Dáil 1993-97. He has been a member of the Dáil since 1987.

Chairman of the Fianna Fáil Parliamentary Party 1992-95.

Member, British-Irish Parliamentary Body, 1991-92; Oireachtas Joint Committee on Women's Rights 1988-89. Oireachtas Joint Committee on State-Sponsored Bodies, 1989-92. Member of Fianna Fáil delegation to Forum for Peace and Reconciliation.

Member, Wicklow County Council 1985-97; Wicklow County Vocational Education Committee 1985-97 (chairman 1991-93); Eastern Health Board; Midlands and Eastern Tourism Organisation; Wicklow Tourism.

Member, Gaelic Athletic Association – player and administrator.

Dick Roche (FF)

Home Address
2 Herbert Terrace, Herbert Road, Bray, Co Wicklow
Telephone
Home (01) 286 3211; *Fax* (01) 286 7666
Birth Place/Date
Wexford. March 1947
Married
Eleanor Griffin. 3 sons, 1 daughter
Education
Wexford CBS; University College, Dublin (BComm, DPA, MPA)
Occupation
Public representative. University lecturer

Dick Roche was previously a Dáil deputy 1987-92. Senator, Administrative Panel 1993-97 and Taoiseach's Nominee November 1992-February 1993.

Fianna Fáil spokesperson on Public Finance in Seanad 1992-97 and on Public Service Reform 1994-97. Chairman, Oireachtas Joint Committee on State-Sponsored Bodies 1989-92.

Member, Wicklow County Council since 1985; Wicklow County Vocational Education Committee since 1985; Greystones Town Commissioners since 1984 (chairman 1986/87). Board member, Eastern Regional Development Organisation. Member, Eastern Health Board 1988; board of Meath Hospital since 1989.

Member, Institute of Public Administration; International Ombudsman Institute; Association of Graduates in Public Administration; Irish Council of the European Movement; Irish Commission for Justice and Peace (chairman 1985/86).

In 1978 he won a United Nations Human Rights fellowship. He is the author of many articles on public administration in Ireland.

Liz McManus (DL)

Home Address
1 Martello Terrace, Bray, Co Wicklow
Telephone
Home (01) 286 8407
Birth Place/Date
Montreal, Canada. March 1947
Married
John McManus. 3 sons, 1 daughter
Education
Holy Child Convent, Killiney, Co Dublin;
University College, Dublin School of
Architecture (BArch)
Occupation
Public representative. Writer

Liz McManus was Minister of State at the
Department of the Environment, with special
responsibility for Housing and Urban Renewal,
1994-97. Democratic Left spokesperson on
Health and Children, Justice, Equality and Law
Reform, Arts, Heritage, Gaeltacht and the
Islands, since 1997.

She has been a Dáil deputy since 1992. She
was the first woman Dáil deputy to be elected
for Democratic Left.

Spokesperson in the Dáil on Agriculture and
Food, Equality and Law Reform, and Health
1993-94.

Chairperson, Task Force on the Needs of the
Travelling Community 1993.

She has served on Wicklow County Council;
County Wicklow Library Committee; County
Wicklow National Monuments Advisory
Committee; Bray Urban District Council
(chairperson 1984/85). Director, Wicklow
Tourism. Founder of Bray Women's Refuge.
Established Bray Economic Action
Committee.

Liz McManus won the Hennessy/New Irish
Writing Award, the Listowel Award, and the
Irish PEN Award for her fiction. In 1990 she
published her first novel, *Acts of Subversion*,
which was nominated for the Aer Lingus/*Irish
Times* Award for new writing.

Billy Timmins (FG)

Home Address
Sruhaun, Baltinglass, Co Wicklow
Constituency Office
Weaver Square, Baltinglass
Telephone
Home/Office (0508) 81655; *Constituency
Office* (0508) 81016
Birth Place/Date
Baltinglass. October 1959
Married
Madeleine Hyland. 1 son, 1 daughter
Education
Patrician College, Ballyfin, Co Laois; University
College, Galway (BA, Diploma in Public
Relations, Marketing and Advertising)
Occupation
Full-time public representative. Formerly
army officer

Billy Timmins is a new Dáil deputy. This was
the first time he contested an election for
public office. He won a seat previously held
by his father, Godfrey Timmins. Fine Gael
spokesperson on Defence, Peacekeeping
and Humanitarian Relief since 1997.

Billy Timmins, as an army officer, served
overseas with UNIFIL in Lebanon and
UNFICYP in Cyprus.

Son of Godfrey Timmins, Dáil deputy for
Wicklow 1968-87 and 1989-97, and a member
of Wicklow County Council since 1950.

Mildred Fox (Ind)

Home Address
Lower Calary, Kilmacanogue, Co Wicklow
Telephone
Home: (01) 287 6386; *Constituency Office*:
(01) 679 0799
Birth Place/Date
Dublin. June 1971
Education
St Kilian's Community School, Ballywaltrim,
Bray, Co Wicklow; University College, Dublin
(BA)
Occupation
Full-time public representative. Formerly hotel
front-office manager

Mildred Fox was first elected to the Dáil in a
by-election in Wicklow in June 1995. The by-
election was caused by the death of her
father, Johnny Fox, who was elected as an
independent deputy in the general election of
1992.

She was the youngest member of the 27th
Dáil, and the only independent woman deputy
in the 27th and 28th Dálaí.

In the vote for Taoiseach in June 1997, she
supported Bertie Ahern, after outlining to the
Dáil various projects that she had secured for
her Wicklow (and East Carlow) constituency.

She has been a member of Wicklow County
Council since May 1995.

Secretary, Wicklow County Board of Ladies'
GAA and playing member of local football and
camogie clubs. Member, Macra na Feirme.

Daughter of Johnny Fox, Dáil deputy for
Wicklow 1992-95.

General Statistics (Dáil General Election 1997)

Constituency	Population	Seats	Electors on Register	Total Votes Cast	%	Invalid Votes	%	Valid Poll	%	Quota	Candidates
Carlow-Kilkenny	111,027	5	85,096	57,140	67.15	691	1.21	56,449	66.34	9,409	11
Cavan-Monaghan	104,089	5	83,005	60,145	72.46	601	1.00	59,544	71.74	9,925	12
Clare	88,074	4	71,491	47,366	66.25	477	1.01	46,889	65.59	9,378	12
Cork East	80,369	4	63,653	43,407	68.19	331	0.76	43,076	67.67	8,616	10
Cork North-Central	100,829	5	71,873	44,416	61.80	408	0.92	44,008	61.23	7,335	14
Cork North-West	60,353	3	47,119	35,164	74.63	401	1.14	34,763	73.78	8,691	6
Cork South-Central	107,608	5	84,288	55,401	65.73	362	0.65	55,039	65.30	9,174	15
Cork South-West	61,210	3	49,382	35,314	71.51	319	0.90	34,995	70.87	8,749	9
Donegal North-East	65,841	3	52,576	35,951	68.38	422	1.17	35,529	67.58	8,883	8
Donegal South-West	62,276	3	51,479	32,894	63.90	454	1.38	32,440	63.02	8,111	9
Dublin Central	87,393	4	64,073	36,282	56.63	541	1.49	35,741	55.78	7,149	14
Dublin North	81,023	4	64,030	41,522	64.85	364	0.88	41,158	64.28	8,232	13
Dublin North-Central	87,600	4	66,559	43,621	65.54	456	1.05	43,165	64.85	8,634	14
Dublin North-East	83,170	4	59,497	37,669	63.31	368	0.98	37,301	62.69	7,461	14
Dublin North-West	87,762	4	60,374	37,203	61.62	504	1.35	36,699	60.79	7,340	15
Dublin South	111,151	5	90,050	58,321	64.77	335	0.57	57,986	64.39	9,665	14
Dublin South-Central	88,858	4	68,146	41,129	60.35	550	1.34	40,579	59.55	8,116	21
Dublin South-East	87,353	4	64,215	37,032	57.67	361	0.97	36,671	57.11	7,335	14
Dublin South-West	110,388	5	75,646	42,292	55.91	440	1.04	41,852	55.33	6,976	15
Dublin West	89,383	4	66,419	40,297	60.67	223	0.55	40,074	60.34	8,015	14
Dún Laoghaire	111,223	5	87,994	54,646	62.10	393	0.72	54,253	61.66	9,043	14
Galway East	80,113	4	61,075	43,368	71.01	451	1.04	42,917	70.27	8,584	11
Galway West	100,251	5	78,064	48,612	62.27	400	0.82	48,212	61.76	8,036	14
Kerry North	61,467	3	51,348	36,063	70.23	284	0.79	35,779	69.68	8,945	6
Kerry South	60,427	3	48,164	35,799	74.33	303	0.85	35,496	73.70	8,875	9
Kildare North	61,970	3	52,388	31,691	60.49	295	0.93	31,396	59.93	7,850	8
Kildare South	60,686	3	47,852	29,173	60.97	365	1.25	28,808	60.20	7,203	8
Laois-Offaly	110,808	5	84,358	58,612	69.48	542	0.92	58,070	68.84	9,679	12
Limerick East	103,441	5	76,705	50,049	65.25	348	0.70	49,701	64.79	8,284	14
Limerick West	61,359	3	47,859	33,979	71.00	365	1.07	33,614	70.24	8,404	9
Longford-Roscommon	82,193	4	63,942	47,843	74.82	563	1.18	47,280	73.94	9,457	11
Louth	90,724	4	71,086	45,611	64.16	603	1.32	45,008	63.31	9,002	15
Mayo	110,713	5	87,719	62,472	71.22	614	0.98	61,858	70.52	10,310	13
Meath	105,370	5	90,125	57,265	63.54	574	1.00	56,691	62.90	9,449	16
Sligo-Leitrim	80,057	4	64,770	45,618	70.43	452	0.99	45,166	69.73	9,034	11
Tipperary North	67,233	3	53,888	40,289	74.76	337	0.84	39,952	74.14	9,989	8
Tipperary South	67,091	3	51,925	35,634	68.63	374	1.05	35,260	67.91	8,816	6
Waterford	90,072	4	69,789	45,464	65.14	667	1.47	44,797	64.19	8,960	13
Westmeath	61,880	3	49,007	33,084	67.51	297	0.90	32,787	66.90	8,197	8
Wexford	102,069	5	83,775	56,364	67.28	678	1.20	55,686	66.47	9,282	10
Wicklow	100,815	5	80,458	52,730	65.54	434	0.82	52,296	65.00	8,717	14
Total	3,525,719	166	2,741,262	1,806,932	65.92	17,947	0.99	1,788,985	65.26		484

Summary of Returns (Dáil General Election 1997)

Constituency	Fianna Fáil		Fine Gael		Labour		PDs		DL		Others	
	No. of 1st prefer-ences	% of 1st prefer-ences	No. of 1st prefer-ences	% of 1st prefer-ences	No. of 1st prefer-ences	% of 1st prefer-ences	No. of 1st prefer-ences	% of 1st prefer-ences	No. of 1st prefer-ences	% of 1st prefer-ences	No. of 1st prefer-ences	% of 1st prefer-ences
Carlow-Kilkenny	23,814	42.19	16,476	29.19	8,573	15.19	3,184	5.64	—	—	4,402	7.80
Cavan-Monaghan	22,887	38.44	20,643	34.67	2,359	3.96	—	—	—	—	13,655	22.93
Clare	23,614	50.36	14,106	30.08	1,684	3.59	3,250	6.93	—	—	4,235	9.03
Cork East	15,696	36.44	12,976	30.12	3,500	8.13	1,830	4.25	4,622	10.73	4,452	10.34
Cork North-Central	15,635	35.53	13,273	30.16	2,321	5.27	3,304	7.51	3,146	7.15	6,329	14.38
Cork North-West	16,166	46.50	14,294	41.12	2,574	7.40	—	—	—	—	1,729	4.97
Cork South-Central	23,455	42.62	16,827	30.57	4,908	8.92	2,304	4.19	—	—	7,545	13.71
Cork South-West	13,667	39.05	15,462	44.18	2,361	6.75	—	—	—	—	3,505	10.02
Donegal North-East	14,855	41.81	6,704	18.87	1,948	5.48	—	—	—	—	12,022	33.84
Donegal South-West	12,339	38.04	7,453	22.97	1,361	4.20	—	—	—	—	11,287	34.79
Dublin Central	15,307	42.83	5,185	14.51	3,035	8.49	—	—	—	—	12,214	34.17
Dublin North	15,908	38.65	7,813	18.98	5,616	13.64	1,431	3.48	—	—	10,390	25.24
Dublin North-Central	20,044	46.44	11,235	26.03	2,848	6.60	1,424	3.30	1,194	2.77	6,420	14.87
Dublin North-East	15,147	40.61	7,050	18.90	6,433	17.25	2,911	7.80	1,381	3.70	4,379	11.74
Dublin North-West	17,263	47.04	5,726	15.60	4,084	11.13	—	—	3,701	10.08	5,925	16.14
Dublin South	22,394	38.62	16,869	29.09	6,147	10.60	5,444	9.39	—	—	7,132	12.30
Dublin South-Central	13,970	34.43	10,125	24.95	4,224	10.41	2,031	5.01	4,586	11.30	5,643	13.91
Dublin South-East	9,456	25.79	10,042	27.38	6,113	16.67	4,022	10.97	—	—	7,038	19.19
Dublin South-West	12,529	29.94	6,487	15.50	4,070	9.72	5,708	13.64	5,094	12.17	7,964	19.03
Dublin West	13,299	33.19	6,788	16.94	4,853	12.11	3,050	7.61	—	—	12,084	30.15
Dún Laoghaire	14,012	25.83	16,799	30.96	4,698	8.66	4,636	8.55	7,534	13.89	6,574	12.12
Galway East	20,858	48.60	13,376	31.17	3,400	7.92	3,182	7.41	—	—	2,101	4.90
Galway West	22,151	45.94	10,710	22.21	4,856	10.07	5,914	12.27	—	—	4,581	9.50
Kerry North	9,412	26.31	8,689	24.29	10,699	29.90	—	—	—	—	6,979	19.51
Kerry South	11,283	31.79	4,888	13.77	4,988	14.05	—	—	—	—	14,337	40.39
Kildare North	10,944	34.86	8,222	26.19	5,964	19.00	2,101	6.69	2,762	8.80	1,403	4.47
Kildare South	10,830	37.59	7,631	26.49	5,834	20.25	3,895	13.52	—	—	618	2.15
Laois-Offaly	28,945	49.85	16,479	28.38	6.741	11.61	3,778	6.51	—	—	2,127	3.66
Limerick East	19,741	39.72	13,176	26.51	4,568	9.19	6,175	12.42	3,403	6.85	2,638	5.31
Limerick West	10,906	32.44	12,502	37.19	1,418	4.22	1,406	4.18	—	—	7,382	21.96
Longford-Roscommon	22,232	47.02	17,452	36.91	699	1.48	2,289	4.84	—	—	4,608	9.75
Louth	18,010	40.02	12,555	27.90	4,725	10.50	2,395	5.32	—	—	7,323	16.27
Mayo	26,571	42.95	30,158	48.75	—	—	—	—	—	—	5,129	8.29
Meath	23,742	41.88	20,933	36.92	3,695	6.52	1,344	2.37	798	1.41	6,179	10.90
Sligo-Leitrim	18,250	40.41	16,545	36.63	4,905	10.86	745	1.65	—	—	4,721	10.45
Tipperary North	16,894	42.29	4,521	11.32	4,126	10.33	1,390	3.48	—	—	13,021	32.59
Tipperary South	13,146	37.28	8,494	24.09	5,681	16.11	—	—	—	—	7,939	22.52
Waterford	16,031	35.79	10,999	24.55	5,271	11.77	2,896	6.46	—	—	9,600	21.43
Westmeath	14,973	45.67	8,484	25.88	8,037	24.51	—	—	—	—	1,293	3.94
Wexford	21,687	38.95	21,481	38.58	9,510	17.08	—	—	1,454	2.61	1,554	2.79
Wicklow	15,619	29.87	10,308	19.71	7,217	13.80	1,726	3.30	5,226	9.99	12,200	23.33
Total	703,682	39.33	499,936	27.95	186,044	10.40	83,765	4.68	44,901	2.51	270,657	15.13

by Emily O'Reilly

'SPRING TIDE' was the headline that screamed from the front page of the now defunct *Irish Press* in November 1992 when Dick Spring's Labour Party won an unprecedented 33 seats in that month's general election.

It was the culmination of almost five years of hard graft by Spring and those around him. They had shaken off the lethargy and depression that had engulfed the party virtually throughout their time in government between 1982 and 1987. They had revamped the party image, replaced the old plough and stars logo with a delicate red rose, moved the policy bank closer to the centre, rid the party of its dissident elements, and exploited the magnificent victory of Mary Robinson at the 1990 presidential election to the full.

Spring had also enjoyed a brilliant few years on the opposition bench. His contributions at times of controversy during the Fianna Fáil/Progressive Democrats administration were noted for their sharpness, for the manner in which they continually outshone the contributions from the leader of the opposition, Fine Gael leader John Bruton.

By 1992 the electorate had been sufficiently seduced by the 'New Labour' vision of cleaner government and a new social deal for the Irish public that they made him kingmaker at the November election.

John Bruton, whose party had lost seats, appeared almost deliberately ignorant of the import of the Labour gains. During the election, he had touted the notion of a rainbow election comprising Fine Gael, Labour and the Progressive Democrats. His presumption deeply angered Spring who was still smarting from his treatment at the hands of his former ministerial colleague, Bruton, during their time together in government.

The post-election negotiations began with Bruton confident that Labour had nowhere else to go. In opposition Spring had demonised Fianna Fáil, wondering aloud how any party could possibly coalesce with them. But after the election, other factors came into play. Labour had little appetite for Bruton's Fine Gael although they taunted him with the suggestion of a scenario whereby Spring and Bruton would share the job of Taoiseach.

Labour also had no desire to coalesce with the PDs and John Bruton had absolutely ruled out Democratic Left from government participation with Fine Gael.

In the early days, Fianna Fáil did not believe either that it had a realistic chance of gaining power. They had dropped seats and party leader Albert Reynolds had had a dreadful election. The outgoing Taoiseach had however managed to secure a huge tranche of structural and cohesion funding from the EU and the party was understandably loath to go out of power at a time when the economy was really turning around.

Fianna Fáil was also helped by the fact that key Labour TDs, notably Ruairí Quinn, had hinted that Fianna Fáil was still the most ideologically compatible party in terms of economic policy, and this overture combined with the other factors mentioned above eventually propelled the two parties into each other's arms. The new Fianna Fáil/Labour coalition was formed in January 1993.

The initial mainstream media reaction was negative. Spring's speech in which he had brought the demonisation of Fianna Fáil to new heights was reprinted and rebroadcast. He was asked, memorably by RTE presenter Olivia O'Leary, whether it was possible to believe anything that Spring said. Later, many in the party came to believe that it had been deeply damaged by the decision to coalesce with Fianna Fáil, even if, at the time, they had felt that they had no other real option.

The next controversy was provoked by the revelations in the *Irish Times* that Labour ministers had appointed a large number of party supporters and family members to positions within their departments. Many of the positions were menial and low paid; some of those appointed had already been working for the particular minister in their constituencies, but the perception nonetheless was of a party doing exactly what it had criticised other parties in the past for doing. It took Labour a long time to recover.

The first policy crisis for the government occurred in 1993 when a currency crisis eventually forced a reluctant, at times dithering, finance minister, Bertie Ahern, to devalue the punt. It turned out to be the right decision even if he came in for much criticism for having waited so long to do it. But the economy, for the next four and a half years, never really looked back as the country entered into a period of unprecedented growth and prosperity.

Meanwhile, much of the main political focus was on the North. Albert Reynolds had stated when he became Taoiseach that it would be his number one priority; British Prime Minister John Major had expressed similar sentiments but few people believed that this was anything more than the familiar political rhetoric about the North.

But throughout 1993 it became clear that something significant was afoot. This came to a head when it was revealed that the leaders of the SDLP and Sinn Féin, John Hume and Gerry Adams respectively, had been holding secret talks.

Towards the end of the summer, the two men went public on the content of their discussions. They had been attempting to develop a bedrock for a nationalist consensus on the way forward for the North, which would lead—although this was not stated explicitly at the time—to an IRA cease-fire.

The revelations led to a great deal of political movement. The British and Irish governments tried to downplay what became known as the Hume-Adams initiative but they too were having many private discussions, also with a view to arriving at a consensus about the way forward.

All of this activity culminated in December 1993 with the signing of the Downing Street Declaration, a set of principles which attempted to set out the parameters of any future settlement in the North. There would be an internal Northern Ireland dimension, a British-Irish dimension and, most crucially, a cross-border dimension.

The reaction was mixed. The Dáil gave Reynolds and Spring a hero's welcome; the British government was more muted and anxious to put as 'orange' a tinge on the document as possible. Ian Paisley's DUP dismissed it out of hand as a sell-out, but the mainstream UUP was more restrained in its response.

Sinn Féin said it needed clarification and the dance of clarification continued for a long period between that party and the British government. All the time, the IRA was being urged to call a complete cease-fire.

In February 1994, John Bruton comfortably survived a leadership challenge, largely due to the assiduous work carried out on his behalf among the backbenchers by TD Michael

Lowry, a man whose actions some years later would cause John Bruton to rue the day he became so personally close to Mr Lowry.

In July 1994, the long-awaited Beef Tribunal report was published. Its publication had been preceded some months earlier by a report in the *Sunday Business Post* which had quoted sources close to Dick Spring as saying that if the report was particularly damning of Mr Reynolds in relation to his handling of the export credit insurance issue some years earlier, then Labour would leave government.

Dick Spring's adviser, Fergus Finlay, later identified himself to his Fianna Fáil programme manager colleagues as the source for the story. Relations were badly damaged and when the report appeared, those relations were put under further strain when Reynolds engineered a positive media 'spin' for himself without any reference to Labour. His claims of exoneration were broadly accurate although the juxtaposition in a statement of two sentences from the report which were several hundred pages apart in the text, was widely criticised.

Spring was furious but effectively bit his lip. What was now called the 'peace process' was at a delicate stage and Spring did not want to do anything to ruffle feathers and disturb the southern political equilibrium.

Things were indeed at a delicate stage in the peace process with major efforts being made by Reynolds in particular to reel in Sinn Féin and the IRA. Success was achieved in August 1994 when the IRA announced a 'complete cessation' of hostilities.

The government, and particularly Reynolds, was jubilant. The Taoiseach moved quickly to welcome a Sinn Féin delegation, led by Adams, to Government Buildings. A Forum based in Dublin Castle was also quickly set up to which all parties North and South were invited to attend. The Unionists refused to take part.

But Reynolds's attempts to embrace Sinn Féin into the democratic fold were not matched by John Major. Under pressure from his tiny House of Commons majority and his dependence on the Unionist MPs for support in real crisis, he kept Sinn Féin at arm's length, insisted they go through a 'decontamination' period of unspecified length and made no commitment to the setting up of all-party talks.

But less than three months later, the focus of domestic political attention was to dramatically shift. A row over the appointment of a President of the High Court was brewing and would come to a head in November. On the surface the argument was indeed over a

difference of opinion over who should be appointed to the post, but the seeds of the battle had been sown some months earlier during the row over the Beef Tribunal report. Many commentators, and indeed many in Fianna Fáil, believed that Labour had very deliberately upped the ante in this row in an attempt to engineer a breakdown.

But whatever the reasons for the row, the result was breakdown. A complex set of developments, centring around the delay in processing the extradition of the paedophile priest Brendan Smyth, led to a walkout by Labour and when it was discovered that Fianna Fáil had allegedly failed to reveal all they knew when Reynolds made a statement on the affair to the Dáil, the government collapsed.

Albert Reynolds immediately resigned from office, just three months after he had played a major role in securing the IRA cease-fire. Very quickly it became clear that none of the Dáil parties had an appetite for another general election and the process of putting together a new administration began.

Bertie Ahern had been elected to succeed Albert Reynolds. A series of intense negotiations between key figures in Labour and Fianna Fáil seemed set to return another coalition between the two parties. Bertie Ahern was so certain of becoming Taoiseach that he had even cobbled together a list of potential cabinet members.

Then came the bombshell; a front-page article by Political Correspondent Geraldine Kennedy which indicated that Fianna Fáil had been guilty of even greater 'duplicity' in relation to the Brendan Smyth affair than Labour had been led to believe. Despite intense denials from Fianna Fáil the fallout from the story was both dramatic and swift. Dick Spring telephoned Bertie Ahern and told him simply that he was breaking off negotiations.

John Bruton, who was by this stage battling for his political life, suddenly found himself within sight of the Taoiseach's office. Negotiations immediately began with Labour and Democratic Left—the party that Bruton had previously refused to have anything to do with. Fine Gael should have been in the driving seat but in the done, conceded key ministries to Labour including Finance, Foreign Affairs, Education and Environment. Labour even managed to keep all their former ministers in office by successfully blocking a second full ministry to Democratic Left. Democratic Left leader Proinsias De Rossa became Minister for Social Welfare while DL TD Pat Rabbitte became what became known as a 'super junior' with access to the cabinet table but no voting rights.

The new Fine Gael/Labour/Democratic Left coalition was formed on 15 December 1994.

A period of intense government cohesion then began which would last until the end of the administration and into the next general election itself. Each of the three parties had very good reasons for maintaining this cohesion. Fine Gael, starved of power for so long, was delighted to be back into power and was determined to stay there; Labour having so shortly vacated one administration, could hardly conduct a repeat performance; and Democratic Left wanted to prove that a small, left-wing party could be trusted with power over a sustained period.

Potential crises were quickly dealt with. The first arose on Budget Day in February 1995, when it emerged that details of the budget had leaked from the office of Fine Gael junior minister Phil Hogan. The details appeared in the *Evening Herald* before finance minister Ruairí Quinn had risen in the Dáil to deliver his budget speech.

Hogan, a very popular figure within the party, promptly resigned. Labour denied that they had requested Hogan's resignation, but the move was seen as a demonstration by John Bruton that he was not going to let anything stand in the way of continued good relations with Labour. It was a pattern that would be repeated on many occasions throughout the next two and half years.

Just three months later, yet another Fine Gael Minister, Hugh Coveney, was forced to retire. A report in the *Sunday Business Post*, detailing how Coveney had apparently sought to ensure that his family firm would be considered for a particular Bord Gáis project, led to a swift meeting with John Bruton and Coveney's resignation almost immediately afterward. Coveney got a junior ministerial appointment and again Labour declared that they had not actively sought his resignation.

In July 1995, there was further evidence of a booming economy with Central Statistics Office figures confirming 7% growth in 1994.

In August Minister Michael Lowry became embroiled in the first of many controversies that would dog his career in office. The *Sunday Times* revealed that Gardaí were investigating claims that Lowry was being followed. Lowry alleged that people linked to Fianna Fáil had arranged the surveillance because, he claimed, of his efforts to get rid of 'cosy cartels' operating in Irish business.

The saga dragged on for several months. It reached its climax when the author of the anonymous letter which had alerted Lowry and others to the alleged surveillance—one

The Election Background

Pat Tuffy—was 'outed.' He told RTE that it was Lowry who had put him up to writing the letters. When this was exposed as a lie, Tuffy recanted.

In November 1995, the long-awaited and long-promised divorce referendum was finally held. The amendment was passed by a hair's breadth and anti-divorce activists blamed bad weather in certain rural constituencies for the failure to secure a No vote. The legislation was subsequently passed through without fuss.

In November, US President Bill Clinton visited the North and Dublin to a rapturous reception in both parts of the island. It was to be a short-lived celebration of the peace.

In January 1996, almost 16 months since the IRA had declared its cease-fire, talks between Sinn Féin and British ministers were held. Little progress was made on two fronts; the now vexed question of decommissioning, and a commencement date for the start of all-party talks. Hints that the IRA might be about to lose patience with the process were ignored and in February 1996, the IRA ended its cease-fire with the bombing of Canary Wharf in London and the murder of two people in the complex.

Sinn Féin blamed the British government for failing to respond generously to the 18-month cease-fire. John Bruton was also attacked on the grounds that he had swallowed the British line on decommissioning and had failed to keep up the momentum injected into the process by his predecessor Albert Reynolds.

Nonetheless, both governments made strides to attempt to inject some life back into the peace process. Within weeks of the bombing, John Major had announced a date for the start of all-party talks but had also insisted that elections should be held to a Northern Ireland forum in order to give the northern parties their respective mandates for the talks. Sinn Féin objected but took part and gained just over 15.5 per cent of the vote.

The forum was convened; the talks process limped into action under the chairmanship of former US senator George Mitchell, but Sinn Féin was barred from participation because of the continuing IRA campaign.

In June 1996, the focus of public attention shifted, tragically, back to the south with the murders of crime journalist Veronica Guerin and Detective Garda Jerry McCabe. The nation was deeply shocked; both the President and the Taoiseach attended Veronica's funeral and the public outrage at her death prompted a series of new legislative measures, including a referendum to tighten up the bail laws, to clamp down on organised crime.

July 1996 saw the start of the Irish EU presidency. It would be a low-key but workmanlike six months with the officials and ministers praised in the end by the EU for the efforts they had made in advancing the EMU agenda and other crucial issues.

Throughout the administration, the hepatitis C scandal had loomed large, with the support group Positive Action pressing the government for a tribunal of enquiry into the affair and for other concessions for the 1,500 victims of contaminated anti-D and other blood products. Health Minister Michael Noonan did make some concessions but adamantly drew the line at the tribunal.

But in early October, the government's hand was finally forced with the death of hepatitis C victim and mother of twelve Brigid McCole. The Blood Transfusion Service Board, it emerged, had settled the case, and admitted to liability, just days before her death. This in turn prompted an official judicial enquiry and the subsequent tribunal was praised for its efficiency and the expert way in which it went about piecing together the chain of events, and the people involved in the contamination of the blood.

In late November, a story in the *Irish Independent* prompted the resignation of another Fine Gael minister. This time it was Michael Lowry who confirmed the report that businessman Ben Dunne had paid for an elaborate extension to Lowry's Tipperary home. The fallout from this, and the revelation about another politician (later found to be the former Fianna Fáil Taoiseach Charlie Haughey) prompted the setting up of another tribunal—this time into the payments to politicians by Dunnes Stores—or, more correctly, by Ben Dunne himself.

In January Ruairí Quinn produced his second budget, announcing an actual budget surplus for 1996. It was clear by now that the countdown to an election was on but there did appear to be some disagreement between the parties as to the best time.

The Dunnes' Payments Tribunal got under way in April 1997 but was adjourned shortly afterwards before hearing either Michael Lowry's or Charlie Haughey's evidence. The government would have liked to postpone the election until after the latter evidence was heard and Bertie Ahern had very loudly cried 'foul'.

John Bruton finally dissolved the Dáil on 15 May and within hours the three rainbow leaders were in the Shelbourne Hotel announcing their joint campaign for re-election, emphasising the cohesion of the outgoing government and claiming that the prosperity currently being enjoyed by the

country would be jeopardised by what they said would be an inherently unstable Fianna Fáil/Progressive Democrats alliance.

Fianna Fáil had prepared well for the campaign and Bertie Ahern in particular had a superb campaign. Images of his very obvious enjoyment at being among the people were used very effectively by the party, leading Fine Gael to complain at one point at RTE's coverage of the Ahern nationwide canvass. Bruton's tour by train lacked impact and it was clear that Ahern was ahead on points in terms of perceived 'likeability'.

But if Fianna Fáil were barnstorming the country, the Progressive Democrats, incredibly, were having a disastrous campaign. They began with very positive ratings for leader Mary Harney and confident predictions that they would win up to 15 seats.

But a series of gaffes left them hugely exposed. Policy statements on single mothers and on proposed cutbacks in the public sector were seized upon by the rainbow parties as evidence of an uncaring 'Thatcherite' grouping who would destroy the social welfare system and put people out of work if they got into power. Despite Bertie Ahern's best efforts to dig his future partners out of the holes they had dug for themselves, the party crashed on polling day, managing to hang on to just four seats—three of them belonging to former members of Fianna Fáil, Harney, Bobby Molloy and Des O'Malley.

But Labour would also crash and, despite the seat gains of Fine Gael, by the time the votes were counted, it was clear that Bertie Ahern would be the next Taoiseach, albeit with the help of independents.

The final result was 81 for the FF/PD block, against 75 for the Rainbow block of FG/Lab/DL with the ten other deputies holding the balance of power.

The new government was formed on 26 June 1997.

Emily O'Reilly is co-presenter of the Radio Ireland 'Daybreak' programme and Political Editor of the *Sunday Business Post*. She is an award-winning political journalist and commentator. She was Woman Journalist of the Year in 1986, completed her Harvard University Journalism Fellowship in 1987 and was winner of the A.T. Cross Golden Pen Award for Supreme Contribution to Irish Journalism in 1994. She has worked with the *Sunday Tribune* and the *Irish Press*. She is a regular commentator on RTE, BBC, ITV and Channel 4 and has published two books.

The 28th Dáil has 166 deputies, the same as the previous Dáil. Of these, 121 (72.89%) were outgoing members of the 27th Dáil, 13 (7.83%) were previously members of the House but not of the 27th Dáil, and 32 (19.28%) are new deputies.

New Deputies

Ardagh, Seán (FF) — Dublin South-Central
Blaney, Harry (Ind) — Donegal North-East
Brady, Johnny (FF) — Meath
Brady, Martin (FF) — Dublin North-East
Burke, Ulick (FG) — Galway East
Carey, Pat (FF) — Dublin North-West
Clune, Deirdre (FG) — Cork South-Central
Collins, Michael (FF) — Limerick West
Cooper-Flynn, Beverley (FF) — Mayo
Fleming, Seán (FF) — Laois-Offaly
Gildea, Thomas (Ind) — Donegal South-West
Gormley, John (GP) — Dublin South-East
Hanafin, Mary (FF) — Dún Laoghaire
Hayes, Brian (FG) — Dublin South-West
Healy-Rae, Jackie (Ind) — Kerry South
Higgins, Joe (SP) — Dublin West
Kelleher, Billy (FF) — Cork North-Central
Lenihan, Conor (FF) — Dublin South-West
McGennis, Marian (FF) — Dublin Central
McGuinness, John (FF) — Carlow-Kilkenny
Mitchell, Olivia (FG) — Dublin South
Moloney, John (FF) — Laois-Offaly
Moynihan, Michael (FF) — Cork North-West
Naughten, Denis (FG)—Longford-Roscommon
Neville, Dan (FG) — Limerick West
Ó Caoláin, Caoimhghín (SF)—Cavan-Monaghan
O'Flynn, Noel (FF) — Cork North-Central
Perry, John (FG) — Sligo-Leitrim
Stanton, David (FG) — Cork East
Timmins, Billy (FG) — Wicklow
Wade, Eddie (FF) — Limerick East
Wall, Jack (Lab) — Kildare South

Ex-TDs Re-elected

Barnes, Monica (FG) — Dún Laoghaire
Belton, Louis J. (FG) — Longford-Roscommon
Cosgrave, Michael J. (FG) — Dublin North-East
Daly, Brendan (FF) — Clare
D'Arcy, Michael (FG) — Wexford
Dennehy, John (FF) — Cork South-Central
Enright, Tom (FG) — Laois-Offaly
Fahey, Frank (FF) — Galway West
Farrelly, John V. (FG) — Meath
O'Kennedy, Michael (FF) — Tipperary North
Reynolds, Gerry (FG) — Sligo-Leitrim
Roche, Dick (FF) — Wicklow
Wright, G.V. (FF) — Dublin North

Women Deputies

20 women won seats in the 1997 general election, the same as in the 1992 general election but three fewer than in the outgoing Dáil.

Election	No. of Women Elected
1997	20
1992	20
1989	13
1987	14
Nov 1982	14
Feb 1982	8
1981	11
1977	5
1973	4
1969	3

Women Elected 1997

Ahearn, Theresa (FG) — Tipperary South
Barnes, Monica (FG) — Dún Laoghaire
Clune, Deirdre (FG) — Cork South-Central
Cooper-Flynn, Beverley (FF) — Mayo
Coughlan, Mary (FF) — Donegal South-West
de Valera, Síle (FF) — Clare
Fitzgerald, Frances (FG) — Dublin South-East
Fox, Mildred (Ind) — Wicklow
Hanafin, Mary (FF) — Dún Laoghaire
Harney, Mary (PD) — Dublin South-West
Keaveney, Cecilia(FG) — Donegal North-East
McGennis, Marian (FF) — Dublin Central
McManus, Liz (DL) — Wicklow
Mitchell, Olivia (FG) — Dublin South
Moynihan-Cronin, Breeda (Lab) — Kerry South
O'Donnell, Liz (PD) — Dublin South
O'Rourke, Mary (FF) — Westmeath
Owen, Nora (FG) — Dublin North
Shortall, Róisín (Lab) — Dublin North-West
Wallace, Mary (FF) — Meath

Deceased Deputies

Four deputies died during the currency of the 27th Dáil:
Blaney, Neil T. (Ind) — Donegal North-East
Fox, Johnny (Ind) — Wicklow
Lenihan, Brian (FF) — Dublin West
O'Sullivan, Gerry (Lab) — Cork North-Central

Resignations

Three deputies resigned their seats during the currency of the 27th Dáil:

Cox, Pat (Ind) — Cork South-Central*
Flynn, Pádraig (FF) — Mayo
O'Connell, John (FF) — Dublin South-Central
*Pat Cox was elected as PD

Retiring Deputies

17 outgoing deputies did not seek re-election in the 1997 election.

Barry, Peter (FG) — Cork South-Central
Bhamjee, Moosajee (Lab) — Clare
Clohessy, Peadar (PD) — Limerick East
Collins, Gerard (FF) — Limerick West
Connolly, Ger (FF) — Laois-Offaly
Gallagher, Pat The Cope (FF) — Donegal South-West
Geoghegan-Quinn, Máire (FF) — Galway West
Hilliard, Colm (FF) — Meath
Hyland, Liam (FF) — Laois-Offaly
Leonard, Jimmy (FF) — Cavan-Monaghan
Nealon, Ted (FG) — Sligo-Leitrim
Noonan, Michael J. (FF) — Limerick West
O'Leary, John (FF) — Kerry South
Ryan, John (Lab) — Tipperary North
Taylor, Mervyn (Lab) — Dublin South-West
Timmins, Godfrey (FG) — Wicklow
Treacy, Seán (Ind) — Tipperary South

Lost Seats

Bhreathnach, Niamh (Lab) — Dún Laoghaire
Bree, Declan (Lab) — Sligo-Leitrim
Burton, Joan (Lab) — Dublin West
Byrne, Eric (DL)* — Dublin South-Central
Connor, John (FG) — Longford-Roscommon
Costello, Joe (Lab) — Dublin Central
Crowley, Frank (FG) — Cork North-West
Doyle, Avril (FG) — Wexford
Fitzgerald, Brian (Lab) — Meath
Fitzgerald, Eithne (Lab) — Dublin South
Fitzgerald, Liam (FF) — Dublin North-East
Flaherty, Mary (FG) — Dublin North-West
Foxe, Tom (Ind) — Longford-Roscommon
Gallagher, Pat (Lab) — Laois-Offaly
Harte, Paddy (FG) — Donegal North-East
Hughes, Séamus (FF) — Mayo (West)§
Kavanagh, Liam (Lab) — Wicklow
Kenny, Seán (Lab) — Dublin North-East
Keogh, Helen (PD) — Dún Laoghaire
Lynch, Kathleen (DL)* — Cork North-Central
McDowell, Michael (PD) — Dublin South-East
Morley, P.J. (FF) — Mayo (East)§
Mulvihill, John (Lab) — Cork East
Nolan, M.J. (FF) — Carlow-Kilkenny
O'Sullivan, Toddy (Lab) — Cork South-Central
Quill, Máirín (PD) — Cork North-Central
Ryan, Seán (Lab) — Dublin North
Walsh, Éamonn (Lab) — Dublin South-West

* Seat won in by-election to 27th Dáil
§ The constituencies of Mayo East and Mayo West were merged into the 5-seat constituency of Mayo

Statistics

Defeated Deputies

Twenty-eight deputies were defeated in the 1997 election: 4 Fianna Fáil, 5 Fine Gael, 3 Progressive Democrats, 13 Labour, 2 Democratic Left, 1 independent. They included the former Minister for Education, Niamh Bhreathnach, and former Ministers of State Joan Burton, Avril Doyle and Eithne FitzGerald.

Narrow Margins

The last seat in nine constituencies was won by one party from the other by less than 500 votes. The narrowest margin was in Dublin South-East, where the fourth and last seat went to John Gormley (GP) from Michael McDowell (PD) by 27 votes. The second-narrowest margin was in Dublin North-West where the fourth and last seat went to Proinsias De Rossa (DL) from Brendan Brady (FG) by 100 votes.

The list below includes close finishes for a seat between candidates from the same party.

Seat	Margin
Dublin South-East	27
John Gormley (GP) from	
Michael McDowell (PD)	
Dublin North-West	100
Proinsias De Rossa (DL) from	
Brendan Brady (FG)	
Dublin South-Central	267
Pat Upton (Lab) from	
Eric Byrne (DL)	
Dublin North-Central	276
Derek McDowell (Lab) from	
Seán Dublin Bay Loftus (Ind)	
Wicklow	277
Mildred Fox (Ind) from	
Liam Kavanagh (Lab)	
Galway East	338
Noel Treacy (FF) from	
John Callanan (FF)	
Louth	381
Michael Bell (Lab) from	
Fergus O'Dowd (FG)	
Tipperary South	435
Michael Ferris (Lab) from	
Seán Healy (Ind)	
Kildare South	439
Jack Wall (Lab) from	
Seán Ó Fearghail (FF)	
Wexford	458
Hugh Byrne (FF) from	
Denis Asple (FF)	
Carlow-Kilkenny	478
Séamus Pattison (Lab) from	
M.J. Nolan (FF)	

Family Seats

Of the 166 deputies in the 28th Dáil, 23 are sons and 7 are daughters of former deputies. A total of 9 deputies are grandchildren of former deputies.

Síle de Valera (FF) and Éamon Ó Cuív (FF) are both niece/nephew and grandchildren of former deputies. Their grandfather was Éamon de Valera (FF), Taoiseach and later President of Ireland, and their uncle was Major Vivion de Valera (FF).

Deirdre Clune (FG), Seán Haughey (FF), Brendan Kenneally (FF), Brian Lenihan (FF), Conor Lenihan (FF) and Gerard Reynolds (FG) are both children and grandchildren of former deputies. Deputy Haughey is both son and grandson of former Taoisigh.

Relationships with Former Deputies

In the following table, where a TD is related to more than one former TD, only the closest relationship is counted.

daughters	7
sons	23
sister	1
brother	1
niece	1
nephews	5
grandson	1
grandniece	1
grandnephew	1

Leading Vote-getters

14 candidates in the 1997 general election got a first-preference vote of more than 10,000. The highest was that of the outgoing Taoiseach, John Bruton (FG), who received 13,037 votes in Meath. Second-highest was Willie O'Dea (FF), who received 12,581 votes in Limerick East. He was followed by Bertie Ahern (FF), who received 12,175 votes in Dublin Central.

Top Ten	Votes
John Bruton (FG)	13,037
Meath	
Wlilie O'Dea (FF)	12,581
Limerick East	
Bertie Ahern (FF)	12,175
Dublin Central	
Liam Aylward (FF)	11,849
Carlow-Kilkenny	
Michael Lowry (Ind)	11,638
Tipperary North	
Caoimhghín Ó Caoláin (SF)	11,531
Cavan-Monaghan	
Ivor Callely (FF)	11,190
Dublin North-Central	
Noel Ahern (FF)	11,075
Dublin North-West	
Brian Cowen (FF)	10,865
Laois-Offaly	
Dick Spring (Lab)	10,699
Kerry North	

While these were the leaders in the actual number of votes, it should be noted that the figures do not in themselves provide the full picture of comparative achievement at the polls. The potential vote of candidates is naturally greatly influenced by the varying sizes of electorates and the varying strengths and numbers of other candidates in the field. One system which makes allowances for constituency factors is the evaluation of performance at the polls by the multiple of the quota received by the candidates. This system provides a different order:

Candidate	Multiple of Quota
Bertie Ahern (FF)	1.703
Dublin Central	
Willie O'Dea (FF)	1.519
Limerick East	
Noel Ahern (FF)	1.509
Dublin North-West	
John Bruton (FG)	1.380
Meath	
Ivor Callely (FF)	1.296
Dublin North-Central	
Liam Aylward (FF)	1.259
Carlow-Kilkenny	
Michael Noonan (FG)	1.218
Limerick East	
Dick Spring (Lab)	1.196
Kerry North	
Michael Lowry (Ind)	1.165
Tipperary North	
Caoimhghín Ó Caoláin (SF)	1.162
Cavan-Monaghan	

24 candidates exceed the quota on the first count: 14 Fianna Fáil, 7 Fine Gael, 1 Labour, 1 Sinn Féin and 1 Independent.

Deputies: When First Elected

Date of Entry	General Election	By-elections
1997	32	—
1992	18	4
1989	21	—
1987	19	—
1982 (Nov)	9	1
1982 (Feb)	9	1
1981	21	—
1977	16	—
1973	2	2
1969	6	—
1965	3	1
1961	1	—
Total	157	9

Dáil Service

Of the 166 deputies in the 27th Dáil, 32 (19.28%) entered the house for the first time in the 1997 general election, another 18 (10.84%) were elected in the 1992 general election plus 4 in by-elections to the 27th Dáil. 21 (12.65%) were elected in the 1989 general election; a further 19 (11.45%) were elected in the 1987 general election. A total of 75 (45.18%) of the present deputies have therefore become members in the last three general elections or by-elections of the ensuing Dálaí. A total of 94 deputies (56.63%) have entered the house in the ten-year period from 1987.

Long-serving Deputies

The longest-serving deputy in the Dáil is Séamus Pattison (Lab, Carlow-Kilkenny), who was first elected in the 1961 general election. He has served continuously in the house since then.

After Deputy Pattison are David Andrews (FF, Dún Laoghaire), Ben Briscoe (FF, Dublin South-Central) and Robert Molloy (PD, Galway West), all of whom were elected to the Dáil for the first time in the general election of 1965. Deputy Molloy was elected as a Fianna Fáil candidate but now represents the Progressive Democrats.

Desmond O'Malley (PD, Limerick East) was elected as a Fianna Fáil deputy to the Dáil in a by-election in 1968.

Relationships among Deputies of the 28th Dáil

There are five pairs of brothers in the 28th Dáil:

Bertie Ahern (FF, Dublin Central)
Noel Ahern (FF, Dublin North-West)

John Bruton (FG, Meath)
Richard Bruton (FG, Dublin North-Central)

Michael Kitt (FF, Galway East)
Tom Kitt (FF, Dublin South)

Brian Lenihan (FF, Dublin West)
Conor Lenihan (FF, Dublin South-West)

Gay Mitchell (FG, Dublin South-Central)
Jim Mitchell (FG, Dublin Central)

Marital Status and Families of Deputies

Of the 166 deputies returned to the 28th Dáil, 22 (13.25%) had not been married and 5 (3.01%) had been separated (one of these married a second time).

The 143 deputies with families have a total of 500 children, an average of 3.5 children. The most common family size is 3 or 4 (38 deputies each).

Number of Children	Number of Deputies
0	13
1	5
2	16
3	38
4	38
5	15
6	7
7	9
8	1
9	1

Occupation of Deputies

Of the 166 deputies elected to the 28th Dáil, 138 can be described as full-time politicians, devoting none of their time (or not a significant amount) to other occupations. This number is made up of 15 Ministers, 17 Ministers of State, the Ceann Comhairle, the Leaders of Fine Gael, Labour and Democratic Left, and 102 other members of the House.

In the list of main occupations in which deputies are or have been engaged, full-time politicians are not given a special category but are included according to their previous occupations. This system has been adopted to give a fuller background to the composition of the House.

Classifying deputies by occupations is considerably complicated by the fact that many of them are involved, or have been involved, in more than one occupation, or indeed have changed occupation following election. For this list, the job making most demands on the time and energy of a deputy was taken as the determining factor for the occupation category.

Candidates' First-Preference Votes

Of the 484 candidates who contested the 1997 general election, 238 had contested the 1992 election. 140 showed major changes (i.e. more than 20% increase or decrease) in their first-preference votes.

Main occupations in which deputies are or have been engaged

Education	38
National Teachers	*10*
Secondary Teachers	*14*
Vocational Teachers	*1*
University and College Lecturers	*6*
Other Teachers	*3*
Farmers and Farm Owners	23
Clerical and Technical	12
Company Directors and Managers	18
Lawyers	15
Solicitors	*10*
Barristers	*5*
Accountants	9
Science and Engineering	9
Health Care	3
Business Interests	5
Trade Union Officials	4
Auctioneers	4
Economists	2
Insurance	2
Journalists	2

Lost Deposits

Of the 484 candidates contesting the 1997 general election, 179 (36.98%) lost their deposits because their votes, after all transfers had been completed, did not exceed one quarter of the quota.

A total of 8 of the 14 candidates in Dublin Central and 12 of the 21 candidates in Dublin South-Central (57.14%) lost their deposit, £300 in each case; 6 of the 12 candidates in Clare and 8 of the 16 candidates in Meath (50%) also lost their deposits.

In Cork North-West, Kerry North and Tipperary South, only 1 candidate in each constituency lost the deposit. However, these are all three-seat constituencies and there were only 6 candidates in each.

The candidates who lost their deposits comprise 1 Fianna Fáil (0.89% of the party's candidates), 8 Fine Gael (8.89%), 6 Labour (13.64%), 9 Progressive Democrats (30.00%), 4 Democratic Left (30.77%), 15 Green Party (57.69%), 3 Sinn Féin (20.00%), 6 Workers' Party (85.71%), 2 Socialist Party (40.00%) and 87 Independent and Non-Party candidates (83.65%). All the candidates of the National Party, the Christian Solidarity Party, the Socialist Workers' Party and the Natural Law Party lost their deposits.

The money from lost deposits is forfeited to the state, to the Central Fund, to be disposed of as directed by the Minister for Finance. It generally goes towards the cost of running elections.

Statistics

Changed Seats

In the 1997 general election, party strengths changed in 32 constituencies and remained unchanged in 9 constituencies (comparison with Dáil at dissolution). In 5 of the unchanged constituencies the same deputies were returned as in the 1992 general election.

Changed (32)

Cavan-Monaghan	SF gain from FF
Clare	FF gain from Lab
Cork East	FG gain from Lab
Cork North-Central	FF gains from PD and DL
Cork North-West	FF gain from FG
Cork South-Central	FF gain from Lab
Donegal North-East	Ind gain from FG
Donegal South-West	Ind gain from FF
Dublin Central	FF gain from Lab
Dublin North	FF gain from Lab
Dublin North-East	FG gain from Lab
Dublin North-West	FF gain from FG
Dublin South	FG gain from Lab
Dublin South-Central	FF gain from DL
Dublin South-East	GP gain from PD
Dublin South-West	FF and FG gains from Lab
Dublin West	SP gain from Lab
Dún Laoghaire	FF and FG gains from Lab and PD
Galway East	FG win extra seat
Kerry South	Ind gain from FF
Kildare North } Kildare South }	Lab win extra seat
Laois-Offaly	FG gain from Lab
Limerick East	FF gain from PD
Limerick West	FG gain from FF
Longford-Roscommon	FG gain from Ind
Mayo East and West	FF lose seat
Meath	FG gain from Lab
Sligo-Leitrim	FG gain from Lab
Tipperary North	Ind and FF gains from FG and Lab
Tipperary South	One seat less: Seán Treacy (Ind), outgoing Ceann Comhairle, did not seek re-election
Wicklow	FF gain from Lab

Number of Candidates Showing Major Change in First-Preference Votes

Party	Increase	Decrease	Total
FF	30	5	35
FG	28	4	32
Lab	2	30	32
PD	2	3	5
DL	4	—	4
GP	6	—	6
SF	9	—	9
SP	1	—	1
WP	2	2	4
NLP	1	—	1
Others	5	6	11
Total	**90**	**50**	**140**

Birth Signs

The most common birth sign of the members of the 27th Dáil is Taurus (23 deputies). The least common is Capricorn and Leo (10 deputies each).

Birth Sign	No of Deputies
Aquarius	17
Pisces	13
Aries	12
Taurus	23
Gemini	16
Cancer	13
Leo	10
Virgo	14
Libra	14
Scorpio	13
Sagittarius	11
Capricorn	10

Variations in Party Support by Constituency

Comparisons between the results of the 1997 and 1992 general elections are not possible in every constituency, as two new constituencies were created as a result of the review of boundaries, and there were substantial changes in the boundaries of other constituencies.

Fianna Fáil

Fianna Fáil increased its share of the vote in 21 constituencies and showed a decrease in 20. The changes given below are in percentage points. The overall increase in the Fianna Fáil share of the vote was 0.22%.

Major Increases

Dublin North-West	13.66%
Limerick East	9.47%
Dublin North-Central	7.47%
Waterford	7.40%
Cork North-Central	7.27%

Major Decreases

Limerick West	14.97%
Kerry South	14.09%
Donegal South-West	10.64%
Kerry North	10.16%
Mayo	7.39%

Fine Gael

Fine Gael increased its share of the vote in 31 constituencies and showed a decrease in 10 constituencies. The overall increase in the party's share of the vote was 3.47%.

Major Increases

Cork South-Central	12.34%
Limerick East	10.90%
Meath	10.45%
Dún Laoghaire	9.41%
Dublin South-West	9.37%

Major Decreases

Tipperary North	16.76%
Donegal South-West	14.76%
Kerry South	6.12%

Labour

Labour increased its share of the vote in 3 constituencies and showed a decrease in 36. In the remaining 2 constituencies the party did not field a candidate in either the 1992 or the 1997 election. The overall decrease in the party's share of the vote was 8.98%.

Increases

Westmeath	4.38%
Galway East	2.47%
Longford-Roscommon	0.17%

Major Decreases

Dublin South-West	24.19%
Dublin North	20.39%
Dublin South-Central	19.22%
Dublin South	18.34%
Cork North-Central	17.02%
Dublin North-Central	16.52%
Waterford	14.37%
Limerick East	14.29%
Dublin North-East	12.83%
Tipperary North	12.42%
Dublin North-West	11.93%
Louth	11.60%
Dublin Central	11.59%
Meath	11.04%
Dublin West	10.49%
Kerry South	10.00%

Progressive Democrats

The Progressive Democrats increased their share of the vote in 8 constituencies and showed a decrease in 12 constituencies. There was no change in the party's overall share of the vote.

Major Increases

Kildare	6.52%
Dublin West	3.58%
Dublin North-East	2.72%

Major Decreases

Limerick East	13.71%
Cork South-Central	8.35%
Galway East	5.94%

Democratic Left

Democratic Left increased its share of the vote in 7 constituencies and showed a decrease in 6 constituencies. The party's overall share of the vote decreased by 0.27%.

Major Increases

Kildare	5.60%
Limerick East	5.12%

Major Decrease

Dublin North-East	5.65%

Green Party

The Green Party increased its share of the vote in 11 constituencies and showed a decrease in 5 constituencies. The party's overall share of the vote increased by 2.76%.

Major Increases

Dublin North	11.09%
Dublin South-East	8.50%

Sinn Féin

Sinn Féin increased its share of the vote in every constituency where a comparison can be made with 1992.

Major Increases

Kerry North	13.54%
Cavan-Monaghan	11.72%
Dublin South-West	6.79%
Donegal North-East	6.76%

Educational Background of Deputies

Level	FF	FG	Party Lab	PD	DL	Others	Total	%
First Level	—	1	—	—	—	3	4	2.41
Second Level	30	14	5	—	—	2	51	30.72
Third Level	47	39	12	4	4	5	111	66.87

Age Groupings of Deputies

(Ages on 6 June 1997, day of the election)

Age	FF	FG	Number of Deputies Lab	PD	DL	Others	Total	%
Over 65	—	1	—	—	—	2	3	1.81
61-65	7	4	2	—	—	—	13	7.83
56-60	8	9	3	2	1	1	24	14.46
51-55	12	14	5	—	—	—	32	19.28
46-50	16	9	2	—	2	2	31	18.67
41-45	18	5	3	1	1	2	29	17.47
36-40	9	8	2	1	—	2	22	13.25
31-35	4	2	—	—	—	—	6	3.61
26-30	3	1	—	—	—	—	4	2.41
21-25	—	1	—	—	—	1	2	1.20

Parties' Performance

Party	Candidates	No. Elected	% Elected	No. lost deposit	% lost deposit	% of 1st Prefs	% of Total Seats
FF	112	77	68.75	1	0.89	39.33	46.39
FG	90	54	60.00	8	8.89	27.95	32.53
Lab	44	17	38.64	6	13.64	10.40	10.24
PD	30	4	13.33	9	30.00	4.68	2.41
DL	13	4	30.77	4	30.77	2.51	2.41
GP	26	2	7.69	15	57.67	2.76	1.20
SF	15	1	6.67	3	20.00	2.55	0.60
NP	19	—	—	19	100.00	1.07	—
SP	5	1	20.00	2	40.00	0.70	0.60
CSP	8	—	—	8	100.00	0.47	—
WP	7	—	—	6	85.71	0.44	—
SWP	4	—	—	4	100.00	0.11	—
NLP	7	—	—	7	100.00	0.08	—
Others	104	6	5.77	87	83.65	6.96	3.61
Total	**484**	**166**	**34.30**	**179**	**36.98**	**100**	**100.00**

Statistics

Interparty Transfers

The transfer of votes in second and succeeding counts is one of the most critical factors in the working of proportional representation voting. In the following tables the transfers are analysed taking into account all counts in all constituencies for which meaningful data are available.

Leakage

One of the most critical aspects of transfers is the ability of a party to ensure that surpluses of its candidates, and votes of eliminated candidates, transfer to other candidates of that party to the maximum extent possible.

The table opposite shows the percentage of transfers from each party to other candidates of the same party, **where at least one other candidate of that party remains in the contest**.

From	To own party	Non-transferable
FF	67.27	5.68
FG	64.46	7.37
Lab	50.77	6.07
PD	61.96	4.41
SF	52.96	3.77

Coalition Parties

The following tables show the transfers within the two coalitions which fought the election (Fianna Fáil-Progressive Democrats and the Rainbow Coalition, Fine Gael-Labour-Democratic Left) **when no other candidate of the party remained in the contest**:

PERCENTAGE OF TRANSFERS

FIANNA FÁIL – PROGRESSIVE DEMOCRATS

From	% to FF	% to FG	% to Lab	% to PD	% to DL	% to Coalition Partner	% to Others	% Non-transferable
FF	—	7.05	7.33	67.69	2.02	67.69	25.15	7.16
PD	56.38	17.33	9.83	—	1.81	56.38	34.20	9.42

RAINBOW COALITION: FINE GAEL – LABOUR – DEMOCRATIC LEFT

From	% to FF	% to FG	% to Lab	% to PD	% to DL	% to Coalition Partner	% to Others	% Non-transferable
FG	8.22	—	57.70	6.30	2.40	60.10	25.20	14.70
Lab	23.76	52.69	—	1.24	4.66	57.35	29.46	13.19
DL	11.41	19.91	41.89	1.04	—	61.79	18.14	20.07

Taking all counts into consideration, **whether another candidate of the same party remained in the contest or not,** the transfers received by each party from their own candidates and from candidates of other parties are as follows:

PERCENTAGE OF TRANSFERS RECEIVED BY:

From	FF	FG	Lab	PD	DL	GP	SF	SP	WP	SWP	NP	CSP	NLP	Ind	% Non-transf.
FF	54.36	8.79	7.99	7.52	1.71	1.41	0.42	0.04	0.14	0.02	0.17	—	0.01	7.80	9.61
FG	13.65	52.75	16.21	1.61	1.96	1.03	0.33	0.06	0.46	—	0.14	0.02	—	2.68	9.08
Lab	16.35	38.05	15.24	2.16	8.46	3.26	0.79	—	—	—	0.13	—	—	1.47	14.09
PD	55.49	15.82	9.00	2.91	2.57	2.03	0.45	0.08	0.15	—	—	—	—	2.02	9.49
DL	11.41	19.91	41.89	1.04	—	2.45	1.73	—	—	—	—	0.14	—	1.36	20.07
GP	16.08	20.50	21.86	7.51	6.38	—	2.39	1.00	—	—	—	—	—	6.65	17.63
SF	29.38	10.46	18.32	2.81	5.82	1.13	1.51	2.48	—	—	0.48	0.58	—	0.26	26.80
CSP	42.58	18.97	5.07	4.72	3.26	7.25	1.27	—	—	—	3.70	—	—	1.56	11.63
NP	26.51	16.81	8.72	12.81	5.34	9.44	1.56	—	—	—	—	—	—	3.09	15.71
WP	13.21	9.75	14.75	2.25	5.61	18.06	9.27	8.66	—	—	3.14	0.42	—	7.86	7.02
Ind	26.26	23.90	10.48	2.23	3.66	5.78	1.59	0.53	0.65	0.04	0.80	0.25	0.04	11.52	12.29

Constituency Profiles

	Highest	Lowest
% Turnout	Longford-Roscommon (74.82%)	Dublin South-West (55.91%)
% Spoiled Votes	Dublin Central (1.49%)	Dublin West (0.55%)
Quota	Mayo (10,310)	Dublin South-West (6,976)
Candidates	Dublin South-Central (21)	Cork North-West, Kerry North, Tipperary South [6 each]
Candidates/Seat	Dublin South-Central (5.25)	Cork North-West, Kerry North, Tipperary South, Wexford [2 each]
Population	Dún Laoghaire (111,223)	Cork North-West (60,353)
Population/Seat	Louth (22,681)	Sligo-Leitrim (20,014)
Electorate	Meath (90,125)	Cork North-West (47,119)
Electorate/Seat	Meath (18,025)	Cork North-Central (14,375)
FF share of 1st Prefs	Clare (50.36%)	Dublin South-East (25.79%)
FG share of 1st Prefs	Mayo (48.75%)	Tipperary North (11.32%)
Lab share of 1st Prefs	Kerry North (29.90)	Longford-Roscommon (1.48%) (1 constituency not contested by Lab)
PD share of 1st Prefs	Dublin South-West (13.64%)	Sligo-Leitrim (1.65%) (13 constituencies not contested by PDs)
DL share of 1st Prefs	Dún Laoghaire (13.89%)	Meath (1.41%) (28 constituencies not contested by DL)
SF share of 1st Prefs	Cavan-Monaghan (19.37%)	Galway West (2.51%) (27 constituencies not contested by SF)
GP share of 1st Prefs	Dublin North (13.64%)	Mayo (1.52%) (15 constituencies not contested by GP)
WP share of 1st Prefs	Waterford (9.24%)	Dublin South-Central (0.73%) (34 constituencies not contested by WP)
SP share of 1st Prefs	Dublin West (16.21%)	Dublin South-Central (0.81%) (36 constituencies not contested by SP)
SWP share of 1st Prefs	Dublin North (1.62%)	Dublin South-Central (0.54%) (37 constituencies not contested by SWP)
NP share of 1st Prefs	Tipperary South (6.03%)	Mayo (1.18%) (25 constituencies not contested by NP)
CSP share of 1st Prefs	Dún Laoghaire (3.69%)	Clare (1.06%) (34 constituencies not contested by CSP)
NLP share of 1st Prefs	Dublin South-East (0.63%)	Dublin South (0.20%) (31 constituencies not contested by NLP)

Seanad Éireann (elected August 1997)

Party	Seats	Party	Seats
Fianna Fáil	29	Progressive Democrats	4
Fine Gael	16		
Labour	4	Others	7

	Senator	Whip	Panel/Constituency
*	Bohan, Eddie	FF	Industrial and Commercial
	Bonner, Enda	FF	Taoiseach's Nominee
*	Burke, Paddy	FG	Agricultural
	Caffrey, Ernie	FG	Industrial and Commercial
	Callanan, Peter	FF	Agricultural
*	Cassidy, Donie	FF	Labour
	Chambers, Frank	FF	Taoiseach's Nominee
	Coghlan, Paul	FG	Industrial and Commercial
	Connor, John	FG	Agricultural
	Coogan, Fintan	FG	Administrative
*	Cosgrave, Liam T.	FG	Industrial and Commercial
	Costello, Joe	Lab	Administrative
	Cox, Margaret	FF	Industrial and Commercial
*	Cregan, Denis (Dino)	FG	Labour
*	Dardis, John	PD	Taoiseach's Nominee
	Doyle, Avril	FG	Agricultural
*	Doyle, Joe	FG	Administrative
*	Farrell, Willie	FF	Industrial and Commercial
	Fitzgerald, Liam	FF	Labour
*	Fitzgerald, Tom	FF	Taoiseach's Nominee
	Fitzpatrick, Dermot	FF	Taoiseach's Nominee
*	Finneran, Michael	FF	Administrative
	Gallagher, Pat	Lab	Industrial and Commercial
	Gibbons, Jim	PD	Taoiseach's Nominee
	Glynn, Camillus	FF	Administrative
	Hanafin, Des	FF	Labour
*	Haughey, Edward	FF	Taoiseach's Nominee
	Hayes, Maurice	Ind	Taoiseach's Nominee
	Hayes, Tom	FG	Agricultural
*	Henry, Mary	Ind	University of Dublin
	Jackman, Mary	FG	Labour
	Keogh, Helen	PD	Taoiseach's Nominee
	Kett, Tony	FF	Administrative
*	Kiely, Dan	FF	Labour
*	Kiely, Rory	FF	Agricultural
*	Lanigan, Mick	FF	Industrial and Commercial
	Leonard, Ann	FF	Taoiseach's Nominee
*	Lydon, Don	FF	Labour
*	McDonagh, Jarlath	FG	Labour
*	McGowan, Paddy	FF	Agricultural
*	Manning, Maurice	FG	Cultural and Educational
*	Mooney, Paschal	FF	Cultural and Educational
	Moylan, Pat	FF	Agricultural
*	Mullooly, Brian	FF	Labour
*	Norris, David	Ind	University of Dublin
*	O'Brien, Francis	FF	Agricultural
	O'Donovan, Denis	FF	Industrial and Commercial
	O'Dowd, Fergus	FG	Administrative
	O'Meara, Kathleen	Lab	Agricultural
	Ó Murchú, Labhrás	FF	Cultural and Educational
*	Ormonde, Ann	FF	Cultural and Educational
*	O'Toole, Joe	Ind	National University of Ireland
	Quill, Máirín	PD	Taoiseach's Nominee
*	Quinn, Feargal	Ind	National University of Ireland
	Ridge, Thérèse	FG	Labour
*	Ross, Shane	Ind	University of Dublin
	Ryan, Brendan	Ind	National University of Ireland
	Ryan, Seán	Lab	Labour
*	Taylor-Quinn, Madeleine	FG	Cultural and Educational
	Walsh, Jim	FF	Agricultural

Voting in the Seanad Elections held as a consequence of the dissolution of the 27th Dáil was for 49 of the 60 seats, the remaining 11 members being nominated later by the Taoiseach. Of the 49 elected members, 43 were returned from the Vocational Panels and 6 from the University Constituencies. Voting was completed on 6 August 1997 for the University Constituencies and for the Vocational Panels.

Of the seats on the Vocational Panels, Fianna Fáil won 23, Fine Gael 16 and Labour 4. Of the University members, none has accepted a party whip. Of the Taoiseach's Nominees, 6 accept the Fianna Fáil Whip, 4 accept the Progressive Democrats Whip, and 1 has not accepted any whip.

Twenty-eight of the members returned to the Seanad were outgoing. Of the 32 newly elected or nominated Senators, 10 were previously members and 8 were Dáil deputies who lost their seats in the 1997 election (1 FF, 2 FG, 3 Lab and 2 PD).

A total of 23 of the Senators were unsuccessful candidates in the 1997 Dáil general election. In the lists of Senators in this section, an asterisk (*) denotes an outgoing member of the 1993-97 Seanad.

Elected (5 Seats)

Ann Ormonde (FF)*
12th Count
Paschal Mooney (FF)*
14th Count
Labhrás Ó Murchú (FF)
15th Count
Madeleine Taylor-Quinn (FG)*
16th Count
Maurice Manning (FG)*
16th Count

Ann Ormonde (FF)

Address 2 Auburn Road, Dublin 4
Tel. *H* (01) 260 1577; *B* (01) 838 0536
b. Kilmacthomas, Co Waterford
Educ. Our Lady's College, Presentation Convent, Clonmel; UCD (BComm, HDipEd, Dip Career Guidance)
Occ. Career guidance counsellor

Senator since 1993. Member, Dublin CC since 1985, now South Dublin CC; Co Dublin VEC. Contested general elections of 1987, 1989, 1992 and 1997.

Paschal Mooney (FF)

Address Carrick Road, Drumshanbo, Co Leitrim
Tel. (078) 41236/41013; *Mobile* (088) 545613; *Fax* (078) 41237
b. Dublin. October 1947
m. Sheila Baldrey. 3s, 2d
Educ. Presentation Bros, Carrick-on-Shannon; Carrick-on-Shannon VEC, Camden Inst, London
Occ. Journalist, broadcaster, public representative

Senator since 1987. Member, Leitrim CC since 1991, Chairman 1994/95. Vice-Chairman Leitrim VEC, Chairman Leitrim Sports Advisory Body.

Labhrás Ó Murchú (FF)

Address An Bóithrín Glas, Caiseal, Co Thiobraid Árann
Tel. (062) 61552; *Fax* (062) 61552
b. Cashel, Co Tipperary. August 1939
m. Úna Ronan
Educ. Cashel CBS
Occ. Director-General, Comhaltas Ceoltóirí Éireann

New senator. Member, Cashel UDC for 18 years; previous chairman

Madeleine Taylor-Quinn (FG)

Address Frances Street, Kilrush, Co Clare
Tel. (065) 51656
b. Kilkee, Co Clare. May 1951
m. George Quinn. 2s
Educ. Conv of Mercy Sec School, Kilrush; UCG (BA, LLB, HDipEd)
Occ. Full-time public representative. Formerly sec school teacher

Senator since 1993 and previously April-November 1982. TD for Clare June 1981-Feb 1982 and Nov 1982-1992. Member, Clare CC since 1979. Daughter of Frank Taylor, TD for Clare 1969-81.

Maurice Manning (FG)

Address 13 Haddington Place, Ballsbridge, Dublin 4
Tel. (01) 6681416
b. Kilkenny. June 1943
m. Mary Hayes. 1s
Educ. De La Salle School, Bagenalstown, Co Carlow; Rockwell College; UCD; Univ. of Strathclyde
Occ. University lecturer

Senator 1981-82 and since 1987; TD for Dublin N-E 1982-87. Leader of FG Group in Seanad since 1987 and Leader of the house 1995-97. Contested Dáil elections of 1981 to 1992. Governing Body, UCD. Senate, NUI.

Candidates

Name	(County, Party)	Vote (1st Pref)
Nominating Bodies Sub-Panel		
Abbott, Henry	(Westmeath, FF)	55
Davis, Gerard	(Dublin, Ind)	8
Feeney, Geraldine	(Sligo, FF)	29
Flynn, Nora	(Waterford, FG)	36
Herity, Michael	(Dublin, Ind)	3
Hillery, John M.	(Clare, FF)	44
Mooney, Paschal	(Leitrim, FF)	91
O Foighil, Pól Báinín	(Galway, FG)	36
Ó Murchú, Labhrás	(Tipperary, FF)	73
O'Reilly, Joe	(Cavan, FG)	75
O'Reilly, Michael	(Dublin, FG)	21
Ormonde, Ann	(Dublin, FF)	121
Walsh, Babette	(Dublin, Ind)	4
Whelan, Noel	(Dublin, FF)	20
Oireachtas Sub-Panel		
Chambers, Frank	(Mayo, FF)	45
Lyons, Denis	(Cork, FF)	26
Manning, Maurice	(Dublin, FG)	93
Taylor-Quinn, Madeleine	(Clare, FG)	82
Walsh, Éamonn	(Dublin, Lab)	112

Agricultural Panel

Elected (11 Seats)

Kathleen O'Meara (Lab)	1st Count
Francis O'Brien (FF)*	9th Count
Paddy Burke (FG)*	17th Count
Tom Hayes (FG)	17th Count
John Connor (FG)	17th Count
Rory Kiely (FF)*	21st Count
Jim Walsh (FF)	23rd Count
Peter Callanan (FF)	23rd Count
Paddy McGowan (FF)*	23rd Count
Pat Moylan (FF)	23rd Count
Avril Doyle (FG)	24th Count

Candidates

Name	(County, Party)	Vote (1st Pref)

Nominating Bodies Sub-Panel

Name	(County, Party)	Vote (1st Pref)
Aird, William	(Laois, FG)	25
Begley, Michael	(Clare, FF)	21
Buckley, Timothy	(Kerry, FG)	15
Burke, Paddy	(Mayo, FG)	50
Callanan, Peter	(Cork, FF)	51
Coonan, Noel J.	(Tipperary, FG)	13
Crosby, Thomas	(Roscommon, FF)	26
Doyle, Avril	(Wexford, FG)	43
Dunne, Joseph	(Laois, FF)	15
Hayes, Tom	(Tipperary, FG)	45
Hilliard, Colm M.	(Meath, FF)	2
Hourigan, Richard V.	(Limerick, FG)	21
Kiely, Rory	(Limerick, FF)	64
Moylan, Pat	(Offaly, FF)	40
Murphy, Gerard	(Cork, FG)	34
O'Brien, Francis	(Monaghan, FF)	78
Ó Fearghail, Seán	(Kildare, FF)	16
O'Reilly, Patrick	(Cavan, FG)	34
Phelan, Kieran	(Laois, FF)	37

Oireachtas Sub-Panel

Name	(County, Party)	Vote (1st Pref)
Berkery, Tom	(Tipperary, FG)	23
Caulfield, Matt	(Monaghan, FF)	9
Connor, John	(Roscommon, FG)	50
Fitzgerald, Tom	(Kerry, FF)	46
Foley, Paddy	(Westmeath, FF)	1
McDermott, Frank	(Westmeath, FG)	34
McGowan, Paddy	(Donegal, FF)	46
O'Meara, Kathleen	(Tipperary, Lab)	87
Walsh, Jim	(Wexford, FF)	57

Kathleen O'Meara (Lab)

Address Lisheen, Portroe, Nenagh, Co Tipperary
Off. 10 Connolly Street, Nenagh
Tel. (067) 34190
b. Roscrea, Co Tipperary. January 1960
m. Kevin Dolan. 1s, 1d
Educ. Sacred Heart College, Roscrea; UCG; NIHE, Dublin
Occ. Public representative. Formerly journalist

New senator. Ministerial adviser with Minister of State Eithne Fitzgerald 1994-97. Candidate in 1997 General Election.

Francis O'Brien (FF)

Address Corwillan, Latton, Castleblayney, Co Monaghan
Tel. H (042) 41152
b. Ballybay, Co Monaghan. April 1943
m. Gertrude Smith. 3s, 1d
Educ. Drumfreehan National School, Co Monaghan
Occ. Farmer, public rep

Senator since 1989. Monaghan CC since 1979 (chairman 1986/87); Monaghan Co Comm of Agr 1985-88 (chairman 1986/87); East Border Region Comm since 1987 (chairman 1991/92).

Paddy Burke (FG)

Address Knockaphunta, Westport Road, Castlebar, Co Mayo
Tel. (094) 22568
b. Castlebar. January 1955
m. Dolores Barrett
Educ. Ballinafad College, Castlebar; Rockwell Agric College, Cashel, Co Tipperary. Franciscan Brothers' Agric College, Mount Bellew, Co Galway.
Occ. Self-employed; public rep

Senator since 1993. Member, Mayo CC since 1979. Former member, Mayo Co Comm of Agric. Mayo-Galway RDO. LAMA since 1991.

Tom Hayes (FG)

Address Cahirvillahow, Golden, Cashel, Co Tipperary
Tel. H (062) 72194; Mobile (086) 810 5016
b. Golden. February 1952
m. Marian Thornton. 3s
Educ. Mount Melleray College, Co Waterford; Tipperary Vocational School
Occ. Farmer

New senator. Member, Tipperary South Riding CC since 1991; Vocational Education Committee; County Enterprise Board; Community School Management Board.

John Connor (FG)

Address Cloonshanville, Frenchpark, Co Roscommon
Tel. *H* (0907) 70143
b. Roscommon. February 1944
Educ. Kilroy's College, Dublin; UCG
Occ. Full-time public representative. Farmer. Formerly local government official

Previously senator 1983-89. TD 1981-82 and 1989-92 for Roscommon constituency and 1992-97 for Longford-Roscommon. Member, Roscommon CC since 1985.

Rory Kiely (FF)

Address Cloncrippa, Feenagh, Kilmallock, Co Limerick
Tel *H* (063) 85033
b. Feenagh. May 1934
m. Eileen O'Connor. 2s, 2d
Educ. CBS, Ráth Luirc, Co Cork
Occ. Public rep, farmer

Senator 1977-82 and since 1983. Limerick CC 1979-85. Contested Dáil election of 1969.

Jim Walsh (FF)

Address Mountgarrett Castle, New Ross, Co Wexford
Tel. *H* (051) 421771
m. Marie Furlong. 1s, 2d
Educ. New Ross CBS
Occ. Company director, farmer

New senator. Member, Wexford CC since 1979 (chairman 1992/93); New Ross UDC since 1974 (chairman 8 times). Chairman, LAMA. Member, Chartered Institute of Transport. Former president, Irish Road Hauliers' Association.

Peter Callanan (FF)

Address Ballymountain, Innishannon, Co Cork
Tel. (021) 775192
b. Kilkern, Castlefreke, Clonakilty, Co Cork
m. Sheila Harrington. 4s, 2d
Educ. Mount Melleray College, Co Waterford
Occ. Farmer

New senator. Member, Cork CC since 1979 (vice-chairman 1989/90); local farming and sporting organisations.

Paddy McGowan (FF)

Address Ballindrait, Lifford, Co Donegal
Tel. (074) 41553
b. Ballybofey. July 1926
Educ. St Eunan's College, Letterkenny
Occ. Public rep, farmer

Senator 1965-81 and since 1987. Donegal CC since 1960. General Cl of CCs. Contested Seanad 1961, 1981 and 1982.

Pat Moylan (FF)

Address Harbour Road, Banagher, Co Offaly
Tel. *H* (0509) 51113; *Fax* (0509) 51858; *Mobile* (087) 574476
b. Banagher. September 1946
m. Mary Dunne. 3s, 1d
Educ. Banagher Vocational School
Occ. Sales representative with concrete firm

New senator. Member, Offaly CC since 1975 (chairman 1991/92, 1992/93); Midland Health Board; Midland Regional Authority; EU Committee of the Regions (Midland Region).

Avril Doyle (FG)

Address Kitestown House, Crossabeg, Wexford
Tel. *H* (053) 42873
b. Dublin. April 1949
m. Fred Doyle. 3d
Educ. Holy Child Convent, Killiney, Co Dublin; UCD
Occ. Public representative

Previously senator 1989-92. TD 1982-89 and 1992-97. Minister of State at the Depts of Finance and Environment 1986-89 and at the Depts of the Taoiseach, Finance and Transport, Energy and Communications 1994-97.

Labour Panel

Elected (11 Seats)

Donie Cassidy (FF)*	1st Count
Don Lydon (FF)*	9th Count
Seán Ryan (Lab)	11th Count
Mary Jackman (FG)	13th Count
Thérèse Ridge (FG)	15th Count
Brian Mullooly (FF)*	17th Count
Des Hanafin (FF)	17th Count
Jarlath McDonagh (FG)*	17th Count
Dan Kiely (FF)*	17th Count
Liam Fitzgerald (FF)	18th Count
Denis (Dino) Cregan (FG)*	25th Count

Candidates

Name	(County, Party)	Vote (1st Pref)

Nominating Bodies Sub-Panel

Name	(County, Party)	Vote (1st Pref)
Bourke, Jack	(Limerick, FF)	52
Bourke, Paddy	(Dublin, Lab)	1
Brennan, Terence	(Louth, FG)	35
Cotter, Bill	(Monaghan, FG)	13
Cummins, Maurice	(Waterford, FG)	38
Jackman, Mary	(Limerick, FG)	45
Kiely, Daniel	(Kerry, FF)	57
Lyons, Seán	(Dublin, Ind)	33
McDonagh, Jarlath	(Galway, FG)	38
McGreal, Michael	(Roscommon, FG)	20
Maloney, Seán	(Donegal)	37
Mullooly, Brian	(Roscommon, FF)	67
Ridge, Therese	(Dublin, FG)	40
Ryan, Seán	(Dublin, Lab)	64

Oireachtas Sub-Panel

Name	(County, Party)	Vote (1st Pref)
Banks, Paddy	(Dublin, FF)	1
Cassidy, Donie	(Westmeath, FF)	83
Cosgrave, Niamh	(Dublin, FG)	15
Cregan, Denis (Dino)	(Cork, FG)	51
Fitzgerald, Liam	(Dublin, FF)	56
Hanafin, Des	(Tipperary, FF)	64
Lydon, Don	(Dublin, FF)	76
O'Kelly, Frank	(Donegal, FG)	25
Sherlock, Joe	(Cork, DL)	58

Donie Cassidy (FF)

Address Castlepollard, Co Westmeath
Tel. (044) 61176
b. Castlepollard. September 1945
m. Anne Geraghty. 4s
Occ. Musical impresario, public representative

Senator since April 1982. Leader of the House since 1997. Westmeath CC since 1985 (chairman 1989/90); MHB since 1985. Substitute member of European Parliament since 1984. Founder of National Wax Museum.

Don Lydon (FF)

Address 34 Clonmore Road, Mount Merrion, Co Dublin
Tel. H (01) 288 8741; B (01) 288 1781
b. August 1938
m. Maeve Ryan
Educ. St Eunan's College, Letterkenny; UCG; UCD
Occ. Psychologist

Senator since 1987. Dublin CC since 1985, now Dún Laoghaire-Rathdown CC. Member, Psychological Associations of Ireland, Britain and America.

Seán Ryan (Lab)

Address 1 Burrow Road, Portrane, Co Dublin
Tel. H (01) 843 6254
b. Dublin. January 1943
m. Patricia Brehony
Educ. College of Technology, Bolton Street, Dublin; College of Industrial Relations, Dublin; School of Management, Rathmines, Dublin
Occ. Full-time public representative

New senator. TD 1989-97. Member, Dublin CC 1983-93; Fingal CC since 1993. Labour Party spokesperson in Dáil on Defence and the Elderly, Labour, Sport and Youth 1989-92.

Mary Jackman (FG)

Address 5 Newtown, Castletroy, Limerick
Tel. H (061) 335511
b. Cappawhite, Co Tipperary. April 1943
m. Nicholas Jackman. 1d
Educ. Convent of Mercy, Doon, Co Limerick; UCC
Occ. Public representative. Secondary school teacher

Previously senator 1989-92, Labour Panel. Member, Limerick CC since 1985; Co Limerick VEC since 1985. Former chairperson, Network. Member, ASTI.

Thérèse Ridge (FG)

Address 4 St Patrick's Avenue, Clondalkin, Dublin 22
Tel. (01) 457 3438; *Mobile* (087) 497479
b. Dublin. March 1941
m. James Ridge. 1s, 2d
Educ. Goldenbridge College, Dublin; St Patrick's College, Maynooth (MA)
Occ. Public representative. Formerly teacher; external tutor, Maynooth Adult Education Department

New senator. Member, Dublin CC 1985-93 (chairman 1992/93); South Dublin CC since 1993 (chairman 1996/97). Former chairman, Irish Pre-School Playgroups Association.

Brian Mullooly (FF)

Address Strokestown, Co Roscommon
Tel. (078) 33550
b. Strokestown, Co Roscommon. February 1935
m. Nancy Kelly. 3s, 5d
Educ. Summerhill College, Sligo; St Patrick's Teachers' Training College, Dublin
Occ. Public representative, national school teacher

Senator since 1981. Cathaoirleach of Seanad since 1997. Roscommon CC since 1974 (chairman 1985-91).

Des Hanafin (FF)

Address Parnell Street, Thurles, Co Tipperary
Tel. *H* (0504) 21338; (01) 660 7361
b. Thurles. September 1930
m. Mona Brady. 1s, 1d
Educ. Blackrock College, Dublin
Occ. Public representative

Previously senator 1969-93, Labour Panel. Chairman, Anti-Divorce Campaign Committee; Pro-Life Amendment Committee. Former member and chairman, Tipperary North Riding CC. Father of Mary Hanafin, TD.

Jarlath McDonagh (FG)

Address Teach Shligigh, Turloughmore, Co Galway
Tel. *H* (091) 97143
b. Galway. June 1945
m. Geraldine Connors. 1s, 3d
Educ. St Jarlath's College, Tuam; UCG (BA, HDipEd)
Occ. Public rep, teacher

Senator since 1993. Galway CC since 1985. Vice-chairman Co Galway VEC. Galway Co Board GAA 1982-90. Executive member, General Cl of CCs. IVEA.

Dan Kiely (FF)

Address Doonard, Tarbert, Co Kerry
Tel. *H* (068) 36163; *B* (068) 47105
b. Tarbert. October 1943
m. 1s, 3d
Educ. St Mary's, Glin, Co Limerick; Fordham Univ, New York
Occ. Businessman, auctioneer, publican

Senator 1981-82 and since 1987. Kerry CC since 1979 (chairman 1992/93). Chairman, General Cl of CCs 1985-87. Dáil candidate in Feb and Nov 1982, and 1987. Chairman, North Kerry GAA, 1968-73.

Liam Fitzgerald (FF)

Address 117 Tonlegee Road, Raheny, Dublin 5
Tel. *H* (01) 847 0632
b. Limerick. September 1949
m. Bríd Lynch. 3s, 2d
Educ. Doon CBS, Co Limerick; St Patrick's Teacher Training College; UCD
Occ. Full-time public representative. Formerly teacher

New senator. TD 1981-Feb. 1982 and Nov. 1982-97. Member, Dublin City Council since 1985. Fianna Fáil Deputy Spokesperson on Education in Dáil 1983-87.

Denis (Dino) Cregan (FG)

Address 7 Elm Grove, Ballinlough, Cork
Tel. *H* (021) 291863; *B* (021) 342333
b. Cork. May 1940
m. Mary Barry. 4s, 3d
Educ. Greenmount NS
Occ. Company director

Senator 1982-87 and since 1993. Member, Cork Corporation since 1979 (Lord Mayor 1991/92). Contested general elections in 1981, February 1982 and 1992.

Industrial and Commercial Panel

Elected (9 Seats)

Pat Gallagher (Lab)	8th Count
Liam T. Cosgrave (FG)*	15th Count
Eddie Bohan (FF)*	22nd Count
Willie Farrell (FF)*	26th Count
Mick Lanigan (FF)*	26th Count
Denis O'Donovan (FF)	26th Count
Paul Coghlan (FG)	26th Count
Margaret Cox (FF)	29th Count
Ernie Caffrey (FG)	29th Count

Candidates

Name	(County, Party)	Vote (1st Pref)
Nominating Bodies Sub-Panel		
Bohan, Eddie	(Dublin, FF)	66
Bridgett, Andrew, G (Gerry)	(Kildare, FF)	6
Callaghan, Vivian	(Cork, FF)	23
Coghlan, Paul	(Kerry, FG)	47
Conroy, Richard	(Dublin, FF)	33
Considine, Peter F.	(Clare, FF)	26
Doolan, Jim	(Galway, FF)	6
Farrell, Willie	(Sligo, FF)	48
Harte, Paddy	(Donegal, FG)	18
Howard, Michael	(Clare, FG)	43
Hughes, Brendan	(Monaghan, FF)	29
Hunter-McGowan, Thomas	(Cork, Ind)	14
Ireland, Billy	(Kilkenny, FG)	39
Kennedy, Michael Joseph	(Dublin, FF)	18
Leyden, Terry	(Roscommon, FF)	31
McCarthy, Desmond Andrew	(Limerick, FF)	0
McPadden, James N.	(Leitrim, FG)	36
O'Donnell, Mícheál	(Louth, FF)	23
O'Donovan, Denis	(Cork, FF)	49
O'Leary, Brian	(Kerry, FF)	15
Reddington, John	(Limerick, FF)	5
Staunton, Myles	(Mayo, FG)	4
Temple, Ciarán	(Westmeath, FF)	26
Tiernan, Joe	(Dublin, FG)	22
Oireachtas Sub-Panel		
Boyle, Daniel	(Cork, GP)	43
Caffrey, Ernie	(Mayo, FG)	37
Cosgrave, Liam T.	(Dublin, FG)	75
Cox, Margaret	(Galway, FF)	33
Dunlea, Nicholas	(Cork, FG)	20
Gallagher, Pat	(Offaly, Lab)	96
Lanigan, Mick	(Kilkenny, FF)	42
Murray, Richard	(Meath, FF)	0

Pat Gallagher (Lab)

Address 8 Hophill Avenue, Tullamore, Co Offaly
Tel: *H* (0506) 52744
b. Dublin. March 1963
Educ. Tullamore CBS; St Patrick's College, Maynooth; UCG
Occ. Full-time public representative. Formerly manager, community training workshop

New senator. TD 1992-97. Member, Offaly CC since 1991; Offaly VEC since 1991 (chairman 1993/94); National Council of National Federation of Youth Clubs 1984-86.

Liam T. Cosgrave (FG)

Address 103 Merrion Park, Blackrock, Co Dublin
Tel. *H* (01) 288 5575; *B* (01) 873 5255
b. Dublin. April 1956
m. Joan Bourke. 2s
Educ. Castleknock College; Incorporated Law Society of Ireland
Occ. Solicitor. Public rep

Senator since 1989; Leas Chathaoirleach since 1997; Cathaoirleach 1996-97. TD for Dún Laoghaire 1981-87. Dublin CC and Dún Laoghaire Corp since 1985. Son of Liam Cosgrave. Grandson of William T. Cosgrave.

Eddie Bohan (FF)

Address 18 Orwell Park, Dublin 6
Tel. *B* (01) 475 4068, 475 3973
b. Longford. November 1932
m. Betty Lambert. 1s, 3d
Educ. Longford Sec School
Occ. Auctioneer, publican

Senator since 1987. Former president of Vintners' Federation of Ireland. Former chairman of Dublin Licensed Vintners' Association.

Willie Farrell (FF)

Address Silverhill, Ballinfull, Co Sligo
Tel. *H* (071) 63119; *B* (071) 63151
b. Cashelgarron, Co Sligo. April 1928
m. Breeda McCullagh. 2s, 1d
Educ. Grange Vocational School
Occ. Farmer, auctioneer, public representative

Senator 1982-83 and since 1987. Sligo CC 1967-97 (chairman 1988/89); NWHB 1972-97 (chairman 1982/83 and 1992/93). Chairman of Association of Health Boards of Ireland 1986-92.

Mick Lanigan (FF)

Address St Jude's, Chapel Avenue, Kilkenny
Tel. *H* (056) 22650; *B* (056) 21247
b. Limerick. January 1938
m. Dorothy Widger. 4s, 2d
Educ. St Peter's, Wexford; De La Salle Coll, Waterford; UCD
Occ. Businessman

Senator since 1977. Leader of Seanad 1987-90. Leader of Fianna Fáil in Seanad 1981-87.

Paul Coghlan (FG)

Address Ballydowney, Killarney, Co Kerry
Tel. *H* (064) 31733; *B* (064) 31892; *Fax* (064) 34652
b. Killarney. June 1944
m. Peggy O'Shea. 2s, 3d
Educ. St Brendan's College, Killarney; De La Salle, Waterford
Occ. Public representative. MIB, MIPAV,MLIA

New Senator. Member, Kerry CC since 1991; Killarney UDC since 1985 (chairman 1992/93); Kerry VEC since 1991; Dingle Harbour Commissioners since 1991.

Ernie Caffrey (FG)

Address Garden Street, Ballina, Co Mayo
Tel. (096) 22352
b. Castleconnor, Co Sligo. October 1936
m. Phyllis Hughes. 2s, 2d
Educ. Regent Institute, London
Occ. Public representative, publican

New senator. Member, Sligo CC 1966; Mayo CC since 1991; Ballina UDC since 1985 (chairman 1994/95); Mayo VEC. Western Regional Authority.

Denis O'Donovan (FF)

Address Montrose House, Slip, Bantry, Co Cork
Tel: *H* (027) 51541; *B* (027) 50808; *Mobile* (087) 543806
b. Bantry. July 1955
m. Mary Murphy. 3s, 1d
Educ. Bantry Secondary School; Carrignavar Secondary College; UCC
Occ. Public representative. Solicitor

Previously senator 1989-93, Taoiseach's Nominee. Member, Cork CC since 1985 (chairman 1989/90).

Margaret Cox (FF)

Address 7 Father Griffin Road, Galway
Tel. *H* (091) 586892; *Mobile* (087) 594273; *Fax* (091) 585070
b. Galway. September 1963
m. Felim McDonnell. 2s
Educ. Meánscoil Mhuire, Galway; UCG; UL
Occ. Managing director, ICE Group, Galway

New senator. Member, Galway City Council since 1995; Western Health Board; Western Regional Health Authority; General Council of County Councils.

Administrative Panel

Elected (7 Seats)

Joe Costello (Lab)	1st Count
Camillus Glynn (FF)	9th Count
Michael Finneran (FF)*	9th Count
Tony Kett (FF)	9th Count
Joe Doyle (FG)*	13th Count
Fintan Coogan (FG)	14th Count
Fergus O'Dowd (FG)	14th Count

Candidates

Name	(County, Party)	Vote (1st Pref)
Nominating Bodies Sub-Panel		
Coogan, Fintan	(Galway, FG)	62
Forde, Margaret G.	(Sligo, FF)	33
Gilbride, Seán	(Dublin, FF)	38
Glynn, Camillus	(Westmeath, FF)	83
Kennedy, Patrick	(Limerick, FG)	60
Kerrigan, Mary	(Dublin, FF)	50
Kett, Tony	(Dublin, FF)	91
McDonald, Charles	(Laois, FG)	34
Mulcahy, Michael	(Dublin, FF)	34
Oireachtas Sub-Panel		
Byrne, Seán	(Tipperary, FF)	33
Costello, Joe	(Dublin, Lab)	129
Doyle, Joe	(Dublin, FG)	79
Finneran, Michael	(Roscommon, FF)	67
Nolan, M.J.	(Carlow, FF)	57
O'Connor, Aidan	(Kerry, FG)	60
O'Dowd, Fergus	(Louth, FG)	64

Joe Costello (Lab)

Address 75 Lr Seán MacDermott Street, Dublin 1
Tel. (01) 836 5698
b. Sligo. July 1945
Educ. Summerhill College, Sligo; St Patrick's College, Maynooth; UCD
Occ. Full-time public representative. Formerly secondary school teacher

Previously senator 1989-92. TD 1992-97. Member, Dublin City Council since 1991; City of Dublin VEC since 1991; Prisoners' Rights Organisation 1973-87 (chairman 1975-85).

Camillus Glynn (FF)

Address Newbrook Road, Clonmore, Mullingar, Co Westmeath
Tel. (044) 40116
b. Westmeath. October 1941
m. Margaret Fallon. 2s, 2d
Educ. St Mary's CBS, Mullingar; St Loman's Nursing School
Occ. Public representative. Formerly psychiatric nurse; substance abuse therapist

New senator. Member, Westmeath CC since 1979 (chairman 1988/89 and 1993/94); Mullingar TC since 1979 (chairman 1990/91); Association of Municipal Authorities of Ireland (president 1989/90); LAMA.

Michael Finneran (FF)

Address Feevagh, Taughmaconnell, Co Roscommon
Tel. (0903) 22245
b. Roscommon. September 1947
m. Elizabeth Walsh. 2s, 2d
Educ. Summerhill College, Sligo
Occ. Health Board officer

Senator since 1989. Member, Roscommon CC since 1979. WHB since 1985.

Tony Kett (FF)

Address 54 Whitethorn Road, Dublin 5
Tel. (01) 831 8821
b. Ballinasloe, Co Galway. June 1951
m. Noreen Kilkenny. 1s, 2d
Educ. St Joseph's College, Garbally Park, Ballinasloe; College of Commerce, Rathmines, Dublin
Occ. Administrator, Central Remedial Clinic, Dublin

New senator. Member, Dublin City Council since 1988 when he was co-opted to fill the vacancy following the retirement of Bertie Ahern, then Minister for Labour.

Joe Doyle (FG)

Address 14 Simmonscourt
Terrace, Donnybrook, Dublin 4
Tel. (01) 269 2391
b. Dublin. June 1936
m. Peggy Maguire. 2s, 1d
Educ. CBS, Westland Row; UCD
(DPA)
Occ. Full-time public rep

Senator 1987-89 and since 1992.
TD for Dublin South-East Nov
1982-87 and 1989-92. Member,
Dublin City Council since 1979.
EHB since 1991. Member, British-
Irish Parliamentary Body 1993-97.

Fintan Coogan (FG)

Address Menlo Park, Galway
Tel. (091) 764282
b. Galway. June 1944
m. Carol Clarke. 1s, 3d
Educ. St Joseph's College,
Galway; UCG
Occ. College lecturer

New senator. TD for Galway
West 1982-87. Member, Galway
County Borough Council since
1988 (Mayor 1994/95); Galway
CC 1988-91.

Fergus O'Dowd (FG)

Address 24 St Mary's Villas,
Drogheda, Co Louth
Tel. (041) 33392;
Mobile (087) 235 2920
b. Thurles, Co Tipperary.
September 1948
m. Agnes Thornton. 3s
Educ. Drogheda CBS
Occ. Full-time public
representative. Formerly teacher

New senator. Member, Louth CC
since 1979; Drogheda
Corporation since 1974 (Mayor
1977/78, 1981/82, 1994/95).
North-Eastern Health Board.
Founding chairman, Droichead
Arts Centre, Drogheda.

Taoiseach's Nominees

Nominated (11 Seats)

Enda Bonner	FF
Frank Chambers	FF
John Dardis	PD
Tom Fitzgerald	FF
Dermot Fitzpatrick	FF
Jim Gibbons	PD
Edward Haughey	FF
Maurice Hayes	Ind
Helen Keogh	PD
Ann Leonard	FF
Máirín Quill	PD

Enda Bonner (FF)

Address Gweedore Road, Dungloe, Co Donegal
Tel. (074) 21722
b. Dungloe. October 1949
m. Phyllis Collins. 1s, 2d
Educ. Franciscan College, Gormanstown; St Eunan's College, Letterkenny; UCG (BComm)
Occ. Accountant in practice. Senior Partner in Bonner, O'Donnell & Co, Accountants and Registered Auditors

New senator. Fianna Fáil candidate, Donegal South-West, 1997 general election. Fianna Fáil National Executive since 1991.

Frank Chambers (FF)

Address Main St, Newport, Co Mayo
Tel. (098) 41145; *Fax* (098) 41777
b. Newport. March 1949
m. Philomena Browne. 2s, 2d
Educ. Newport Secondary School
Occ. Auctioneer and farmer

New senator. Mayo CC since 1976. Former chairman, Mayo Arts Advisory Council. Former director of Ara Mhara Teo.

John Dardis (PD)

Address Belmont House, Newbridge, Co Kildare
Tel. (045) 431665
b. Newbridge. July 1945
m. Beatrice Lane. 1s, 2d
Educ. Dominican College, Newbridge; UCD (BAgrSc)
Occ. Farmer, agricultural journalist. Public representative

Senator, Agricultural Panel since 1993, Taoiseach's Nominee 1989-93. PD candidate for Leinster, European Elections 1989, 1994; for Kildare, general election 1992; for Kildare South, general election 1997. Kildare CC since 1991.

Tom Fitzgerald (FF)

Address Ballinaboola, Dingle, Co Kerry
Tel. *H* (066) 51543
b. Tralee, Kerry. March 1939
m. Bridget O'Dowd. 2s, 1d
Educ. Cloonacurra, Lispole NS
Occ. Full-time public representative. Formerly fisherman

Senator 1981-83 and since 1987. Asst Chief Whip to the Fianna Fáil Group in last Seanad and spokesperson on the Marine 1995-97. Kerry CC 1974-85 (chairman 1979/80).

Dermot Fitzpatrick (FF)

Address 80 Navan Road, Dublin 7
Tel. (01) 838 7515
b. Dublin. April 1940
m. Mary Wallace. 1s, 3d
Educ. Coláiste Mhuire, Dublin; UCD (MB, BCh, BAO, BDS)
Occ. Family doctor

Dáil deputy, Dublin Central, 1987-89. Dublin Corporation since 1985, Alderman. Former member, Eastern Health Board.

Jim Gibbons (PD)

Address St Anne's, Athy Road, Carlow
Tel. *H* (0503) 43657; *Fax* (0503) 33383
b. Dunmore, Co Kilkenny. April 1954
m. Sonia MacMahon. 3s, 1d
Educ. Cistercian College, Roscrea; UCD (BAgrSc, MSc)
Occ. Landscape architect

New senator. Candidate for PDs in Carlow-Kilkenny 1997. Son of Jim Gibbons, TD and Minister. Brother of Martin Gibbons, TD 1987-89.

Edward Haughey (FF)

Address Ballyedmond Castle, Rostrevor, Co Down
Tel. (016937) 38706; *Fax* (016937) 38749; *O* (01693) 69824
Occ. Company director

Member of last Seanad, Taoiseach's Nominee. Chairman of Norbrook Laboratories and Norbrook Holdings. He is a director of Bombardier Shorts plc, Bank of Ireland Management (NI). He was a member of the Forum for Peace and Reconciliation. DBA, OBE

Maurice Hayes (Ind)

Educ. Queen's University, Belfast; University of Dublin and National University of Ireland Hon. degrees
Occ. Writer, author, commentator

New Senator. Former Northern Ireland Ombudsman; retired Northern Ireland civil servant; member, Board of Independent Newspapers plc and Chairman of Ireland Funds. Member of Senate of Queen's University; Governor of Linenhall Library; former chairman of Northern Ireland Community Relations Council.

Helen Keogh (PD)

Address 12 Beech Court, Killiney, Co Dublin
Tel. (01) 285 8433
b. Dublin. June 1951
m. Paddy Hayes. 2d
Educ. Loreto Convent, Beaufort, Rathfarnham; UCD (BA, HDipEd, Dip Career Guidance Counselling)
Occ. Public representative

Dáil deputy (Dún Laoghaire) 1992-97. Senator 1989-92 (Taoiseach's Nominee). Former PD Chief Whip in Dáil. Dún Laoghaire Borough Corp and Dublin CC 1991-93; Dún Laoghaire-Rathdown CC since 1993. Pres, WPA 1985/86.

Ann Leonard (FF)

Address Stranagarvagh, Smithsboro, Co Monaghan
Tel. (047) 57020
b. Smithsboro. January 1969
Educ. St Louis Sec. School, Monaghan; Our Lady's Hosp. for Sick Children, Crumlin; Irish Institute of Reflexologists; Rotunda Hosp.; The Missionary Training Hosp., Drogheda;
Occ. Paediatric nurse

New Senator. Fianna Fáil candidate, Cavan-Monaghan, 1997. Daughter of Jimmy Leonard, former TD.

Máirín Quill (PD)

Address 1 Wellesley Terrace, Wellington Road, Cork
Tel. (021) 502099
b. Kilgarvan, Co Kerry. Sept 1936
Educ. St Mary's College, Mountmellick; Mary Immaculate College of Education, Limerick; UCC (BA, HDipEd)
Occ. Full-time public representative. Formerly secondary school teacher

Dáil deputy, Cork North-Central 1987-97. Founder member of Progressive Democrats. Cork Corp since 1979, Alderwoman 1985-91. Former chairperson of Prog Dem Parl Party.

University of Dublin

Elected (3 Seats)

David Norris (Ind)*   1st Count
Mary Henry (Ind)*   5th Count
Shane Ross (Ind)*   6th Count

Electorate	31,210
Total Poll	13,383
Spoiled Votes	9
Valid Poll	13,374
Quota	3,344

First Count

Ivana Bacik	885
Seán Barrett	1,491
Brian Caul	149
Mary Henry	2,410
Nigel Hutson	74
Prabhu Kulkarni	218
David Martin	345
Henry Mountcharles	461
David Norris	4,866
Shane Ross	2,475

Mary Henry (Ind)

Address 12 Burlington Road, Dublin 4
Tel. *H* (01) 6683663; *B* (01) 6602532
b. Cork. May 1940
m. John McEntagart. 2s, 1d
Educ. Rochelle School, Cork; Alexandra College, Dublin; TCD (MD, MB, BCh, MA)
Occ. Medical practitioner

Senator since 1993. Member, Comhairle na nOspidéal since 1992. President, Cherish. Board member, Well Woman Centre. Former member, EHB. Member, Rape Crisis Centre.

David Norris (Ind)

Address 18 North Gt George's Street, Dublin 1
Tel. *H* (01) 8724614; *B* (01) 6772941
b. Leopoldville, Belgian Congo. July 1944
Educ. St Andrew's College; High School, Dublin; TCD (BA [Mod])
Occ. Former university lecturer

Senator since 1987. Member, Irish Council for Civil Liberties. Chairman, Campaign for Homosexual Law Reform. Chairman, North Great George's Street, Dublin, Preservation Society since 1979. Chairman, Board of James Joyce Cultural Centre.

Shane Ross (Ind)

Address Askefield House, Dublin Road, Bray, Co Wicklow
Tel. *H* (01) 282 1896
b. Dublin. July 1949
m. Ruth Buchanan. 1s, 1d
Educ. Rugby School; TCD (BA [Mod])
Occ. Business editor, national paper. Former stockbroker

Senator since 1981. Member, Wicklow CC since 1991. Son of Senator John N. Ross (Univ of Dublin panel).

National University of Ireland

Elected (3 Seats)

Joe O'Toole (Ind)*   6th Count
Feargal Quinn (Ind)*   6th Count
Brendan Ryan (Ind)   7th Count

Electorate	93,309
Total Poll	34,102
Spoiled Votes	24
Valid Poll	34,078
Quota	8,520

First Count

William Binchy	6,736
Tommy Francis	3,111
Ann Mary Ó Cléirigh	873
Linda O'Shea Farren	1,601
Joe O'Toole	7,492
Brendan Price	444
Feargal Quinn	6,964
Brendan Ryan	5,885
Eamon Ryan	972

Feargal Quinn (Ind)

Address Sutton Cross, Dublin 13
Tel. (01) 832 5700
b. Dublin. 1936
m. Denise Prendergast. 3s, 2d
Educ. Newbridge College; UCD (BComm)
Occ. Supermarket chain owner

Senator since 1993. Former chairman of An Post, Irish Management Inst, Irish Quality Assoc, Finance Comm of Dublin Archdiocese. Governor, Dublin Skin and Cancer Hospital since 1972.

Joe O'Toole (Ind)

Address Kilsallaghan, Co Dublin
Tel. *H* (01) 835 1338
b. Dingle, Co Kerry. July 1947
m. Joan Lynam. 2s, 3d
Educ. CBS, Dingle; St Patrick's Teachers' Training College, Dublin; Maynooth College; UCD (BA, HDipEd)
Occ. General secretary, INTO. Formerly teacher

Senator since 1987. General secretary, INTO since 1992; Executive Council member, ICTU.

Brendan Ryan (Ind)

Address 16 The Orchards, Middle Glanmire Road, Cork
Tel. (021) 502213
b. Athy, Co Kildare. August 1946
m. Clare O'Connell. 1s, 2d
Educ. Athy CBS; St Patrick's Seminary, Roscommon; UCD (BE)
Occ. Lecturer in Chemical Engineering, Cork RTC

Previously senator 1981-93, National University of Ireland Panel. Chairman, Cork Simon Community 1975-80; now president. Member, Cork Council of Trade Unions 1980-81. Vice-president, Irish Campaign for Nuclear Disarmament.

Dublin South-Central (9 June 1994)

The Dublin South-Central by-election was caused by the resignation of John O'Connell (FF) on 24 February 1993. The seat was won by Eric Byrne (DL) on the ninth count.

Voting		%
Electorate	62,300	
Valid Poll	26,775	42.98
Quota	13,388	

1st Count		%
Byrne, Eric (DL)	**7,445**	**25.56**
Connolly, Joe (Lab)	2,643	9.08
Cooney, Benny (Ind)	152	0.52
Gavin, Éamonn (Ind)	972	3.34
Gibney, Martina (SF)	781	2.68
Goodwillie, John (GP)	1,752	6.02
Hayes, Brian (FG)	4,637	15.92
Keane, Cáit (PD)	1,881	6.46
Kelly, Shay (WP)	595	2.04
Mulcahy, Michael (FF)	5,642	19.37
Park, Michael (Ind)	275	0.94

Mayo West (9 June 1994)

The Mayo West by-election was caused by the resignation on 4 January 1993 of Pádraig Flynn (FF) on his appointment as European Commissioner. The seat was won by Michael Ring (FG) on the second count.

Voting		%
Electorate	45,932	
Valid Poll	29,123	63.40
Quota	14,562	

1st Count		%
Cooper-Flynn, Beverley (FF)	10,967	37.66
Cowley, Jerry (Ind)	388	1.33
McGuinness, Paddy (Ind)	6,275	21.55
Mee, Johnny (Lab)	1,103	3.79
Ring, Michael (FG)	**10,390**	**35.68**

Cork North-Central (10 November 1994)

The Cork North-Central by-election was caused by the death of Gerry O'Sullivan (Lab). The seat was won by Kathleen Lynch (DL) on the eighth count.

Voting		%
Electorate	70,142	
Valid Poll	37,348	53.25
Quota	18,675	

1st Count		%
Burke, Colm (FG)	6,035	20.72
Burns, Michael (PD)	1,628	5.59
Duffy, Gerry (Ind)	426	1.46
Homan, Jimmy (WP)	1,082	3.72
Kelleher, Billy (FF)	9,528	32.72
Luck, Nora Anne (NLP)	162	0.56
Lynch, Kathleen (DL)	**9,843**	**33.80**
O'Leary, Con (Ind)	1,036	3.56
O'Leary, Don (SF)	1,304	4.48
O'Leary, Donie (Ind)	445	1.53
O'Sullivan, Lisa (Lab)	4,003	13.75
Power, Jane (GP)	1,856	6.37

Cork South-Central (10 November 1994)

The Cork South-Central by-election was caused by the resignation of Pat Cox (Ind – elected as PD). The seat was won by Hugh Coveney (FG) on the sixth count.

Voting		%
Electorate	78,420	
Valid Poll	42,134	53.73
Quota	21,068	

1st Count		%
Boyle, Dan (GP)	6,677	22.93
Coveney, Hugh (FG)	**13,128**	**45.08**
Dennehy, John (FF)	13,316	45.72
Ellard, Alan (PD)	1,719	5.90
Kelly, Catherine (CSP)	1,704	5.85
McCarthy, Seán (WP)	813	2.79
McEnery, Brian George (NLP)	219	0.75
O'Flynn, Joe (Lab)	1,940	6.66
Ryan, Brendan (Ind)	2,618	8.99

Wicklow (29 June 1995)

The Wicklow by-election was caused by the death of Johnny Fox (Ind). The seat was won by his daughter, Mildred Fox (Ind), on the eighth count.

Voting		%
Electorate	81,525	
Valid Poll	43,589	53.47
Quota	21,795	

1st Count		%
Collins, Tim (Lab)	5,064	17.39
Fox, Mildred (Ind)	**11,724**	**40.26**
Garrett, Desmond (NLP)	104	0.36
Hayes, Frank (WP)	211	0.72
Honan, Tom (FG)	5,503	18.90
Keddy, Charlie (Ind)	254	0.87
Kelly, Nicky (Ind)	4,556	15.64
McManus, John (DL)	2,841	9.76
Philips, Susan (Ind)	1,627	5.59
Roche, Dick (FF)	10,060	34.54
Singleton, Emer (GP)	1,565	5.37
Tallon, Jim (Ind)	80	0.27

Donegal North-East (2 April 1996)

The Donegal North-East by-election was caused by the death of Neil T. Blaney (Ind). The seat was won by Cecilia Keaveney (FF) on the fourth count.

Voting		%
Electorate	50,443	
Valid Poll	30,625	60.71
Quota	15,313	

1st Count		%
Blaney, Harry (Ind)	8,943	30.71
Doherty, Pat (SF)	2,340	8.03
Keaveney, Cecilia (FF)	**9,872**	**33.90**
Maloney, Seán (Lab)	3,791	13.02
Sheridan, Jim (FG)	5,679	19.50

Dublin West (2 April 1996)

The Dublin West by-election was caused by the death of Brian Lenihan (FF). The seat was won by his son, Brian Lenihan (FF), on the eleventh count.

Voting		%
Electorate	65,534	
Valid Poll	28,410	43.35
Quota	14,206	

1st Count		%
Casey, Gerard (CSP)	768	2.64
Cooney, Benny (Ind)	21	0.07
Gogarty, Paul (GP)	1,286	4.42
Higgins, Joe (Ind)	6,743	23.15
Jackson, Vincent Ballyfermot (Ind)	1,131	3.88
Lenihan, Brian (FF)	**6,995**	**24.02**
Lyons, Seán (Ind)	514	1.76
McCann, John (SF)	1,574	5.40
Mac Giolla, Tomás (WP)	2,909	9.99
Morrissey, Tom (FG)	3,728	12.80
O'Donovan, Michael (Lab)	1,058	3.63
O'Halloran, John (Ind)	369	1.27
Terry, Sheila (PD)	1,314	4.51

The Cabinet appointed 15 December 1994

FROM LEFT TO RIGHT

Seated: Mervyn Taylor (Minister for Equality and Law Reform), Ruairí Quinn (Minister for Finance), John Bruton (Taoiseach), (President Mary Robinson), Dick Spring (Tánaiste and Minister for Foreign Affairs), Michael Noonan (Minister for Health), Michael D. Higgins (Minister for Arts, Culture and the Gaeltacht).

Standing: Dermot Gleeson (Attorney General), Hugh Coveney (Minister for Defence and Minister for the Marine), Enda Kenny (Minister for Tourism and Trade), Richard Bruton (Minister for Enterprise and Employment), Proinsias De Rossa (Minister for Social Welfare), Nora Owen (Minister for Justice), Niamh Bhreathnach (Minister for Education), Brendan Howlin (Minister for the Environment), Michael Lowry (Minister for Transport, Energy and Communications), Ivan Yates (Minister for Agriculture, Food and Forestry), Seán Barrett (Chief Whip), Pat Rabbitte (Minister of State to the Government).

The Rainbow Coalition Government (15 December 1994 - 26 June 1997)

Taoiseach	John Bruton
Tánaiste and Minister for Foreign Affairs	Dick Spring
Minister for Finance	Ruairí Quinn
Minister for Health	Michael Noonan
Minister for Equality and Law Reform	Mervyn Taylor
Minister for Arts, Culture and the Gaeltacht	Michael D. Higgins
Minister for the Environment	Brendan Howlin
Minister for Education	Niamh Bhreathnach
Minister for Justice	Nora Owen
Minister for Social Welfare	Proinsias De Rossa
Minister for Tourism and Trade	Enda Kenny
Minister for Enterprise and Employment	Richard Bruton
Minister for Agriculture, Food and Forestry	Ivan Yates
Minister for Transport, Energy and Communications	Michael Lowry (to 30.11.96; resigned) Alan Dukes (from 3.12.96)
Minister for Defence and Minister for the Marine	Hugh Coveney (to 23.5.95; resigned) Seán Barrett (from 23.5.95)
Attorney General	Dermot Gleeson

Ministers of State in the Rainbow Coalition Government 1994-97

The Ministers of State were appointed on 20 December 1994

Seán Barrett	Taoiseach and Defence: Chief Whip, 20.12.94 - 23.5.95, when he was appointed Minister for Defence and Minister for the Marine
Pat Rabbitte	Government and Enterprise and Employment: Commerce, Technology and Consumer Affairs
Emmet Stagg	Transport, Energy and Communications: Energy
Brian O'Shea	Health: Mental Handicap, Health Promotion, Food Safety and Public Health
Eithne Fitzgerald	Office of Tánaiste, Enterprise and Employment: Labour Affairs
Joan Burton	Foreign Affairs and Justice: Overseas Development Aid
Toddy O'Sullivan	Tourism and Trade
Gay Mitchell	Taoiseach, Foreign Affairs: Local Affairs, European Affairs
Bernard Allen	Education, Environment: Youth and Sport, Local Government Reform, Urban Traffic Management
Bernard Durkan	Social Welfare: Integration of the Taxation and Social Welfare Codes, Customer Information Programmes
Jimmy Deenihan	Agriculture, Food and Forestry: Rural Development, the LEADER Programme, An Bord Bia, the Food Industry
Phil Hogan	Finance: Public Expenditure, Office of Public Works, 20.12.94 - 9.2.95 (resigned)
Jim Higgins	Finance: Office of Public Works (10.2.95 - 23.5.95); Taoiseach and Defence: Chief Whip (from 24.5.95)
Hugh Coveney	Finance: Office of Public Works, Cabinet Budget Committee, Ministerial Team for Peace Process (from 24.5.95)
Austin Currie	Health, Education and Justice: Child Care, Children's Policy, Special Education
Éamon Gilmore	Marine: Port Development, the Law of the Sea
Liz McManus	Environment: Housing and Urban Renewal
Avril Doyle	Taoiseach, Finance, Transport, Energy and Communications: Strategic Management Initiative in the Public Service, Consumer Guarantee Programmes in the Public Service and Famine Commemoration from 27.1.95
Donal Carey	Taoiseach, Arts, Culture and the Gaeltacht: Gaeltacht, Western Development from 27.1.95

The Government held office from 15 December 1994 to 26 June 1997. It was a three-party Coalition of Fine Gael, Labour and Democratic Left (the Rainbow Coalition). Hugh Coveney resigned as Minister for Defence and Minister for the Marine on 23 May 1995 and was replaced by Seán Barrett on the same day. Michael Lowry resigned as Minister for Transport, Energy and Communications on 30 November 1996 and was replaced by Alan Dukes on 3 December 1996. The portfolio was held by the Taoiseach, John Bruton, 30 November to 3 December 1996.

Constitutional Referenda 1937-97

Date	Subject	Electorate	Total Poll	%	Spoiled Votes	%	Total Valid Poll	%	Yes Votes	%	No Votes	%	% of Elect. Yes	% of Elect. No
1/7/37	Plebiscite	1,775,055	1,346,207	75.8	134,157	10.0	1,212,050	68.3	685,105	56.5	526,945	43.5	38.6	29.7
17/6/59	Straight Vote	1,678,450	979,531	58.4	39,220	4.0	940,311	56.0	453,322	48.2	486,989	51.8	27.0	29.0
16/10/68	Formation of Dáil Consts	1,717,389	1,129,477	65.8	48,489	4.3	1,080,988	62.9	424,185	39.2	656,803	60.8	24.7	38.2
16/10/68	Straight Vote	1,717,389	1,129,606	65.8	48,212	4.3	1,081,394	63.0	423,496	39.2	657,898	60.8	24.7	38.3
10/5/72	EEC Membership	1,783,604	1,264,278	70.9	10,497	0.8	1,253,781	70.3	1,041,890	83.1	211,891	16.9	58.4	11.9
7/12/72	Voting Age	1,783,604	903,439	50.7	47,089	5.2	856,350	48.0	724,836	84.6	131,514	15.4	40.6	7.4
7/12/72	Position of RC Church	1,783,604	903,669	50.7	49,326	5.5	854,343	47.9	721,003	84.4	133,340	15.6	40.4	7.5
5/7/79	Adoption	2,179,466	623,476	28.6	15,517	2.5	607,959	27.9	601,694	99.0	6,265	1.0	27.6	0.3
5/7/79	Seanad University Seats	2,179,466	622,646	28.6	24,562	3.9	598,084	27.4	552,600	92.4	45,484	7.6	25.4	2.1
7/9/83	Protection of Unborn	2,358,651	1,265,994	53.7	8,625	0.7	1,257,369	53.3	841,233	66.9	416,136	33.1	35.7	17.6
14/6/84	Voting for Non-citizens	2,399,257	1,138,895	47.5	40,162	3.5	1,098,733	45.8	828,483	75.4	270,250	24.6	34.5	11.3
26/6/86	Divorce	2,436,836	1,482,644	60.8	8,522	0.6	1,474,122	60.5	538,279	36.5	935,843	63.5	22.1	38.4
24/5/87	Single European Act	2,461,790	1,085,304	44.1	4,904	0.5	1,080,400	43.9	755,423	69.9	324,977	30.1	30.7	13.2
18/6/92	Maastricht Treaty	2,542,840	1,457,219	57.3	7,488	0.5	1,449,731	57.0	1,001,076	69.1	448,655	30.9	39.4	17.6
25/11/92	Right to Life	2,542,841	1,733,309	68.2	81,835	4.7	1,651,474	64.9	572,177	34.6	1,079,297	65.4	22.5	42.4
25/11/92	Travel	2,542,841	1,733,821	68.2	74,454	4.3	1,659,367	65.3	1,035,308	62.4	624,059	37.6	40.7	24.5
25/11/92	Information	2,542,841	1,732,433	68.1	74,494	4.3	1,657,939	65.2	992,833	59.9	665,106	40.1	39.0	26.2
24/11/95	Divorce	2,628,834	1,633,942	62.2	5,372	0.3	1,628,570	62.0	818,842	50.3	809,728	49.7	31.1	30.8
28/11/96	Bail	2,659,895	777,586	29.2	2,878	0.4	774,708	29.1	579,740	74.8	194,968	25.2	21.8	7.3

Fine Gael Front Bench
(Appointed September 1997)

Leader and Northern Ireland: John Bruton, TD
Deputy Leader, Enterprise, Trade and Employment: Nora Owen, TD
Finance: Michael Noonan, TD
Whip: Seán Barrett, TD
Public Enterprise and Fine Gael Policy Development: Ivan Yates, TD
Justice, Equality and Law Reform: Jim Higgins, TD
Foreign Affairs: Gay Mitchell, TD
Agriculture and Food: Hugh Coveney, TD
Defence and Promotion of Women within Fine Gael: Frances Fitzgerald, TD
Environment and Local Government: Alan Dukes, TD
Social, Community and Family Affairs: Jim O'Keeffe, TD
Arts, Heritage, Gaeltacht and the Islands: Enda Kenny, TD
Health and Children: Alan Shatter, TD
Tourism, Sport and Recreation: Bernard Allen, TD
Marine and Natural Resources: Michael Finucane, TD
Education, Science and Technology, Relations with the Social Partners: Richard Bruton, TD
Parliamentary Party Chairman, Organisational Development and Preparation for Local Elections: Phil Hogan, TD

Fine Gael Junior Spokespersons
(Appointed September 1997)

Criminal Law Reform, Northern Ireland, Party Leader on British-Irish Parliamentary Body: Charles Flanagan, TD
Aquaculture and Forestry, Assistant Whip: P.J. Sheehan, TD
Equity and Disabilities: Theresa Ahearn, TD
Health - Food Safety and Older People: Paul Bradford, TD
Islands, Gaeltacht and Western Development: Donal Carey, TD
Environmental Information and Protection: Deirdre Clune, TD
Agriculture - Food: Paul Connaughton, TD
Energy: Austin Currie, TD
Office of Public Works: Jimmy Deenihan, TD
Overseas Development Assistance and Human Rights: Bernard Durkan, TD
Housing, House Prices, Urban Renewal: Brian Hayes, TD
Local Development, National Drugs Strategy, Dublin Traffic: Olivia Mitchell, TD
Adult Education, Youth Affairs and School Transport, Liaison with Young Fine Gael and Promotion of Young People within Fine Gael: Denis Naughten, TD
Children: Dan Neville, TD
Science, Technology, Small Business and Enterprise, Border Counties: John Perry, TD
Agriculture - Livestock Breeding and Horticulture: Michael Ring, TD
Labour Affairs, Consumer Rights and Trade: David Stanton, TD
Defence, Peacekeeping and Humanitarian Relief: Billy Timmins, TD

Labour Party Spokespersons
(Appointed July 1997)

Foreign Affairs and Northern Ireland: Dick Spring, TD
Finance: Ruairí Quinn, TD
Environment: Brendan Howlin, TD
Equality and Law Reform: Breeda Moynihan-Cronin, TD
Agriculture: Willie Penrose, TD
Natural Resources: Michael Ferris, TD
Health and Children: Derek McDowell, TD
Science and Technology, Consumer Affairs: Pat Upton, TD
Public Enterprise: Emmet Stagg, TD
Enterprise and Employment: Tommy Broughan, TD
Arts and Heritage: Jim Kemmy, TD
Defence: Brian O'Shea, TD
Tourism, Sport and Recreation: Jack Wall, TD
Education, Gaeltacht and the Islands: Michael D. Higgins, TD
Justice: Róisín Shortall, TD
Social Welfare: Michael Bell, TD

Democratic Left Spokespersons
(Appointed July 1997)

Taoiseach, Foreign Affairs, Social, Community and Family Affairs, Defence: Proinsias De Rossa, TD
Enterprise, Trade and Employment, Finance, Education, Tourism and Sport: Pat Rabbitte, TD
Environment, Marine, Agriculture and Public Enterprise: Éamon Gilmore, TD
Health and Children, Justice, Equality and Law Reform, Arts, Heritage, Gaeltacht and the Islands: Liz McManus, TD

General Elections 1923-97 (Party Seats and % of First-Preference Votes)

Year of Election	Total Seats	Fianna Fáil (Anti-Treaty to 1927)		Fine Gael (Cumann na nGaedheal to 1937)		Labour		Farmers, Clann na Talm-han	Other Parties* and Inde-pendents	Government	Taoiseach (President of Executive Council to 1937)
		Seats	% Votes	Seats	% Votes	Seats	% Votes	Seats	Seats		
1923	153	44	27.6	63	38.9	14	12.4	15	17	C na nG	W.T. Cosgrave
June 1927	153	44	26.1	47§	27.5	22	13.8	11	29	C na nG	W.T. Cosgrave
Sept 1927	153	57	35.2	62§	38.7	13	9.5	6	15	C na nG	W.T. Cosgrave
1932	153	72	44.5	57§	35.3	7	7.7	4	13	FF	E. de Valera
1933	153	77§	49.7	48	30.5	8	5.7	—	20	FF	E. de Valera
1937	138	69§	45.2	48	34.8	13	10.3	—	8	FF	E. de Valera
1938	138	77§	51.9	45	33.3	9	10.0	—	7	FF	E. de Valera
1943	138	67§	41.9	32	23.1	17	15.7	14	8	FF	E. de Valera
1944	138	76§	48.9	30	20.5	12§§	11.5	11	9	FF	E. de Valera
1948	147	68§	41.9	31	19.8	19	11.3	7	22	Inter-Party	J.A. Costello
1951	147	69§	46.3	40	25.7	16	11.4	6	16	FF	E. de Valera
1954	147	65	43.4	50	32.0	19§	12.0	5	8	Inter-Party	J.A. Costello
1957	147	78	48.3	40	26.6	12§	9.1	3	14	FF	E. de Valera to 1959 S. Lemass
1961	144	70	43.8	47	32.0	16§	11.6	2	9	FF	S. Lemass
1965	144	72	47.8	47	33.9	22§	15.4	—	3	FF	S. Lemass to 1966 J. Lynch
1969	144	75§	45.7	50	34.1	18	17.0	—	1	FF	J. Lynch
1973	144	69§	46.2	54	35.1	19	13.7	—	2	Coalit. (FG/Lab)	L. Cosgrave
1977	148	84	50.6	43	30.5	17§	11.6	—	4	FF	J. Lynch to 1979 C.J. Haughey
1981	166	78§	45.3	65	36.5	15	9.9	—	7	Coalit. (FG/Lab)	G. FitzGerald
Feb 1982	166	81	47.3	63	37.3	15	9.1	—	4§	FF	C.J. Haughey
Nov 1982	166	75	45.2	70	39.2	16	9.4	—	3§	Coalit. (FG/Lab)	G. FitzGerald
1987	166	81	44.2	51§	27.1	12	6.4	—	4	FF	C.J. Haughey
1989	166	77	44.2	55	29.3	15	9.5	—	6§	Coalit. (FF/PD)	C.J. Haughey to 1992 A. Reynolds
1992	166	68	39.1	45	24.5	33	19.3	—	6§	Coalit. (FF/Lab) to 1994 Coalit. (FG/Lab/DL)	A. Reynolds to 1994 J. Bruton
1997	166	77	39.3	54	28.0	17	10.4	—	18	FF/PD	B. Ahern

*Other parties:

1927 (June):	National League 8, Sinn Féin 5
1927 (Sept):	National League 2
1933:	Centre Party 11, later merged with Fine Gael
1948:	Clann na Poblachta 10
1951:	Clann na Poblachta 2
1954:	Clann na Poblachta 3
1957:	Sinn Féin 4, Clann na Poblachta 1
1961:	National Progressive Democrats 2, Clann na Poblachta 1
1981:	SFWP 1, SLP 1
1982 (Feb):	SFWP 3
1982 (Nov):	WP 2
1987:	PD 14, WP 4, DSP 1
1989:	WP 7, PD 6, DSP 1
1992:	PD 10, DL 4
1997:	PD 4, DL 4, GP 2, SF 1, SP 1

§ includes outgoing Ceann Comhairle returned without contest
§§ includes National Labour 4. In 1943 Labour divided into Labour and National Labour.

Fianna Fáil

Áras de Valera
13 Upper Mount Street
Dublin 2
Tel. (01) 676 1551
Fax (01) 678 5690

General Secretary Pat Farrell

Fine Gael

51 Upper Mount Street
Dublin 2
Tel. (01) 676 1573
Fax (01) 662 5046

General Secretary Jim Miley

The Labour Party

17 Ely Place
Dublin 2
Tel. (01) 661 2615
Fax (01) 661 2640

General Secretary Ray Kavanagh

Progressive Democrats

25 South Frederick Street
Dublin 2
Tel. (01) 679 4399
Fax (01) 679 4757

General Secretary Garvan McGinley

Democratic Left

69 Middle Abbey Street
Dublin 1
Tel. (01) 872 9700
Fax (01) 872 9238

General Secretary John Gallagher

The Green Party/Comhaontas Glas

51 Upper Fownes Street
Dublin 2
Tel. (01) 679 0012
Fax (01) 679 7168

Co-ordinator Mary Bowers

Natural Law Party

39 Pembroke Lane
Ballsbridge
Dublin 4
Tel. (01) 874 1133
Fax (01) 668 1513

Chairman Thomas Mullins

Sinn Féin

44 Parnell Square
Dublin 1
Tel. (01) 872 6932
Fax (01) 873 3441

General Secretary Lucilita Bhreatnach

The Workers' Party

86 Parnell Street
Dublin 1
Tel. (01) 874 0716
Fax (01) 874 8702

General Secretary Pat Quearney

Comhar Críostaí/The Christian Solidarity Party

54a Booterstown Avenue
Blackrock
Co Dublin
Tel. (01) 288 0273
Fax (01) 299 0420

National Secretary Patrick D. Smyth

National Party

16 Revington Park
North Circular Road
Limerick
Tel. (061) 364172
Fax (061) 364114

National Secretary Maureen Normoyle

Socialist Party

141 Thomas Street
Dublin 8
Tel. (01) 677 2592

General Secretary Dermot Connolly

The Communist Party of Ireland

43 East Essex Street
Dublin 2
Tel. (01) 671 1943

General Secretary James Stewart

The new team: Taoiseach and Tánaiste congratulate each other on the formation of the Fianna Fáil-Progressive Democrats coalition.

The fifth elections to the European Parliament were held in June 1994. The results are summarised on this page and details of the counts in each of the four constituencies are given in the following pages.

Connacht/Ulster

Elected

Pat The Cope Gallagher (FF)
Mark Killilea (FF)*
Joe McCartin (FG)*

	Number	%
Electorate	496,352	
Total Poll	237,601	47.87
Spoiled Votes	4,971	2.09
Valid Poll	232,630	46.87
Seats	3	
Quota	58,158	
Candidates	9	

Voting by Party

1st Pref	Number	%	% 1989
Fianna Fáil	98,809	42.47	32.70
Fine Gael	68,986	29.65	28.00
Labour	19,826	8.52	1.59
Green Party	8,628	3.71	—
Prog Democrats	21,219	9.12	12.96
Sinn Féin	13,939	5.99	4.99
Workers' Party	—	—	2.84
Others	1,223	0.53	16.92

Seats

FF	2
FG	1

FF gain from Ind

Dublin

Elected

Patricia McKenna (GP)
Niall Andrews (FF)*
Mary Banotti (FG)*
Bernie Malone (Lab)*

	Number	%
Electorate	755,486	
Total Poll	280,761	37.16
Spoiled Votes	2,917	1.04
Valid Poll	277,844	36.78
Seats	4	
Quota	55,569	
Candidates	15	

Voting by Party

1st Pref	Number	%	% 1989
Fianna Fáil	57,925	20.85	29.06
Fine Gael	66,169	23.82	17.22
Labour	39,093	14.07	12.76
Green Party	40,388	14.54	8.32
Prog Democrats	8,212	2.96	8.11
Democratic Left	24,133	8.69	—
Sinn Féin	8,190	2.95	2.58
Workers' Party	15,830	5.70	15.84
Others	17,904	6.44	6.06

Seats

FF	1
FG	1
GP	1
Lab	1

GP gain from DL

Leinster

Elected

Liam Hyland (FF)
Alan Gillis (FG)
Jim Fitzsimons (FF)*
Nuala Ahern (GP)

	Number	%
Electorate	624,561	
Total Poll	269,044	43.08
Spoiled Votes	6,599	2.45
Valid Poll	262,445	42.02
Seats	4	
Quota	52,490	
Candidates	12	

Voting by Party

1st Pref	Number	%	% 1989
Fianna Fáil	87,823	33.46	36.92
Fine Gael	72,784	27.73	26.89
Labour	40,567	15.46	13.18
Green Party	30,997	11.81	6.28
Prog Democrats	12,591	4.80	8.37
Sinn Féin	6,523	2.49	2.64
Workers' Party	—	—	4.38
Others	11,160	4.25	1.32

Seats

FF	2
FG	1
GP	1

GP gained added seat

Munster

Elected

Brian Crowley (FF)
Gerard Collins (FF)
John Cushnahan (FG)*
Pat Cox (Ind)*

	Number	%
Electorate	755,176	
Total Poll	369,890	48.98
Spoiled Votes	5,319	1.44
Valid Poll	364,571	48.28
Seats	4	
Quota	72,915	
Candidates	16	

Voting by Party

1st Pref	Number	%	% 1989
Fianna Fáil	153,509	42.11	28.83
Fine Gael	68,156	18.69	17.56
Labour	25,486	6.99	8.86
Green Party	10,033	2.75	—
Prog Democrats	31,674	8.67	17.30
Democratic Left	15,573	4.27	—
Sinn Féin	5,171	1.42	—
Workers' Party	6,270	1.72	5.43
Others	48,699	13.36	22.00

Seats

FF	2
FG	1
Ind	1

PD loss, one seat less

European Parliament Election (June 1994) — Connacht/Ulster

Seats 3
Quota 58,158

	1st Count	2nd Count Transfer of **Douthwaite's** and **Lacey's** Votes	3rd Count Transfer of **Doherty's** Votes	4th Count Transfer of **Molloy's** Votes	5th Count Transfer of **Gallagher's (Ann)** Votes
DOHERTY, Pat (SF)	13,939	+726 14,665	−14,665 —		
DOUTHWAITE, Richard (GP)	8,628	−8,628 —			
GALLAGHER, Ann (Lab)	19,826	+2,369 22,195	+3,108 25,303	+2,572 27,875	
GALLAGHER, Pat The Cope (FF)	53,171	+951 54,122	+3,535 57,657	+1,715 59,372	
HIGGINS, Jim (FG)	30,947	+1,153 32,100	+668 32,768	+4,367 37,135	+5,018 42,153
***KILLILEA**, Mark (FF)	45,638	+807 46,445	+1,055 47,500	+5,530 53,030	+6,743 59,773
LACEY, Mary (NLP)	1,223	−1,223 —			
***McCARTIN**, Joe (FG)	38,039	+822 38,861	+600 39,461	+4,435 43,896	+5,475 49,371
MOLLOY, Bobby (PD)	21,219	+1,565 22,784	+754 23,538	−23,538 —	
NON-TRANSFERABLE		1,458	4,945	4,919	10,639

Seats 4
Quota 55,569

	1st Count	2nd Count Transfer of Burns's Votes	3rd Count Transfer of Madigan's Votes	4th Count Transfer of O'Toole's Votes	5th Count Transfer of Braiden's Votes	6th Count Transfer of O'Byrnes's Votes	7th Count Transfer of Murphy's Votes	8th Count Transfer of Stafford's Votes	9th Count Transfer of MacGiolla's Votes	10th Count Transfer of Guerin's Votes	11th Count Transfer of McKenna's Surplus	12th Count Transfer of Rabbitte's Votes
*ANDREWS, Niall (FF)	36,877	+58 36,935	+618 37,553	+580 38,133	+3,139 41,272	+499 41,771	+1,024 42,795	+10,671 53,466	+1,312 54,778	+2,126 56,904		
*BANOTTI, Mary (FG)	38,053	+107 38,160	+738 38,898	+86 38,984	+873 39,857	+2,142 41,999	+462 42,461	+504 42,965	+874 43,839	+2,682 46,521	+511 47,032	+6,865 53,897
BRAIDEN, Olive (FF)	8,237	+37 8,274	+145 8,419	+154 8,573	−8,573 —							
BURNS, John (NLP)	1,705	−1,705 —										
GUERIN, Orla (Lab)	16,674	+91 16,765	+197 16,962	+341 17,303	+674 17,977	+334 18,311	+216 18,527	+402 18,929	+1,296 20,225	−20,225 —		
Mac GIOLLA, Tómas (WP)	15,830	+135 15,965	+284 16,249	+1089 17,338	+209 17,547	+216 17,763	+448 18,211	+368 18,579	−18,579 —			
McKENNA, Patricia (Green)	40,388	+540 40,928	+1,620 42,548	+2,800 45,348	+710 46,058	+1,493 47,551	+2,448 49,999	+880 50,879	+4,054 54,933	+2,816 57,749	−2,180 55,569	
MADIGAN, Paddy (NP)	6,903	+203 7,106	−7,106 —									
*MALONE, Bernie (Lab)	22,419	+91 22,510	+368 22,878	+515 23,393	+695 24,088	+725 24,813	+444 25,257	+1,012 26,269	+2,479 28,748	+7,976 36,724	+628 37,352	+10,344 47,696
MITCHELL, Jim (FG)	28,116	+64 28,180	+647 28,827	+154 28,981	+262 29,243	+1,461 30,704	+1,495 32,199	+838 33,037	+1,969 35,006	+1,031 36,037	+173 36,210	+5,902 42,112
MURPHY, Éamonn (Ind)	9,296	+89 9,385	+583 9,968	+392 10,360	+71 10,431	+136 10,567	−10,567 —					
O'BYRNES, Stephen (PD)	8,212	+42 8,254	+485 8,739	+89 8,828	+111 8,939	−8,939 —						
O'TOOLE, Larry (SF)	8,190	+38 8,228	+128 8,356	−8,356 —								
RABBITTE, Pat (DL)	24,133	+86 24,219	+426 24,645	+561 25,206	+254 25,460	+1,176 26,636	+418 27,054	+478 27,532	+3,968 31,500	+2,177 33,677	+533 34,210	−34,210 —
STAFFORD, John (FF)	12,811	+27 12,838	+340 13,178	+483 13,661	+1,298 14,959	+211 15,170	+1,179 16,349	−16,349 —				
NON-TRANSFERABLE		97	527	1,112	277	546	2,433	1,196	2,627	1,417	335	11,099

European Parliament Election (June 1994) — Leinster

Seats 4 / Quota 52,490	1st Count	2nd Count — Transfer of **Mullins's** and **Sweetman's** Votes	3rd Count — Transfer of **Bhreathnach's** Votes	4th Count — Transfer of **Fitzsimons's** (Jack) Votes	5th Count — Transfer of **Dardis's** Votes	6th Count — Transfer of **Pattison's** Votes	7th Count — Transfer of **Bell's** Votes
AHERN, Nuala (GP)	30,997	+1,305 / 32,302	+1,547 / 33,849	+1,863 / 35,712	+2,234 / 37,946	+1,351 / 39,297	+6,524 / 45,821
BARNES, Monica (FG)	29,958	+277 / 30,235	+213 / 30,448	+501 / 30,949	+2,743 / 33,692	+1,378 / 35,070	+4,448 / 39,515
BELL, Michael (Lab)	22,987	+199 / 23,186	+629 / 23,815	+627 / 24,442	+924 / 25,366	+9,560 / 34,926	-34,926 / —
BHREATHNACH, Lucilita (SF)	6,523	+104 / 6,627	-6,627 / —				
DARDIS, John (PD)	12,591	+328 / 2,919	+133 / 13,052	+420 / 13,472	-13,472 / —		
FITZSIMONS, Jack (NP)	6,752	+510 / 7,262	+540 / 7,802	-7,802 / —			
***FITZSIMONS**, Jim (FF)	41,375	+236 / 41,611	+905 / 42,516	+1,168 / 43,684	+1,118 / 44,802	+824 / 45,626	+4,637 / 50,263
GILLIS, Alan (FG)	42,826	+330 / 43,156	+190 / 43,346	+447 / 43,793	+3,319 / 47,112	+1,199 / 48,309	+2,587 / 50,896
HYLAND, Liam (FF)	46,448	+289 / 46,737	+518 / 47,255	+983 / 48,238	+998 / 49,236	+2,307 / 51,543	+2,618 / 54,161
MULLINS, Thomas (NLP)	1,180	-1,180 / —					
PATTISON, Séamus (Lab)	17,580	+289 / 17,869	+271 / 18,140	+338 / 18,478	+475 / 18,953	-18,953 / —	
SWEETMAN, Peter (Ind)	3,228	-3,228 / —					
NON-TRANSFERABLE		541	1,681	1,455	1,661	2,336	14,112

Seats 4
Quota 72,915

	1st Count	2nd Count Transfer of Crowley's Surplus	3rd Count Transfer of Riordan's, Moloney's and Luck's Votes	4th Count Transfer of McCarthy's Votes	5th Count Transfer of O'Regan's Votes	6th Count Transfer of Boyle's Votes	7th Count Transfer of Lynch's Votes	8th Count Transfer of Lane's Votes	9th Count Transfer of Bennis's Votes	10th Count Transfer of Collins's Surplus	11th Count Transfer of Kemmy's Votes	12th Count Transfer of Raftery's Votes
BENNIS, Nora (Ind)	18,424	+547 18,971	+321 19,292	+513 19,805	+460 20,265	+1,598 21,863	+2,374 24,237	+745 24,982	−24,982 —			
BOYLE, Dan (GP)	10,033	+289 10,322	+339 10,661	+734 11,395	+576 11,971	−11,971 —						
COLLINS, Gerard (FF)	49,677	+4,722 54,399	+131 54,530	+517 55,047	+475 55,522	+724 56,246	+1,018 57,264	+13,570 70,834	+4,693 75,527	−2,612 72,915		
*COX, Pat (Ind)	27,920	+1,149 29,069	+264 29,333	+408 29,741	+659 30,400	+1,505 31,905	+1,983 33,888	+1,903 35,791	+3,975 39,766	+909 40,675	+7,858 48,533	+3,962 52,495
CROWLEY, Brian (FF)	84,463	−11,548 72,915										
*CUSHNAHAN, John (FG)	36,906	+413 37,319	+129 37,448	+105 37,553	+283 37,836	+652 38,488	+843 39,331	+1,113 40,444	+2,282 42,726	+389 43,115	+3,774 46,889	+25,129 72,018
KEMMY, Jim (Lab)	25,486	+616 26,102	+157 26,259	+444 26,703	+1,139 27,842	+1,606 29,448	+3,707 33,155	+772 33,927	+2,197 36,124	+409 36,533	−36,533 —	
*LANE, Paddy (FF)	19,369	+1,681 21,050	+81 21,131	+299 21,430	+212 21,642	+372 22,014	+334 22,348	−22,348 —				
LUCK, Stewart (NLP)	890	+44 934	−934 —									
LYNCH, Kathleen (DL)	15,573	+554 16,127	+155 16,282	+328 16,610	+706 17,316	+1632 18,948	−18,948 —					
McCARTHY, Kieran (SF)	5,171	+114 5,285	+106 5,391	−5,391 —								
MOLONEY, Conor (Ind)	858	+43 901	−901 —									
O'MALLEY, Des (PD)	31,674	+613 32,287	+153 32,440	+156 32,596	+332 32,928	+988 33,916	+2,041 35,957	+1,221 37,178	+1,987 39,165	+351 39,516	+5,855 45,371	+4,284 49,655
O'REGAN, Martin (WP)	6,270	+97 6,367	+157 6,524	+457 6,981	−6,981 —							
RAFTERY, Tom (FG)	31,250	+646 31,896	+116 32,012	+118 32,130	+268 32,398	+525 32,923	+1,709 34,632	+802 35,434	+2,284 37,718	+314 38,032	+2,649 40,681	−40,681 —
RIORDAN, Denis (Ind)	607	+20 627	−627 —									
NON-TRANSFERABLE		—	353	1,312	1,871	2,369	4,939	2,222	7,564	240	16,397	7,306

EC Commission

The European Commission operates at the very heart of the European Union. Its role as the source of policy initiatives is unique; yet this role is not always clearly understood. The Commission has used its right of initiative to transform the framework provided by the Union's founding treaties into today's integrated structures. The benefits for citizens and companies throughout the Union have been considerable: more freedom to travel and trade, more prosperity, much less red tape.

But the Commission has not done this alone. It works in close partnership with the other European institutions and with the governments of the Member States. Although the Commission makes proposals, all the major decisions on important legislation are made by the ministers of the Member States in the Council of the European Union, after taking account of the advice of (or, in some cases, in codecision with) the democratically elected European Parliament.

The Commission consults widely with interested parties from all sectors and all walks of life when preparing draft legislation. In addition to its power of proposal, the Commission acts as the EU executive body and as guardian of the Treaties.

The Commission represents the common interest and embodies, to a large degree, the personality of the Union. The key theme of the Commission under Mr Jacques Santer is to defend the interests of Europe's citizens. The 20 members of the Commission are drawn from the 15 EU countries, but each one swears an oath of independence, distancing himself or herself from partisan influence from any source.

The Commission's job is to ensure that the European Union can attain its goal of an ever-closer union of its peoples. A principal task is to ensure that goods, services, capital and persons can move freely throughout the territory of the Union. It must see to it too that the benefits of integration are balanced between countries and regions, between business and consumers and between different categories of citizens.

The Commission fulfils three main functions. Because of its right of initiative, the Commission is charged with making proposals for all new legislation. It does so on the basis of what it considers best for the Union and its citizens as a whole rather than on behalf of sectoral interests or individual countries.

The scope of these activities is laid down in the Treaty and ranges from trade, industry and social policies to agriculture, the environment, energy, regional development, external relations, overseas development and others.

Before it issues an item of draft legislation, the Commission carries out extensive preliminary soundings and discussions with representatives of governments, industry, the trade unions, special interest groups and, where necessary, technical experts. It tries to take account of these often competing interests when it prepares its proposals.

In preparing legislation, the Commission also takes account of the prevailing economic, political and social realities. In its initiatives, the Commission takes the principle of subsidiarity into account so that it initiates legislation only in areas where the European Union is better placed than individual Member States to take effective action.

Once a Commission proposal has been submitted to the Council of Ministers and the European Parliament, the three institutions work together to produce a satisfactory result. In agreement with the Commission, the Council can amend a proposal by a qualified majority (if the Commission does not agree, the change requires unanimity) and the Commission is always open to amendments from the European Parliament.

The European Parliament shares the power of codecision with the Council in a number of policy areas and has the right of amendment in others. In revising its proposals, the Commission is bound to take the Parliament's amendments into consideration.

In cases where the Commission can only secure agreement in the Council by making what it considers unacceptable amendments, it may withdraw the proposal rather than accept a bad agreement which is not in the interests of the Union as a whole.

The draft Treaty on the reform of the European Union to prepare the way for enlargement which was agreed in Amsterdam in June 1997 states that at the date of entry into force of the first enlargement of the Union the Commission shall comprise one national of each Member State provided that by that date, the weighting of the votes in the Council has been modified in a manner acceptable to all Member States.

It also states that at least one year before the membership of the European Union exceeds twenty, a conference of the Member States shall be convened to carry out a comprehensive review of the provisions of the Treaties on the composition and functioning of the institutions.

European Commission
Representation in Ireland
European Union House
18 Dawson Street
Dublin 2
Tel. +353-1-6625113
Fax +353-1-6625118
e-mail frank.meates@ireland.dg10-bur.cec.be

Jacques Santer. President. Responsible for Secretariat-General; Legal Service; Security Office; Forward Studies Unit; Inspectorate-General; Joint Interpreting and Conference Service; Spokesman's Service; monetary matters (with Mr de Silguy); common foreign and security policy and human rights (with Mr van den Broek); institutional matters and Intergovernmental Conference (with Mr Oreja). Luxembourg member. Doctor of law. Christian Social Party. Former Prime Minister. Former Vice-President, European Parliament. Born 1937.

Manuel Marín. Vice-President. External relations with southern Mediterranean countries, the Middle East, Latin America and Asia (except Japan, China, Korea, Hong Kong, Macao and Taiwan), including development aid. Spanish member. Law degree. Spanish Socialist Party. He served as Member of Parliament, European Parliament, State Secretary. Born 1949.

Karel van Miert. Competition. Belgian member. Degree in diplomatic sciences. European Commission since 1989. Socialist Party. He served as member of the European Parliament, Belgian Chamber of Representatives, as vice-president of the Socialist International, lecturer on the European institutions. Born 1942.

João de Deus Rogado Salvador Pinheiro. External relations with African, Caribbean and Pacific countries and South Africa, including development aid; the Lomé Convention. Portuguese member. PhD in chemical engineering, DSc. Commission since 1993. He served as Minister for Education and Culture and as Minister for Foreign Affairs. Born 1945.

Leon Brittan. Vice-President. External relations with North America, Australia, New Zealand, Japan, China, Korea, Hong Kong, Macao and Taiwan; common commercial policy; relations with OECD and WTO. British member. MA (Cambs). Conservative Party. Member of Commission since 1989. Member of Parliament 1974-88 and served as Chief Secretary to the Treasury, Home Secretary, Secretary of State for Trade and Industry. Born 1939.

Martin Bangemann. Industrial affairs; information and telecommunications technologies. German member. Doctor of law. Free Democratic Party (FDP). He served as Member of Bundestag, European Parliament, Federal Minister of Economic Affairs, Chairman of FDP, Chairman of the Liberal and Democratic Group in the European Parliament. Born 1934.

Hans van den Broek. External relations with the countries of Central and Eastern Europe, the former Soviet Union, Mongolia, Turkey, Cyprus, Malta and other European countries; common foreign and security policy and human rights (in agreement with the President); external missions. Dutch member. Doctor of law. Christian Democratic Party. Commission since 1993. He served as member of Lower House of Parliament. Minister for Foreign Affairs. Born 1936.

Pádraig Flynn. Employment and social affairs; relations with the Economic and Social Committee. Irish member. Former teacher. Fianna Fáil Party. He served as Dáil deputy and as Minister for the Gaeltacht, Minister for Trade, Commerce and Tourism, Minister for the Environment, Minister for Justice and Minister for Industry and Commerce. Commission since 1993. Born 1939.

EC Commission

Marcelino Oreja Aguirre. Relations with the European Parliament; relations with Member States (transparency, communication and information); culture and audiovisual policy; Office for Official Publications; institutional matters. Spanish member. Doctor of Law. Commission since 1994. He served in Congress, as Secretary General of the Council of Europe, European Parliament. Born 1935.

Édith Cresson. Science, research and development; Joint Research Centre; human resources, education, training and youth. French member. Doctorate in demography. Socialist Party. She was Prime Minister 1991-92. She was a Member of the European Parliament, Minister for Agriculture, Minister for Foreign Trade and Tourism, Minister for Industrial Redeployment and Foreign Trade, Minister for European Affairs. Born 1934.

Monika Wulf-Mathies. Regional policies; relations with the Committee of the Regions; Cohesion Fund (in agreement with Mr Kinnock and Mrs Bjerregaard). German member. PhD. She served on Executive Committee and as chairperson of ÖTV (Public Service and Transport Union), Deputy Chairperson of the Supervisory Board of Deutsche Lufthansa AG. Born 1942.

Mario Monti. Internal market; financial services and financial integration; customs; taxation. Italian member. Degree in economics and management. He was Professor at the University of Turin and Professor, rector and President of Bocconi University. Member of Treasury Committee on Debt Management, Treasury Committee on Banking Law Reform. Born 1943.

Anita Gradin. Immigration, home affairs and justice; relations with the Ombudsman; financial control; fraud prevention. Swedish member. Degree in social work and public administration. Commission since 1994. She served as Member of Parliament, Council of Europe, Minister for Immigrant and Equality Affairs and Minister for Foreign Trade, Ambassador of Sweden to Austria and Slovenia. Born 1933.

Ritt Bjerregaard. Environment; nuclear safety. Danish member. Former teacher. Social Democratic Party. She served as Minister for Education, Minister for Social Welfare, Leader of the Parliamentary Social Democratic Party, member of the Council of Europe, President of the Danish European Movement, Vice-President of Socialist International Women. Born 1941.

Neil Kinnock. Transport (including trans-European networks). British member. BA. Labour Party. Member of Parliament for Bedwellty and Islwyn in South Wales from 1970 until his appointment to the Commission. Leader of Labour Party 1983-92. Vice-President of Socialist International. Privy Councillor. Born 1942.

Franz Fischler. Agriculture and rural development. Austrian member. Agriculturalist. He was a member of the National Parliament (Nationalrat), Federal Minister of Agriculture and Forestry, Director of Chamber of Agriculture. Born 1946.

Emma Bonino. Fisheries; consumer policy; European Community Humanitarian Office (ECHO). Italian member. Degree in foreign languages and literature. Radical Party. She was a member of Italian Chamber of Deputies (first elected in 1976) and European Parliament. Founder member of 'Food and Disarmament International'. Promoter of international human, civil and political rights campaigns in Eastern European countries. Born 1948.

Erkki Antero Liikanen. Budget; personnel and administration; translation and in-house computer services. Finnish member. Master's degree in political science. He has served as Member of Parliament; Member of Nordic Council; Secretary-General of Social Democratic Party; Minister for Finance; Minister in the Ministry of the Interior; Head of the Finnish Mission to the European Union. Born 1950.

Yves-Thibault de Silguy. Economic and financial affairs; monetary matters (in agreement with the President); credit and investments; Statistical Office. French member. Law degree. He served in French Embassy in Washington (Counsellor, economic affairs), in Prime Minister's office (adviser, European, economic, financial affairs), Secretary-General of Interdepartmental Committee on Economic Cooperation in Europe. Born 1948.

Christos Papoutsis. Energy and Euratom Supply Agency; small business; tourism. Greek member. Economist. PASOK. He has served as member of the European Parliament (Leader of the PASOK delegation and Vice-Chairman of European Socialist Parties), as a special adviser to the Government on public administration, former President of Greek National Union of Students. Born 1953.

Index

Advertisers